D0045323

Advance Praise for
The Riches of This Land

"Surprising and enlightening and timely. *The Riches of This Land* turns our understanding of why America once had an economy that delivered prosperity on its head. Only when black men, women of all races, and immigrants broke through blockades of oppression did their gains flow out to everyone. And, now, as Americans seek to find their way out from another devastating economic crisis, Tankersley exposes the true heroes of American prosperity—and why they are the source of our future renewal."

—Ibram X. Kendi, National Book Award–winning
and #1 New York Times–bestselling author

"*The Riches of This Land* is that rare combination of compassionate narrative and trenchant economic analysis to examine the often-misunderstood history of the American middle class and prescribe policies to revive it. Through great storytelling and a firm grasp on economics, Jim Tankersley gives us powerful insight on the key economic question of our time."

—David Wessel, director, Hutchins Center on Fiscal &
Monetary Policy at the Brookings Institution

"Globalization, the movement of manufacturing from America to China, and the current pandemic have shredded the American middle class. If we are to ever regain an economy that works for all people—not just a sliver of the economic elite—we need to understand who made America great in the first place. In his brilliantly written *The Riches of this Land*, Jim Tankersley tells the fascinating stories of the men and women who were the force behind the widespread prosperity we once enjoyed and who can lead us back to the promised land."

—Andy Stern, president emeritus, Service Employees
International Union, and author of Raising the Floor

"A heartfelt, warm, and often moving book about working men and women and the troubles they face. It unites sharply observed stories with trenchant accounts of cutting-edge research to open up a conversation about systemic discrimination that could lay the foundation for an entirely new way of thinking about rebuilding both the working class and our economy."

—*Rebecca Henderson, John and Natty McArthur University Professor, Harvard University, and author of* Reimagining Capitalism in a World on Fire

"An essential book from an essential reporter taking on the most pressing political question of our age. *The Riches of This Land* is a brilliant, searing, and human-centered examination of the American middle class, what it could be, and what it must be."

—*Annie Lowrey, staff writer for the* Atlantic *and author of* Give People Money

"*The Riches of This Land* is the inspiring story of the American economy's unsung heroes, and a manual for building a better future together as one nation."

—*Arthur Brooks, professor of the practice of public leadership, Harvard Kennedy School, and author of* Love Your Enemies

THE
RICHES
OF THIS
LAND

THE
RICHES
OF THIS
LAND

The Untold, True Story of
America's Middle Class

JIM TANKERSLEY

PUBLICAFFAIRS

New York

PublicAffairs
Hachette Book Group
1290 Avenue of the Americas, New York, NY 10104
www.publicaffairsbooks.com
@Public_Affairs

Printed in the United States of America

First Edition: August 2020

Published by PublicAffairs, an imprint of Perseus Books, LLC, a subsidiary of Hachette Book Group, Inc. The PublicAffairs name and logo is a trademark of the Hachette Book Group.

The Hachette Speakers Bureau provides a wide range of authors for speaking events. To find out more, go to www.hachettespeakersbureau.com or call (866) 376-6591.

The publisher is not responsible for websites (or their content) that are not owned by the publisher.

Print book interior design by Amy Quinn

Library of Congress Control Number: 2020939475

ISBNs: 978-1-5417-6783-6 (hardcover); 978-1-5417-6784-3 (e-book)

LSC-C

10 9 8 7 6 5 4 3 2 1

For Max and Lily, the riches of my land

Look with pity, O heavenly Father, upon the people in this land who live with injustice, terror, disease, and death as their constant companions. Have mercy upon us. Help us to eliminate our cruelty to these our neighbors. Strengthen those who spend their lives establishing equal protection of the law and equal opportunities for all. And grant that every one of us may enjoy a fair portion of the riches of this land.

—The Book of Common Prayer

Contents

Prologue

This is a story about the greatest middle class in human history, how it was built more than a half century ago, and how America could rebuild it today from the ruins of a historic economic collapse. Its heroes are black men, immigrants, and women of all races. They are the key to restoring prosperity that is broadly shared among all workers, and not confined largely to the rich and elite.

It is also a story about white men who suffered when the middle class fell into decline, some of whom put Donald Trump in the White House. It is about Trump's promises to those workers, which he did not keep. But it is not a story about Trump, not really. It is bigger than he is. It predates his election by decades. It runs up and down family trees. It sprawls across cotton fields and factory floors and tin cans that fly to the moon.

For much of my life, starting in childhood in what was once a timber town, I've chased that story. I've tried to solve the mystery of how America lost so many good jobs, why so many workers lost the comfortable lives their parents once enjoyed. The pursuit of that story grew to become my career as a journalist traversing the country, most recently in the Washington bureau of the *New York Times*, chronicling the nation's economic and political dysfunction and, as I write this, its spiral into a virus-induced recession.

My reporting uncovered lies that have poisoned our national economic debate for decades, long before this latest recession, but which left us weak and vulnerable when that recession hit. Politicians and business leaders and other powerful men have peddled an incomplete origin story for the middle class, one that put white men at the center and shoved the real heroes to the side. Those omissions have changed economic policymaking for the worse. As we struggle to rebuild the economy again, those lies, left unchallenged, could once again thwart our efforts to deliver shared and sustainable prosperity to all Americans. No matter who they are or where they live or what unique skills they bring to their communities.

The real story of the middle class reveals itself through statistics and deep economic research. But it is foremost a human story.

In the pages ahead there are no charts. Instead, there are people I have been lucky enough to encounter in more than a decade of reporting and writing about the economy, who taught me what cutting-edge economic analyses look like in the flesh. No one taught me more than several generations of black Americans in a single, industrious family, led by one of the most extraordinary people I have ever met, a multiple-job-juggling highway worker named Ed Green. You'll meet him soon. You'll like him.

The book skips back and forth across time and geography, but it roughly follows my journey as a reporter. I didn't always cover economics. Early in my career I wrote about politics, chasing candidates across Oregon and Colorado and Ohio, drinking in a stream of empty answers to real problems. The platitudes changed and the winning messages changed, but the problems didn't go away. I watched voters grow numb to those promises, lose faith in those politicians, and throw their hands up in helplessness with the political system. I threw my hands up, too, and went searching for real answers to the real human problems that seemed to be getting only worse.

The answers I found are hopeful, even in a time of great turmoil. They apply to black women who tend nursing homes in the suburbs of Richmond, Virginia; to white men who mine coal in West Virginia or work the once-great factories along the Ohio River; to Mexican immigrants who run hair salons in Chicago. They apply to nurses and grocery clerks and delivery drivers, the essential workers of the COVID-19 pandemic, who fed and supplied and cared for the country as it rapidly shut its economy down. And they apply to bartenders, paralegals, saleswomen, and millions of others who were thrown out of work by the virus and into the deep pool of fear that has become all too common for American workers this century.

If you are someone, anyone, who feels as though the economy and the culture have left you behind and there's no way to get ahead anymore, I am here to tell you it does not have to be that way. It was not always that way. It can get better. I strongly believe that it will.

The road to renewal starts with a retelling of the origin story of America's great postwar boom, focused on people whom historians and journalists have too often overlooked. I am going to show you how the simple, radical act of reducing discrimination against women and nonwhite workers was the reason America experienced its first great middle-class expansion, turning a good economy for workers into a transcendent one. It's a wild, true story. And it's the source of my faith that America can build such an economy again.

—Alexandria, Virginia, Spring 2020

1

Winston-Salem, 1943

"I'M WITH THEM"

Theodosia Simpson silenced the tobacco-cutting machines of plant 65 on June 17, shortly after returning from lunch. She worked on the top floor, the machines stretching out around her like crops ready for harvest. Three rows, each separated by a wide aisle. Twenty-two machines per row. Three women at each machine, synchronized. Every fifteen minutes a man would push a big rolling cart over, lift a box off it, and drop it on the machine. One woman would pull bundles from the box and lay them down. The second woman would spread out the contents. The third woman would feed them into the machine. They did this for eight hours a day, five and a half days a week, with no breaks except for lunch and, at most, five minutes to use the toilet. They had no vacation days, no sick days, not even a day granted for pregnant women to give birth. Their machine fed other machines, which performed other tasks, on the lower floors of plant 65. Theodosia's machine was number 13. When she refused to turn it on and the women around her followed suit, it was like cutting an oxygen line. Work stopped on the floor below, then the floor below that. Within five minutes, plant 65 was off-line.

Within a few days, the entire R.J. Reynolds company was, too.

It was 1943, nearly 177 years after a group of white men in Pennsylvania declared a self-evident truth, that all men are created equal and endowed by their creator with certain unalienable rights. War was raging across the cobblestones of Europe and the sand islands of the Pacific, and there were boys in uniform who needed their cigarettes. The white men who ran the company knew it was no time for the largest tobacco factory in northwestern North Carolina to lurch to a halt.

So did the black women who made the factory run.

Theodosia had gone to work for R.J. Reynolds in the depths of the Great Depression when she was sixteen years old. She began as a temporary worker in the cigarette plant, hired to help meet the extra demand that came with the summer months. That fall she moved to plant 12, then later to plant 65. Those plants were the stemmeries, where workers began the long and arduous process of ripping tobacco leaves from their stems and rolling them into smokes, for soldiers and everyone else. The women who worked in the plants would go home at night and wash the dust out of their ears. Their dresses would stink worse than any barroom.

There was a hierarchy among the workers, with the black women at the bottom. The untier, who pulled the tobacco leaves from the box, earned a few cents per hour less than the spreader, who arranged the leaves to be fed into the machine. The spreader earned a few cents less than the machine operator. On the day of the work stoppage, Theodosia was working as a spreader, earning less than thirty cents an hour, which would be several dollars per hour less than minimum wage today.

Theodosia and several of her former colleagues at the factory recalled their experience there, decades later, in interviews with a historian named Robert Rodgers Korstad. Their memories have been archived and made public by the Southern Oral History Program at the University of North Carolina. When you sift through them, a narrative emerges of discrimination, determination, and what would become a victory not only for the black women and men who toiled for R.J. Reynolds but for thousands of white workers, too.

It is an allegory of worker empowerment. A preview of how a long-repressed group of Americans would kick open new doors of opportunity and lead the nation to a Golden Era of shared prosperity. It is also a blueprint for the nation today, as it climbs out of the pit of a recession that exposed how weak and unjust the economy became after that Golden Era died.

The foremen in the plant were white men, often with little formal education. They would scream at women for not working fast enough. They would scold black women in particular for reading on their lunch break. "What are you doing with a newspaper?" Theodosia recalled one telling her. "You came here to work." They would pat women and hold some of them at their desks for hours, just to amuse themselves. If a woman talked back, or slowed down, or complained in any way, a foreman would often point toward the door, which he called "the hole the carpenter left." Go ahead, he was saying. Find yourself a new job. He knew there wasn't a better one, not in those days, not for a black woman in the city of Winston-Salem.

On the morning of June 17, 1943, a black woman at the machine next to Theodosia's burst into tears. She was a widow, a mother of five. She had fallen sick, as workers often did in the Reynolds factory, but she was still working, because there were no sick days on the stemming line. The women at each machine were expected to feed through an entire box of tobacco every quarter of an hour. The previous month, the foremen had doubled the number of leaves stuffed into each box, but they had kept the same expectations: four boxes an hour, every hour. The sick woman was falling behind that pace, and a foreman had just walked over to tell her to hurry up. He pointed to the carpenter's hole. "And she started crying, almost went into hysteria," Theodosia recalled, "because she had these children to rear and nobody working but her."

Leaders of a labor union had come to Winston-Salem months before, to try to organize tobacco workers, and Theodosia had been going to their meetings. One day that spring she had tried to fasten her dress with union pins, but the foreman sent her home to change clothes, and the next day the plant changed its dress code to outlaw pins of any kind. She had been looking for the right moment to act on what she was hearing about banding workers together. The crying woman had stirred her to it. She beckoned some friends she could trust over to the bathroom. They decided that the next day, Friday, they would stage a sit-in work stoppage. Somehow a foreman caught wind of their plan, and the ladies learned that he had learned about it, and so at lunch they decided to move faster. They returned to their machines. Someone pulled the whistle that signaled it was time for work to start again.

What came next sounds like a story from the scriptures.

Theodosia and her trusted friends sat down on their stools. They stared at the machines. They did not turn them on.

Other women, who had not heard about the plan at lunch, turned their machines on.

A black man came by with a cart full of tobacco boxes. He, too, had been sick all week. He had asked repeatedly to see a nurse. She kept sending him back to work, telling him he was fine. Theodosia, who would later rise to work in the X-ray laboratory of a hospital, realized decades after the fact that the man was probably showing signs of hypertension. The man paused near Theodosia and looked around at all the machines that were stopped. "And he said," Theodosia told her interviewer, "'If these women'll stand up for their rights, I'm with them,' and just dropped on the floor"—dead.

When the women who were still working heard that man and saw him fall, they turned off their machines too.

Days later, when the machines roared back to life, the workers of the Reynolds factory had a union, and that union had won promises of more humane treatment from the white men who ran the company. The workers would soon have sick days, paid vacation, and holidays. They would have a retirement plan and profit sharing. Their wages would jump. For some workers, pay would double. The gains spread to all the workers, regardless of race or gender or job title.

Every Reynolds cigarette was a joint venture, powered by the sweat of thousands of white workers and thousands of black workers. Most of the white workers were not foremen or managers. They did slightly less debilitating jobs on the production line, for higher pay, than black workers. Some of them joined in the sit-down stoppage and the union drive that followed, but whether they did or not, each white worker reaped the benefits.

Every single employee of the Reynolds factory took a huge step toward a middle-class American life in the summer of 1943. All thanks to the black women of plant 65.

Today, as we close in on 250 years of the American republic, the idea of the "middle class" is deeply entrenched in American life. Politicians pander to it. Polls show that nearly every worker thinks he or she is a part of it. That group includes people who live wealthier, more comfortable lives than almost anyone in Winston-Salem in the 1940s could have dreamed of, all the way up to the white men who owned the tobacco factories.

But the middle class, as we know and love and understand it, is a relatively recent development in the United States. It was born in the twentieth century, long after the settling of the American continent by white people. It has been a popular phenomenon for maybe three-quarters of a century. In cultural consciousness, it eased onto the scene around World War I, began to really catch on in the 1940s—around the time of the Reynolds factory strikes—and peaked in 1971, at almost the exact same time as hippies.

In technical terms the nation has always had something you could call a middle class. For a long time, it was limited to a shifting group of white-collar workers, who almost always were white. As the historian Stuart M. Blumin has detailed, the term referred to a particular type of salesclerk in the Jacksonian 1820s. To Walt Whitman, it meant a slightly different type of office-working suburbanite when he extolled the virtues of the middle class in newspaper editorials before the Civil War. Later in the 1800s it referred to exceedingly narrow groups of workers, like Boston streetcar operators; in the twentieth century, at times, it seemed to encompass everyone in the country who worked. "Americans use the term with remarkable imprecision," Blumin wrote in his book *The Emergence of the Middle Class*, "yet, we seem to represent something very important about our culture and society by doing so."

The middle class as we understand it now is not limited to one color of collar, or to any color of the skin. It unites salaried professionals like teachers and paralegals with highly trained, blue-collar factory workers who get paid by the hour. It includes a growing number of service workers like home health aides. The broad middle class sprawls across cities, suburbs, and rural America. It was forged in the national mobilization to supply and fight the Second World War, it flourished in that war's aftermath, and it has dwindled in the last several decades.

It is perhaps the most American of aspirations, a shared national myth that has the virtue of being true.

We are losing it, in part because we have lost sight of what made it in the first place: American people, working together, to secure better lives not just for themselves but for their neighbors.

That's an origin story you don't often hear. For a reason.

In recent years the middle-class mythos has been co-opted and narrowed by powerful white men who, in the time-honored tradition of ruling elites attempting to keep a crumbling hold on power, have convinced one group of distressed workers to blame their troubles on another group of distressed workers. They have taken little responsibility for the policies they have pushed that hurt working families, killing jobs and stifling wage growth. The stories they tell workers now cast immigrants and other "outsiders" as thieves of economic opportunity, stealing prosperity from the hardworking white men who built America's industrial belt and, with it, the middle class.

Those stories are incomplete, incorrect, and a threat to the economic, social, and moral health of our nation. They miss the lessons of plant 65 and the women who brought a factory to its knees, and of the thousands of workers those women helped guide toward the middle class. The real story, the one that white male elites have tried to crumple back into the carton and toss to the side of the road, is more hopeful. More unifying.

The real story of America's middle class, as I have discovered in more than a decade of writing about economic change for national newspapers, and in a lifetime of worry and wonder about workers who could not seem to get ahead no matter how hard they tried, is not a story of theft by outsiders. It does not pit one group of struggling laborers—be they men of color or immigrants or women across all races—against a similar, white, male group.

The real story, revealed in cutting-edge economic research, a retracing of centuries of American history, and conversations with the women and men who make our market-based economy hum today, is that workers need each other. They hold in their hands—be they calloused or manicured—the ability to lift one another to better pay, better treatment, and a better quality of life.

Let's be clear up front: this story grapples, in great detail, with the economic trials of white, working-class American men, whose fortunes have declined in recent decades and whose anger has in many ways reshaped the country's social and political landscape. But unlike a lot of what you read or see or hear about the middle class, this is not a story *about* those men. It is a story about the false promises they have been sold, and about the unlikely allies they and other workers need to reclaim the prosperity that all Americans expect and deserve to enjoy.

I have spent more than a decade of reporting on the trail of the country's lost middle class, from a scrappy newsroom in Toledo, Ohio, to the Washington, D.C., bureau of the *New York Times*. I went looking for an explanation for why middle-class jobs vanished from factory towns along the Ohio River, for the rocket men and women of Southern California, for the grandchildren of R.J. Reynolds employees in the Carolinas. I poured myself into the question of why so many American workers have given themselves over to anger and finger-pointing, to a government-by-grievance mentality that seems to care less about solving problems and more about scorching their perceived enemies, even if they burn themselves in the process. I went looking for the source of their anger and the path to their renewal.

What I found was a story of hope, even in the bleak days of a recession. A story that should unite black women who drive buses and deliver mail with white men who tune engines in garages, that shows the shared fate of newly arrived immigrants and Americans whose ancestors made land on the *Mayflower*. A truth that can revive a middle class that has been scorched, for far too long, by the lies of elite white men.

The great American middle-class boom is actually a story of men of color and women breaking shackles that had held them back from before the birth of the nation. Their progress lifted everyone in the country, including white men. The reason so many Americans have slipped out of the middle class in recent decades is that the economy stopped opening as many new opportunities for those workers, and even started pushing some of them backward. Fixing that problem is the answer to reviving America's middle class. For women, for black men, for immigrants. Even for white men like the ones whose livelihoods were left to rot in the forests of my youth, in Western Oregon, which is where this journey begins.

2

McMinnville, 1978

THE CLEAR-CUT AMERICAN DREAM

The fur trade brought white people to Yamhill County, a conifer corner of the Pacific Northwest where beavers dammed the creeks flowing down the back side of the Coast Range. Forests kept the settlers there, kept them busy, and kept them alive. Pioneers fresh off the Oregon Trail felled Douglas firs to build their homes along the Yamhill River. They tied the logs into skiffs that carried their crops downriver to Portland and the sea. For generations after the first whites arrived, most men in the county either tilled the soil or worked in the woods. The shadow of the industry slowly receded only after Oregon became a state. Other sectors grew up slowly but surely around it. Still, on the eve of the Second World War, half of the land in the county—221,525 acres in all—was either standing timber or growing back from recent cuts. There were twenty-nine sawmills slicing logs, a plywood plant near the western county line, and a pulp plant on the eastern edge.

When I was born there in 1978, in the county seat of McMinn-ville, in a hospital that has since been knocked down and replaced by a chain drugstore, timber was still king—or at least, still calling the shots. Roughly one out of every six private-sector workers in Yamhill County worked as a logger, or in the sawmills, or in some other connection to the woods. If you counted employment at paper mills and trucking compa-nies that hauled logs, the share would be even higher.

I still draw comfort from the trees. They greet you when you drive to-ward McMinnville, whether from the mountains that lie to the west or the farmland that lies to the south or the sprawling suburbs that lie to the north and east. Hemlock and red cedar and Sitka spruce, but above all the Doug firs, tall and green, with layers of branches angled skyward at sharp and repeated angles. Like a Christmas tree lot, as far as you can see.

I grew up understanding that those trees weren't just yuletide dec-orations or some sort of museum collection for Portlanders to admire, though they were both. They gave jobs to our neighbors. In the boom after World War II, Yamhill County's mills churned out hundreds of thousands of board feet of lumber each year, and they put thousands of children—mostly sons—of war veterans to work. My parents were chil-dren of veterans, and they were white migrants to Oregon, though their wagon was a Buick and their trail was the I-5 freeway running north from California. My father hung long crosscut saws on the walls of his first law office, where he helped small timber outfits buy and sell land to harvest. Our church friends included a forester who cruised timber, sizing up the forests for how much wood they could yield, clad in a preferred brand of jeans called Wild Ass. (He also occasionally wore them to services.) Fa-thers of school friends worked in the mills, or managed them, or carried thick round logs from the forests on long truck beds in a low, straining gear.

As a child I saw the forests of Yamhill County lure kids out of our high school and other high schools in the smaller towns around us. For a long time, they lifted those kids into the middle class. Well into the mid-1980s, the typical worker in Oregon's forest-products industry earned nearly one and a half times the salary of the typical worker in all the state's other industries combined, according to statistics from the Oregon Office of Economic Analysis. We didn't know those stats as kids. We just knew that other kids said working in the woods was a good job. A job to be proud of. A job to aspire to.

It seems almost impossible to imagine now, as lattes and wine and microchips have taken over the state economy, but as recently as the late 1970s, one out of every ten jobs in Oregon—from the city streets of Portland to the high desert of Burns to the fishing fleets in Depoe Bay— grew out of the timber industry. Those workers didn't need an expensive college degree to earn what was at the time a solidly middle-class wage. A graduate of McMinnville High School could walk off the commencement lawn at Wortman Stadium and into a job cutting trees in the Coast Range, with reasonable expectation that after a few years of risking his neck and wrenching his back, he could buy a home and a car and afford to raise a family in a mostly rural, mostly white county. Some kids didn't even need to graduate. The money in the industry seemed good enough—and the freedom even more so—that they just walked out of class one day and left high school behind.

Until the day that connection splintered.

This was my introduction to the rotting of the American middle class—or at least, one rugged, rural, overwhelmingly white sliver of it. It is where my journey to understanding decades of struggle for workers truly begins. It is not the full picture of the middle class, not even close. But it was the picture I woke up to every day as a kid.

From the time I entered elementary school through the time I left home for college, a national recession, an automation proliferation, and an overhaul in federal forest management ravaged the wood-products industry. Officials in Washington, D.C., curtailed the amount of federal land available for logging. Companies bought new tools and technologies that allowed them to fell the same number of trees with far fewer workers. Harvest levels dropped in Yamhill County. Nearly half the timber jobs went away.

It is a strange and horrible and scarring thing to watch, even if you don't realize at the time exactly what it is you are seeing: an economic ladder snapping out from under a cluster of workers, trapping older ones in the middle of their careers and leaving young ones to wonder if they will ever get their lives off the ground. It can traumatize a community, scramble its politics, leave its leaders struggling for answers. Some communities manage to bounce back, as mine did, but many workers never really do.

I have seen many an economic ladder snap in the decades since I left home, none so fiercely and quickly as in the spring of 2020. A deadly virus swept the country and millions of Americans lost their jobs overnight. The carnage was carried live on cable. No one could miss it.

That wasn't true in Oregon in the eighties. The spread of the damage was slower and, for many people, harder to see. Probably because I was a kid trying to make sense of what was happening around me, it was terrifying. It was also formative. Living through the downfall of the timber industry taught me how the economy could crush workers with almost no warning.

In order to tell you the story of the middle class, I need to tell you that story, which means I need to tell you my story, and my hometown's.

Yamhill County sits in the upper left corner of Oregon, near the top of the Willamette Valley, with the Pacific Coast Range as its back fence and the Cascades looming to the east. Its boundaries run long and rectangular at the bottom, with an offset hammerhead on top. Like a mallard at rest on a pond, his head at attention and his beak dipping forward. Or, for a child of the Game Boy era, like the backward-Z-shaped Tetris piece, fit satisfyingly snug into a scoring row. The northeast corner—the top of the beak—lies close enough to the state's largest city, Portland, to count as a far-flung exurb. The southwestern edge laps tantalizingly close to the Pacific Ocean, just nine miles over the county line. On the rare summer day when the sun is hot in the valley and warm-for-the-Pacific-Northwest on the beach, a teenager borrowing his dad's car can make the drive up and down the wide passes on Highway 18 to the sands of Lincoln City in less than an hour, depending on how aggressively he's willing to pass log trucks on the way over the ridge.

It is the cradle of Beverly Cleary, the beloved author of the *Ramona* books and other children's literature, who signed a book of mine when I was a boy and she had been honored at the McMinnville Public Library. Cleary was born in McMinnville but raised in nearby Yamhill, which is also the hometown of my colleague Nicholas Kristof, a *New York Times* columnist who has twice won the Pulitzer Prize. "The 1970s," Kristof and Sheryl WuDunn, his wife, wrote in their book *Tightrope*, "were an optimistic time in Yamhill, a town southwest of Portland with one flashing red light, four churches, and, at that time, 517 people, almost all of them white." For a broader picture of the country, I am partial to the maps made by my best friend from high school, Mike McDaniel, who left Oregon to earn a master's degree in geography and now roams the Willamette Valley charting cropland for growers of hazelnuts, alfalfa, and pinot noir. "Yamhill County," he told me, when I asked him to sum up his maps in a few words, "is a uniquely beautiful little corner of Oregon, a classic example of European American settlement of the western frontier that still clings to a mostly white, agrarian past and struggles with growth and transition to a more urban, diverse, and complicated future."

It still astonishes me that my parents found it. They were a librarian and a lawyer who had spent the ends of their childhoods and the tumult of college in the late 1960s in Southern California. My mother was born in Seattle but had moved to the Golden State as a young girl. My father was an Air Force brat whose parents retired to northern Arizona soon after he finished high school. Mom earned a master's from the University of Southern California and then went to work for the Los Angeles Public Library, answering phones on the reference desk, sometimes to settle bar bets, a human search engine before anyone had thought of the electronic kind. Dad finished law school at the University of California at Los Angeles, spurned some big-firm offers in L.A. and Denver, and took a year-long clerkship at the Oregon Supreme Court in Salem, one of the sleepiest state capitals in America.

When my brother and I were kids, I asked incredulously how they could have possibly denied their future children a lifetime of beach trips and Dodger games in favor of a town that did not, when they moved there, possess a single McDonald's. The way they told the story was, it was the right mixture of happenstance and lifestyle choice. Near the end of his clerkship, my father was connected by a friend to a two-lawyer shop with an opening for a junior associate, located in a town of ten thousand that neither of my parents had ever heard of. He interviewed a couple of times, including once with one of the partners on a steelhead fishing trip on the Nestucca River, and they offered him the sort of job he had held in his mind as ideal. It was not at a big firm with a fast track to a federal judgeship, as some of his law school classmates landed. But it was in a town small enough that he could join the Water & Light board, in a firm relaxed enough that he could take weeks off in the fall to hunt deer and elk. He could be home early enough on spring evenings to coach Little League games.

My mother was a slower sell. The first time my father took her to McMinnville, she cried. "What am I going to do here?" she said. The way she ended up answering that question, I would later realize, was a clue to solving America's middle-class puzzle.

They arrived in 1976. Five years later, with two very young boys in tow, they bought a house. They paid $91,000. The same house would cost a young family in McMinnville about $400,000 today, an increase of more than 50 percent after you adjust for inflation. My parents still live in that house. From the balcony of my old bedroom on the second floor, where I would fall asleep to the voice of Dodger broadcaster Vin Scully wafting in from stations in Bakersfield or Las Vegas, you can see the foothills of the Coast Range, swathed in evergreens.

I wanted to be the second baseman for the Dodgers, a dream hampered by the fact that I couldn't hit, field, or throw well. One day in the early 1990s, in an overcrowded middle school, I stumbled onto what the guidance counselors called a career track. Perhaps influenced by my grandfather, who wrote for the *Washington Post* and several other outlets in the 1940s, I had signed up for a student newspaper club. My first contribution was a column attacking the school ban on baseball caps, which landed me in the principal's office. "What are we going to do with you?"

he asked, and "journalism" seemed like a pretty fun answer. I joined the high school paper as a freshman. That summer, I somehow landed a job at the thrice-weekly *News-Register*, our local paper, mostly writing obituaries and wedding announcements. It grew into a full-time reporting gig, every summer of high school.

All the while, McMinnville was coping with the shock of the timber decline. High school social studies classes were bitterly divided over the existence of a bird known as the spotted owl. Almost none of us had personally seen it, but politicians had offered the owl up as a convenient (and ultimately misplaced) target for outrage over the lost jobs, it being an endangered species that had been discovered in forests across the state. We argued a lot about spotted owls, and old-growth timber, in factions that I now realize foreshadowed the American electoral divide in the years ahead.

The timber shock also stirred a question somewhere in the back of my aspiring-journalist brain. That question would linger and mutate and eventually consume much of my professional life, which would take me to faraway places working for national publications you could rarely buy in those days on Third Street or anywhere else in my town.

The early version of that question, the one that would later animate me as a reporter whose entire job is covering economic policymaking in Washington, was some version of this: When will the economy start working again for the guys I went to school with? The guys I played hoops with at the community center, the ones I wrote about for the local paper, who smacked me with dodgeballs in gym? The ones I lost touch with when I chased my own dreams all the way out of town?

I have since come to see the bigger, scarier, more informed version of that question. It is the most important question in American public life today. It was so amid the rise of populism in the early 2010s that swept Donald Trump to the presidency in 2016, and it is especially so now that the country has fallen into the swiftest recession in its history—one that laid bare the fragility of the vast majority of workers' lives and dreams in the twenty-first century.

That fundamental question is this: Where did the good jobs go for the American middle class, and where will we find new ones?

Answering that question has taken me all over the country, to big cities and sleepy suburbs and towns so small they make McMinnville feel like Metropolis. Unlike so many of my classmates, I was desperate to leave town after graduation. I wrote my college admissions essay on my love for newspapers and baseball box scores. It helped get me into Stanford, where I joined the student paper, scored a string of summer internships, and landed a job at the big paper in Portland, *The Oregonian*, upon graduation.

It was June of 2000, and the popping of a stock market bubble was about to hurt a lot of American workers, journalists and otherwise. Donald Trump had recently ruled out a run for president.

In the two decades since, McMinnville has found a way to thrive in spite of the timber crash. Its population has tripled since my parents moved there. There are now two McDonald's, one on either end of town. There are boutique hotels downtown, one with a brewpub on the first floor and what I am fairly certain is the only bar in the world that has ever displayed one of my newspaper stories in a frame on its wall. (The important thing is the subject, a local World Series hero named Scott Brosius, and not the byline.) In the hills outside of town grow some of the most valuable wine grapes in North America, whose juice has helped fuel the growth that McMinnville and Yamhill County have experienced over the last forty years.

You can look at that growth and say, wow, that little spot has done well for itself, in spite of everything. And you'd be partly right.

What you'd miss is the change in who has been helped by that growth, the structural realignment of an economy that used to do well for a certain group of workers, but then, very rapidly, stopped working for them at all.

That is the change I investigated as a reporter who first covered politics, then economics, for publications including the *Rocky Mountain News*, *The Blade* newspaper in Toledo, the *Chicago Tribune*, *National*

Journal, the *Washington Post*, *Vox*, and now the *New York Times*. This book draws on reporting I have done for all those publications, some of which I wrote about in newspaper, magazine, and digital stories.

I have long been consumed by the question of when the economy will start working again for the guys I went to high school with. But in my travels I have found that the problem is bigger than those guys, who were largely white and who frequently did not go to college. And I have found that the solution is entwined with a very different group of workers—ones who have become a convenient target for politicians hoping to harness worker anxiety to advance their own careers.

My profession has missed large parts of that story. National reporters have mostly overlooked the diverging fortunes of workers in Oregon, which was a presidential swing state in 2000 but has trended solidly toward the Democratic Party since then. One consequence of that shift is that national news reporters don't spend nearly as much time as they otherwise would in the state, interviewing undecided voters about the struggles, concerns, and aspirations that guide them in choosing a candidate. We have a bias in newsrooms toward stories about conflict; in political reporting, that shows up as bias toward seeking out internally conflicted voters, in the areas where, thanks to America's collect-the-set-and-win system for electing presidents, those ultimate decisions will decide who wins the White House.

We missed those disaffected Oregon voters, as a national news media, in the most recent election cycles. But we missed a lot more than that. By focusing on the prosperity of places like Portland, San Jose, and Austin, or on the perennial swing-voting white workers of Pennsylvania, Ohio, Michigan, and Wisconsin, we missed entire classes of workers who were much more quietly punished by the seismic economic shifts of the last forty years.

I think my dad, who loves wordplay more than anyone I've ever met, would like me to say that by focusing on the economic forest for the last several decades, we've missed the trees.

The most important story in America right now is a story about the trees.

Nurturing them again will help the economy grow out of the ashes of the COVID-19 pandemic, but not if the country falls back into the politics of vilification, discrimination, and exclusion that have denied us another Golden Era for far too long.

I have learned in my reporting that the United States economy thrived after World War II in large part because America made it easier for people who had been previously shut out of economic opportunity—women, minorities, immigrants—to enter the workforce and climb the economic ladder, to make better use of their talents and potential. They were the unsung engine of what most Americans now think of as the time when the economy worked best for an expanding middle class.

But today, new barriers have risen up to block those workers from advancement, from inadequate parental leave policies to federal limits on imported brainpower. Overt racial discrimination persists.

Those barriers don't just hurt women and men of color. They also hurt working-class white people. In order to get its middle class back on track—and to help the country build a better and stronger economy from recession—America needs to restore its upward flow of talent, which was broken over the last forty years. It needs better opportunities for women who went to college, for immigrants with coding skills, for black men who have struggled to land jobs and start businesses. It needs to revitalize crumbling cities and dying small towns across the country, with new and stronger infusions of talent. It needs to weave a new safety net to cushion people against economic shocks that they did not cause and, when the economy recovers, launch those people back into the jobs that bring the most value to the country.

The United States also needs to break down the unearned advantages that allow a single group to capture so much of the nation's prosperity. That group does not include all the highest-skilled or most productive workers in the country. But it is the group that has long set the rules of the economy and has used those rules to divert prosperity for its own gain. In overly broad terms, we call that group "elite white men with college degrees."

People like Donald Trump, and like me.

What Trump carried with him to Washington was something more dangerous and damaging, to the white workers who delivered him the presidency, than another broken promise from a politician. He peddled a false alliance that will never deliver for those workers, and a false enemy to hold it together. He and his political allies want white workers, particularly white men, to believe that their economic, political, and cultural survival requires teaming up with some of the most powerful white men in the country—elites of Wall Street and Washington who have fashioned themselves, improbably, as anti-elitist—against a cresting demographic tide led by (nonwhite) immigrants and economically empowered women. The peddlers of that alliance want white workers to buy the idea that a rise of "cosmopolitan" values has undermined their national foundations and eroded their power. Their calls to make America great again, to shut off its intake of immigrants and refugees, to send those who challenge them "back to where you came from" are unmistakably a demand to restore a bygone era, which was whiter and more patriarchal than the country is today.

That vision rests on a misreading of history and, at best, a misunderstanding of the economic currents that have pushed America and the world to a digitized, specialized set of interlocking value chains that skip easily across national borders. It minimizes the ways in which America's middle class was built by more than just white men.

It is a cynical, time-honored, and deeply effective way to distract hardworking voters from the real villains in their economic saga. And it is profoundly self-defeating, for workers and elites alike.

I have learned in my career that one wonderful and challenging thing about living in new places and expanding your horizons is it helps you see the parts of your own, home world that you did not fully appreciate as a child. We did not learn, in my mostly white high school, about Oregon's ugly racial history. I don't recall any history lessons on the Indian-killing exploits of Phil Sheridan, an army officer who would go on to Civil War heroics after terrorizing tribes in the Oregon Territory, and who is still celebrated every summer in the Yamhill County town that bears his name. We did not learn about the racial exclusion laws that made it illegal for African Americans to move to the state until 1926. When that question about jobs going away, and what comes next, started gnawing at me as a kid, I didn't spend nearly enough time thinking about the sorts of people who didn't go to my high school, whose paths to the middle class were also being wiped away. The more I did, the more I saw the answer to my original question emerging before my eyes.

Sometimes, of course, even a relatively homogenous hometown can give you a window on that much broader world, with its much bigger problems. My family's church while I was growing up was named St. Barnabas; through it, my mother organized a statewide donation drive for drought relief in Africa. We prayed each week for congregations in countries I'd never dreamed of visiting. And in the back of the small leather handbooks that held the service rites—the Book of Common Prayer—I found appeals for divine intervention on a truly global scale. They were eye opening, those prayers for special circumstances. They were poetry.

One of them was called the Prayer for the Oppressed. I think about it often, after I've talked with the workers who feel squeezed and diminished in America today. They are not oppressed in the way enslaved African Americans were in the United States before the Civil War, or the way the Israelites were in Egypt. They're oppressed by an economy that has been designed, intentionally and unintentionally, to work largely for one select group of Americans at the expense of almost everyone else. Oppressed by political leaders who are responsive to the concerns of the elite and powerful far more than they are to workers in cubicles, on factory floors, and behind store counters. Oppressed by the illusion of opportunity, the stories of an American Dream they have struggled to experience in the flesh.

Oppressed, most of all, by a sense of betrayal. Even when the American economy grew and thrived over the last forty years, those workers were left in the slow lane. When it slammed to a halt, they were the ones who hurt most. That's not the deal those workers were promised. Americans expect society to progress and technology to advance, in slow and fast bursts, but never to go backward. They expect, in the words of

President John F. Kennedy, relentlessly repeated by President Ronald Reagan, a rising tide to lift all boats. They're smart and savvy enough to feel the weight of injustice when they see the water coming in and a select few rising high on the waves while they themselves struggle to keep from slipping under.

The pandemic recession plunged millions of people deep underwater. But the richest Americans rode out the storm in their telework bunkers, with wine and fresh produce delivered by the disproportionately young, female, nonwhite "essential" workers who risked infection to keep the country running but didn't earn enough to afford even a hovel of their own. That is the story of the American economy in the twenty-first century: long stretches of middle-class malaise, ending in two—two!—once-in-a-lifetime economic crises, which gutted most workers but left elites unscathed.

The Prayer for the Oppressed goes like this: "Look with pity, O heavenly Father, upon the people in this land who live with injustice, terror, disease, and death as their constant companions. Have mercy upon us. Help us to eliminate our cruelty to these our neighbors. Strengthen those who spend their lives establishing equal protection of the law and equal opportunities for all. And grant that every one of us may enjoy a fair portion of the riches of this land."

I went forth in the world, as an economics journalist, to learn why so many Americans are not enjoying their fair portion of our land's riches, whether they toil in the fields or the woods or the factories or the office parks. I came back understanding that those Americans, in so many ways, are themselves the riches. And we are hiding them—to paraphrase a warning about human capability issued in the Sermon on the Mount—under a bushel. To show you the truth in that story, the riches of those Americans, I first need to tell you the middle-class story that white men have been getting all wrong, for far too long now.

3

Ohio, 2006

THIS IS NOT YOUR LIFE

My family played a lot of board games when I was a kid. One of them sold me a promise of how the economy was supposed to work. It came with little plastic minivans, brightly colored cash, and a game board that mapped your journey to the middle class and beyond. It was a Milton Bradley classic: The Game of Life.

The driving idea behind Life (literally—you drove your minivan around the board, picking up money and game cards and the occasional infant) was to amass as much economic security as possible. You got a job, with or without going to college first. You got married, bought a house, stockpiled insurance policies, racked up paydays, and built your nest egg as high as it would go. The winner was the one who retired with the most money. We played it often at my house. Disturbingly so, in retrospect, especially because of how much my dad loved the game's penultimate transaction, when you earned a payout for every child in your car. "Selling your kids," he called it.

The game was everything America told itself about how the economy delivered for all workers, down to the smiling players depicted on the box. Unless you hit an extremely bad-luck run of spins—losing turns, paying penalties, having other players basically steal your cash with cards marked "Revenge"—you came out okay in the end. Pretty much everyone did. There was a baseline level of security that most players enjoyed, most of the time. You won by getting filthy rich, but even if you fell short of that, you still had a relatively comfortable tour around the board. That, to me, is the best way of articulating what most people mean when they talk about being middle class, or wanting to be. What they're aspiring to is security. The ability to own a home and a car, save enough to retire, provide for a family, and give any kids they might have (and definitely do not get to sell) the opportunity and resources to enjoy a life at least as successful as their own—and hopefully a better one.

If there was a single state that embodied those aspirations, it was Ohio. When it wasn't picking our presidents (no one since John F. Kennedy has won the White House without it) or vetting the things we buy (Columbus has long been known as a test market, the diversity of its population almost perfectly representing the demographics of the United States as a whole), Ohio was selling the rest of the country a model of the middle-class lifestyle that generations of Americans grew to expect from their vibrant, capitalist economy. It was a factory-made fairy tale. The Milton Bradley ideal, brought to life.

And when I arrived there, years before the Great Recession, it was clear the game in Ohio had gone terribly wrong.

At the start of the 1990s, before President Bill Clinton signed on to the North American Free Trade Agreement (NAFTA), or the World Trade Organization voted to admit China as a member, or before any of the other major trade disturbances that economists blame to varying degrees for damage to manufacturing in the United States, more than one million Ohioans worked in a factory. More than one out of every five jobs in the state were manufacturing jobs, a significantly higher rate than in the nation as a whole. Factory employment had peaked in America, in raw job totals, around 1980, and had been sliding since. As a share of all jobs, manufacturing was in steady decline nationwide, stretching all the way back to the mid-1950s.

Ohio, along with its industrial midwestern neighbors, was attempting to defy those trends. Throughout the Clinton administration, it remained a manufacturing-employment powerhouse. If you or someone in your family did not work in a factory, odds were your jobs were linked to one anyway. If you worked in a factory, you probably enjoyed what economists called the "manufacturing wage premium": your job paid more per hour than a service-sector job would, which increased your odds of affording the comforts of a middle-class life. It was a great deal for workers, until, suddenly, it wasn't available anymore.

I began to understand what Ohio's middle class lost, and what that loss meant for its politics, only after I moved to the state for a job. It was a sunny April day in a downtown that looked like it had been abandoned in an air raid. The Ohio River, a passage back to the glory days of the industrial Midwest, sparkled a few blocks away. Vacant storefronts crumbled on almost every corner.

The country was midway through what would go down as the worst decade for the American middle class since the Great Depression, though nobody knew at the time just how bad it would be. A small crowd was waiting to hear another political candidate promise, against evidence and fading hope, that he would bring back the good-paying jobs that had floated away.

I had moved to Toledo in 2005 to join *The Blade*, a newspaper that was ambitious beyond its circulation in a time of constant, savage newsroom cutbacks nationwide as the internet carved the beating heart out of local print journalism. It sent me across the state to cover two nationally watched elections at once: one of America's most expensive and competitive contests for the United States Senate, and a wide-open race to replace arguably the most unpopular governor in the history of the state. I was new to the newsroom and a foreigner in the Midwest, having never lived more than a few miles east of the Rocky Mountains. My title at the paper was "political writer," but my job, I quickly discovered, was all about economics.

In the short time I had lived in Northwest Ohio, the state had lost sixteen thousand manufacturing jobs. It had lost nearly two hundred thousand over the previous five years, even though the national economy had been growing at what economists consider a strong rate of more than 3 percent per year.

In Toledo, where I arrived in the summer of 2005, workers talked of passing job openings at the local auto plants down to their children, in a sort of chain migration into the middle class. Everyone saw how the flow was being choked off. The city had just over three hundred thousand people then, and about fifty thousand manufacturing jobs, but both the jobs and the population were declining. Those declines fed into a civic culture that was equal parts pride and resentment, with a strong dose of self-deprecation on top. The first question someone had asked me when I'd moved into town was why: Why would anyone move here? The next question was what school I'd gone to—meaning which high school. Meaning, did you grow up here and attend the same private Catholic school that my family did? McMinnville High School, I said, and the questioner shook his head. A better answer, like "St. John's" or "St. Francis," would have explained the first question, too.

The truth is, I moved to a declining industrial town for the politics. I had covered federal campaigns and the state legislature as a reporter in Denver, where I learned the value of chatting regularly with the state economists who worked in a basement office in the Capitol building and mining their spreadsheets for stories. (It yielded more scoops than you'd think.) I wanted a job in a crucial state for the 2008 presidential election, and I found one in Toledo. It had many charms. Housing prices were far more affordable than they were in Denver. When I visited I saw leafy neighborhoods with cute older homes, a brand-new downtown ballpark for a hallowed minor-league team, the Mud Hens, and a local political establishment that generated constant, absolutely wild news stories, like union officials blowing dues money at strip clubs, or a party chairman conning state officials into investing pension funds in his rare-coin business. The people I met were friendly and they worked hard.

The local economy was making all of them nervous.

Toledo boomed with the railroads in the late 1800s and soon became a hub for glass manufacturers. Other factories rose to join them, building scales and ships and, above all, cars. Its peak was arguably the 1920s, before the Great Depression landed the first of what would be many blows to the city's industrial base. More came in the seventies, the eighties, and even the nineties, as affluent white residents increasingly fled to the outlying suburbs and Fortune 500 companies packed up and left town. The 2001 recession, which was relatively light in comparison to what lay ahead, cost the city another tenth of its remaining factory jobs. By the middle of that decade, the city, and Ohio around it, was gripped by what you might call us-against-them economics. The city fought its suburbs for shopping-mall developments and new corporate headquarters. The state fought right-to-work states in the South, and its neighbor Indiana, for jobs. Everyone saw America in a zero-sum competition with the rest of the world, most notably Mexico but increasingly China.

The state line with Michigan was a short drive away, and Detroit lay another forty-five minutes beyond. The freeway heading north to the Motor City ran past one of Toledo's remaining jewels, a Jeep plant that had been scheduled to shut down before civic leaders—and a daily pressure campaign on the front pages of The Blade—succeeded in keeping it in town. Soon after moving in I needed a new car, and my editor gave me some advice, which sounded a lot like an order. Buy a Jeep, he said. One of the ones they make here. If you have to buy something else, make sure it's American. Under no circumstance was I to show up at a union hall or a political rally, representing the newspaper, driving a foreign car. I bought a Ford SUV. But most of the time when I raced around the state for stories, it was in a dark-green, company-owned, Toledo-made Jeep.

In April of 2006, that Jeep took me to Steubenville, at the eastern edge of the state, an area that had been losing about one thousand factory jobs a year. The economy wasn't the only thing candidates talked about there—George W. Bush had won Ohio just two years earlier by focusing heavily on national security and gay marriage—but it was the dominant topic. No one in this part of Ohio had to guess whether the economy was working for them. Their eyes and ears and neighbors told them it was not.

Along the Ohio River in that election cycle, there was still hope for a turnaround, largely because so many people remembered when everything was humming. You could see from the buildings in Steubenville that it used to be bigger and stronger and more important in the economic machinery of America than it was when I first encountered it. The city used to support a more vibrant middle class. It was the site of America's first woolen mill, built in the early 1800s. For much of its history, it was a hub for the steel and coal industries. Its decline was an early warning to factory workers around the state. Steel jobs started to fall away in Steubenville in the 1980s, and with them the population and condition of the town.

You could hear those memories from the people who came to question the politician on that April day. They'd had something, and they'd lost it, and they wanted to know why it went away. They still believed someone might help them get it back.

But things were only going to get worse. Much worse.

Two years later, in the midst of what was then the worst national recession in several generations, the county that includes Steubenville would break narrowly for Barack Obama, helping him win Ohio and the White House. On Obama's watch, the area lost more than one out of every ten of its jobs. Eight years later, the region stampeded to Donald Trump. He won with 65 percent, collecting the most raw votes of any presidential candidate in that county in nearly thirty years. His victory was powered by a combination of forces, including racial resentment and backlash to rapid social change, which Trump inflamed and harnessed to more powerful effect than any presidential candidate had since the segregationist George Wallace in 1968.

Underpinning his victory was the frustration that had built among white workers without a college degree—the men and women who live and work and suffer and seethe in communities like this all over America—from decades of economic decline and a seemingly endless parade of politicians pledging, and failing, to reverse it. Those workers have experienced, to paraphrase the populist pioneer Ross Perot, the great whooshing of *fifteen million* good-paying jobs that should have appeared in America, but did not, over the course of a decade. The economy has changed, and it has taken many of their jobs with it, and they are rightly angry.

Long before Trump escalatored onto the political scene in his eponymous tower in New York City, everyone in Ohio knew there was only one real question that a winning presidential candidate needed to answer: How will you bring the jobs back? It was the first thought you'd hear from a union boss in Youngstown, an autoworker outside Cleveland, or a steakhouse-fed consultant in Columbus. It was the first sentence of the stump speeches delivered by almost every candidate, from city council hopefuls to the men running for Senate. And you could see it—you couldn't miss it, really—on any drive across the state, on the turnpike or back roads, through cities and suburbs and especially the small towns along the river, the bombed-out ruins of what had been the world's greatest middle-class success story, now a wellspring for what would become the Trump movement.

Pennsylvania, Wisconsin, and Michigan were the shock states that tipped the presidency to Trump in November of 2016. Ohio was his hammer blow. He won it by eight points, he won nearly every county, and his opponents underestimated him. "Hillary Clinton is going to win Ohio," the state's lone Democratic statewide officeholder told me a little more than a month before the election, as we sat in a minor-league baseball park in Columbus. "Fairly easily." The misjudgment was all the wilder because that Democrat, a United States senator named Sherrod Brown, had built his career championing the aggrieved workers that a New York real estate developer was about to ride to victory.

No one saw Trump, or anyone like him, coming in the spring of 2006. Ohio's Republican candidates were pitching a traditional conservative blend of tax cuts and rollbacks of business regulation. Democrats criticized trade agreements they said had fattened corporate profits and left workers fighting for scraps.

Economic appeals were all the rage for politicians, particularly chal-
lengers. Democratic presidential candidate John Kerry made them repeatedly across the state in 2004, when he lost to Bush by two percentage
points. Kerry had promised a "fair playing field" in trade and told Ohioans, in a speech in Toledo during primary season, that "it's not hard to
see why so many people think they are working for the economy, but the
economy is not working for them." All the 2006 candidates offered some
version of that message: a promise to get the economy working for Ohio
workers again.

I was listening to one version of those promises, from the Democrat
who would go on to win the governor's race, on that sunny day in Steubenville, company Jeep parked nearby. But my attention was drifting. I
was deep into a multiday reporting swing, chasing candidates from the
state's northeast corner to its southern border, before cutting back toward
home through long stretches of farms and factories. I had heard a lot of
speeches on the trip already, and had conducted a lot of interviews, and
they were all bleeding together. My gaze wandered toward the economic
wreckage that lay up and down the street. What in the world happened
here? I wondered. The candidate was talking. Heads were nodding in the
crowd.

That boyhood question, about the guys I went to school with and
when they might get a better shake from the economy, came tumbling
back, fused with the realities of my new midwestern life. The candidate
had his answers—they all did—and, I realized, I didn't really buy any of
them.

From that realization came a crazy idea, which I would spend the next
several months pursuing in tandem with one of my *Blade* colleagues, Josh
Boak. Instead of just writing day after day about campaign sloganeering,
we decided to try to figure out some answers ourselves.

Let's pause for a moment to talk about the term "middle class." The
phrase means something different to everyone, which is where we should
start. The ranks of the self-reported middle class in America are large.
Somewhere between one-half and two-thirds of the country thinks of

itself that way, with the share growing larger in years when the economy is stronger, according to the Gallup polling organization. If you add in the people who call themselves "working class," you get to about nine out of every ten Americans, which is nearly everyone. Of the one-tenth of Americans who do not identify as middle or working class, most think of themselves as lower class, or poor. Almost no one thinks of themselves as rich, or at least will admit to pollsters that they do.

Economic statistics help us see the divide between groups of workers more precisely. They divide Americans into five groups, called "income quintiles." The top quintile includes the highest-earning 20 percent of households. The bottom quintile is the lowest-earning 20 percent. The 60 percent of households in the middle are what is sometimes referred to as the broad middle class. It's important to note that those quintiles don't march upward in even intervals, like the staircase in a two-story house. They're like a strange funhouse staircase, where the first four steps rise modestly, and the last one makes you reach up and jump just to climb up it. To get to the top quintile, you have to earn dramatically more than the group right below you.

The people in the top quintile, the richest 20 percent of Americans, earn as much between them every year as everyone in the bottom four quintiles combined. *One-fifth of the country earns more than half its income.* It wasn't always that way, and that's important to bear in mind as we explore what's gone wrong for the folks in the middle.

Even a strict income test of "middle-class" status is complicated by other factors. Geography, for one. A growing amount of America's economic activity is being concentrated in a handful of large metropolitan areas, which some economists call "superstar cities." They're places like San Francisco, Los Angeles, Austin, Chicago, and Manhattan. They attract big businesses, which demand highly skilled workers, who command high salaries and drive up the cost of living in the area for everyone. As a result, it's more expensive to live in America's most economically vibrant locales, which means it takes a lot more money to be a middle-income earner there than elsewhere. The median income—the middle of the middle class—in 2018 for a household in Yamhill County, Oregon, where

I was born, was just under $62,000 a year. In Santa Clara County, California, where I went to college, the median income that year was about $126,000. By that definition, you have to earn twice as much money to be middle class in Palo Alto than you do in McMinnville.

There's another gulf when it comes to race. White Americans earn, as a group, substantially more than nonwhites. So a minority worker can be counted as middle class in her or his racial group, but still be nowhere near middle class for the country as a whole. For non-Hispanic white households in America—the group I'm going to shorthand as "white" for the duration of this book—the income range that gets you into that broad middle class starts at about $30,000 and runs all the way up to about $140,000. For Hispanics, the range goes from $22,000 to about $100,000. For black Americans, the most economically disadvantaged racial group in the country, the broad middle-class cutoff starts at just under $16,000 and ends just below $90,000. The way the math works is this: a married pair of black workers can each put in forty hours a week, earning exactly the federal minimum wage of $7.25 an hour, and comfortably qualify as middle class among their fellow black households. Very few things unite our country across party, income, and racial lines today, but I've yet to talk to a worker who says earning minimum wage is enough to make you middle class.

Income is a useful tool for tracking middle-class progress, partly because it's one of the best-documented, longest-running economic data points that we have. It will come up again and again in these pages as a way of showing what's changed for American workers over time. But it's not the only measure and, in truth, probably not the best one. Researchers at the Brookings Institution have tallied a dozen different ways to define "middle class," all of them defensible. There is a whole subculture in Washington of people who argue over the "correct" definition of the middle class.

I like the "Game of Life" definition myself. I measure the size of the middle class by the number of Americans who can afford the basic economic security promised to them on the game board.

The Obama administration came up with a similar definition, minus the Milton Bradley product placement. It created a Middle Class Task

Force, chaired by Joe Biden, who was then the vice president, several months before the Great Recession ended. Like most pleasant-sounding initiatives in Washington, the task force produced almost no tangible improvements for middle-class families; neither did the Obama economy, until well into his second term. But it did produce a helpful version of what you might call a "consumption-based measure" of the middle class: a set of things that Americans need to be able to afford in order to feel economically secure. (It's not a partisan list; many of its goals, like home-ownership and retirement security, echoed policy priorities of President George W. Bush, a Republican, who preceded Obama.) "Middle-class families are defined by their aspirations more than their income," Biden's report said. It assumed that those aspirations included owning a home and a car; having health insurance; saving for retirement and for their children's college educations; and taking occasional family vacations. It wasn't a Monopoly list of luxuries. It was a Game of Life list of basic American comforts. A list that is increasingly unaffordable for the typical American worker.

The middle-class model that Ohio sold to the rest of America for decades was based on a similar list of economic security blankets, with the exception of money for college. Like the kids flocking to the woods in Oregon, you didn't need a degree to build a good-paying career in the Buckeye State. You just needed a job in a factory. Until those jobs started to vanish, and no one running the state knew why.

In the spring of my first full year in Ohio, shortly after my colleague and I decided to look for the economic answers that were eluding the state's political elite, I called a friend from college. He had gone on to study economics in a doctoral program at the Massachusetts Institute of Technology, one of the most prestigious departments in America. I asked him which economists could best help with our quest. He sent me to a friend at the Federal Reserve Bank of Cleveland, one of the twelve regional branches of America's central bank. The regional Fed banks all run their own research departments, which often use local economies as laboratories for learning about national trends in job creation, productivity, wages, and, in that oh-so-competitive way that so many people think about the economy, the differences that cause some places do better than others. A pair of researchers in Cleveland had recently completed such a study. It set out, immodestly, to be the definitive word on why some states grew faster than their peers over the longest time frame they could find good data on: seventy-five years of American capitalism.

Josh and I drove to Cleveland, ate in the Fed building's cafeteria, marveled at the marble columns in the lobby, talked at length with the economists, came home, and wrote up a proposal for our editor. It was dated May 18, 2006, and titled "What Happened to Ohio?" It started like this:

> There was a time when Ohio's factories hummed a little louder than the average American mill, a time when its economy grew a little faster, its people earned a little more money. That was 1969. It's been downhill since.

> Ohio today lags the nation in job growth, per-capita income, and nearly every measure of higher education—a chasm that widened permanently in the mid-1990s, when the dot-com wave that buoyed so much of the nation rolled right past Ohio without so much as a splash. The state lost 200,000 jobs in the last seven years, while adding population, as America gained 3.5 million jobs. Politicians blame a decline in American manufacturing and say the state must create "new generation" jobs in technology to pull from its slump.

> They're wrong. This fall, we need to show voters why. State and federal economic data reveal Ohio's decades-long economic slide for what it is: a set of failures by its leaders.

Our goal, we wrote in conclusion, was to force the candidates for Ohio's highest offices "to face the harsh reality of the state's economy and address it with bold solutions, not gimmicks or platitudes."

Our editors said yes, if we could handle the juggling. Josh would still need to cover county government elections. I needed to stay on the

Senate and gubernatorial races. To solve the puzzle of what had gone wrong for workers in Ohio, we were going to have to work a lot more ourselves.

Josh, like me, was a recent *Blade* arrival, a preacher's son and Princeton grad from Canton, Ohio, who was similarly consumed with solving the economic puzzle of his home state. He had risen fast at the paper in part because, in the midst of a developing political scandal that was wrapped up in shady financial transactions, he knew more than anyone else on the staff about hedge funds. We divided the tasks for what we knew would be a multipart series, juggling the research with our day jobs. We compiled gigabytes of spreadsheets and government reports. We interviewed business leaders, academics, more economists. We came to some pointed conclusions about what ailed the Ohio economy—about what had gone wrong in the state—and found human stories to illustrate them. We wrote on weekends and at night. My son was born that August; in the final days before we published in September, Josh and I would take turns at my kitchen table, one of us honing the draft on the laptop, the other holding the baby.

We published our stories six weeks before the election. They featured an octogenarian venture capitalist, a shuttered Huffy bike factory, the two Cleveland Fed economists, and, in the final installment, a pair of immigrant entrepreneurs, Ping Jia and Charu Ramanathan, who had come to Ohio to earn their doctorates, developed a novel new way of mapping the human heart, patented it, and started a company based on their ensuing invention. The state, our reporting had determined, suffered from a shortage of innovation, investment, and brainpower. It relied too heavily on government subsidies to businesses. Those subsidies were poorly targeted, and state officials weren't using the right measures to gauge their success, so it was hard for them to see where their efforts proved ineffective.

Most importantly, we concluded that Ohio had started sputtering long before most of the factories had shut down, because it had lost its innovative edge. The home of the Wright brothers, a longtime cradle for inventions and new business development, had fallen behind the curve over the course of half a century of nursing its incumbent businesses along. Policymakers were so busy counting "jobs created" by tax credits, and promising to bring back the young people who had moved out of the state, that they missed what should have been two blaring warnings about the direction of their economy. The first was that Ohio had tumbled down the ranks of the most innovative, industry-spawning states, as measured by patent production, which the Cleveland Fed economists had identified as the single best predictor of which states prospered more than others over seventy-five years of the American economy. The second was the state's inability to attract and retain the most valuable workers in some of the most innovative industries in the world, like medicine and technology: people with doctorates or other advanced degrees who were educated in the United States but born abroad. If policymakers wanted to get Ohio's economy humming again, we concluded, they should find ways to attract more highly skilled immigrants.

It's hard to imagine how we could have written anything more diametrically opposed to the campaign appeal Donald Trump brought to Ohio in 2016. Trump stampeded the state with promises of quick solutions and easy-to-blame villains. He told Ohioans it was not their fault that their economy had fallen behind. Bad trade deals killed factory jobs, he said. Those jobs, no matter how long they'd been gone, could come back. Immigrants weren't a solution; they were a big part of the problem.

His arguments bore no resemblance to what Josh and I had learned to be true about Ohio and its economy. But they played well with the white, working-class voters who had exhausted their patience with other politicians after subsisting on the economic equivalent of coffee and sugar packets through expansion and recession and what felt like a recovery in name only.

Those voters responded to Trump's insults of America's leaders and his assertions, without evidence, that foreign governments were flooding the United States with drugs and criminals. "Our politicians are stupid," he told an audience in Cleveland in August 2015 at a televised debate among Republican candidates. "And the Mexican government is much smarter, much sharper, much more cunning. And they send the bad ones over because they don't want to pay for them. They don't want to take care of them. Why should they when the stupid leaders of the United States will do it for them?"

Trump's pitch was simple and binary and exculpatory for workers. You didn't fail, he was saying. Someone did this to you. You may have lost, but you aren't the losers. "Our country is in serious trouble," he said in his closing statement at that Cleveland debate. "We don't win anymore. We don't beat China in trade. We don't beat Japan, with their millions and millions of cars coming into this country, in trade. We can't beat Mexico, at the border or in trade."

I saw Trump's arguments unfold in 2016 as a visitor to Ohio, while I was retracing the steps of what turned out to be my relatively short stint in the state. *The Blade* had been engulfed in labor tension in the fall of 2006, and an editor pulled me into his office one day shortly after my son was born in one of the great acts of kindness I have experienced. We might lock out the union, he told me. You need health care for your baby. We'd hate to lose you, but if I were you, I'd start looking for another job. A few months later, the *Chicago Tribune* hired me to join what was then a dozen-person bureau in Washington, D.C. I would return to Ohio in 2008 for the primaries and the general election, always focused on the economy, and each time I returned, I found voters growing more and more numb to politicians' promises of renewal. The state fell with the nation into recession. I had to short sell my house in Toledo for two-thirds of what I paid for it.

Obama won the state in the midst of financial crisis with a plateful of technocratic policies for escaping the recession and some tough talk on trade. During the primaries he told a crowd near Cleveland that "if we're honest with ourselves, we'll acknowledge that we can't stop globalization in its tracks and that some of these jobs aren't coming back." Then he went on to bash NAFTA. He promised to end tax breaks for companies that shipped jobs overseas. After his victory that November, Democrats were clobbered in Ohio's 2010 statewide elections, which allowed voters to vent their anger at the brutality of the recession and the state's feeble recovery from it. Obama won a more narrow reelection in 2012, but working-class white voters were already drifting away from him and his party in Ohio and other industrial states. By 2014, a typical family in Ohio and nationwide was still earning less income after adjusting for inflation than it had before the crisis hit.

As Donald Trump once again toyed with running for president, voters across the industrial states were looking for someone, anyone, to solve their frustrations. They were waiting for someone who would restore their place in the tale that white Americans have long told each other about the middle class. About the people and places that made it strong.

They were waiting for someone to bring their jobs back.

4

Southern California, 2013

THE JOBS ARE NOT COMING BACK

We'd like to give a special thanks to all those Americans who built those spacecraft. Who did the construction, design, the tests, and put their hearts and all their abilities into those craft. To those people, tonight we give a special thank you. And to all the other people that are watching and listening tonight, God bless you. Goodnight from Apollo 11.

—Neil Armstrong, July 23, 1969, on the
eve of splashing down on Earth

Bob Thompson still remembers the day of the landing, clear as a crater through a telescope. He recalled it for me from his office, a shrine to the Space Age with green shag carpeting. I had flown from Washington, D.C., to see him. Years after I left Ohio, I was still chasing the question of what it would take to bring back good jobs for the middle class. I'd decided to retrace the country's steps, to go back to the time before everything went wrong. I wanted to hear about Apollo and how it rocketed a young man with no college education straight into the middle class.

The landing was on a Sunday afternoon, Pacific time. Weather records note that the temperature had climbed into the eighties, and only a trace of rain had fallen that week. It was the sort of Southern California summer day Jan and Dean sang about, all blue skies and palm trees and short sleeves. Bob told me he spent it in a dark room with a thin crowd and a chipped bar and a black-and-white television hanging overhead, watching a hunk of metal, which once had passed through his little corner of a cavernous factory floor, twirl around the surface of the moon.

Bob worked nights, and he often drank in the afternoon at a bar called the EZ Inn. It's gone now, cleared for a freeway by men who cared more about efficiency than the sentimental attachments of America's industrial past. Bob still has a sign from the bar next door that sold pitchers of beer for two bucks and a quarter. He also has a batch of souvenirs from the factory, which was known as North American Rockwell when Bob and thousands of other workers fashioned the spacecraft that would fly on the mission known as Apollo 11.

On this particular afternoon, July 20, 1969, only a few people filled the bar. Bob isn't sure, but he thinks there might not have been anyone else there from the North American plant. They were mostly home with their families watching on color TV sets. For company, Bob had the EZ Inn's owner, Buzz, who was tending the bar himself that day. He was a rotund man, mopped in gray hair, who spent some of his off hours teaching Bob to play golf. Bob called him Buzzy. He served a lot of Budweiser in his place, on account of so many of the regulars being guys who worked at the Anheuser-Busch bottling plant up in Van Nuys, in the San Fernando Valley, north of downtown. The EZ Inn was south of downtown, almost halfway between Disneyland and Dodger Stadium, in a city named Downey. You might think of it as a rocket suburb.

At least you might have back then.

I flew to Downey because if we want to know how to revive the middle class, we need to understand how it boomed in the aftermath of World War II. There is a story white America has told itself about how and where that boom occurred. We need to start with it—with the classic white tale of the Golden Era for American workers—in order to fill in the parts it leaves out and correct the lies it tells us now.

Bob's story is a first corrective step, set not in the industrial heartland but in a sunny Southern California suburb, toasting its role in a national triumph.

Bob and Buzzy were drinking longneck Buds when Neil Armstrong and Buzz Aldrin broke orbit and guided their ship toward the surface of the moon. The lander was named *Eagle* and built by the Grumman Corporation in Bethpage, New York, on Long Island. It looked like a sort of camp stove you can buy now at an outdoor store, with fold-down metal feet and a spherical top. It detached from a conical command module named *Columbia*, piloted by an astronaut named Michael Collins, which was built in Southern California, at the North American plant in Downey. Armstrong stepped out of the lander and radioed back to mission control in Houston and a rapt audience of television viewers. That's one small step, he said, and in the bartender's eyes, Bob Thompson saw tears.

I never thought I would live to see this, Buzzy said. Bob agreed. He was much younger, in his mid-twenties, and there was a time when he never really thought he'd see it either. But now he had, right there in black and white over the bar, and his mind hurtled back through time and space to books he'd read and stories he'd heard. Back to something even more amazing, perhaps, than the achievement itself, for a young man who had grown and studied and worked in one town for nearly all his life.

Bob was thinking about the moon, humankind's constant and cyclical companion. All the heroes we've had in this world, he thought. Kings and queens and Jesus Christ himself. They all stared up at that moon. And when the time finally came for people to make the trip to that moon, nearly 240,000 miles from surface to surface, it started right here. In Downey, California. With a vehicle that Bob Thompson himself had helped assemble.

When America celebrated the half-century anniversary of the moon landing in 2019, Bob Thompson was seventy-seven years old and well into a second career as the chief caretaker of an industrial legacy that has all but vanished from Southern California. He is a white man, with shock-white stringy hair, a Santa Claus beard, and pinkish skin that has tanned but not browned in the California sunshine. He smiles wide, and he laughs, and like more than a few grandfathers in this country, his voice takes on a whimsical tone when he talks about something "neat." These days he tells stories about space to schoolchildren. They visit him in the green carpeted hut that is the Downey Historical Society, next door to a playground called Apollo Park. They ask him about the capsules and the shuttles and everything else the workers of the North American plant crafted for the United States government to blast into orbit and beyond. He tells them what their town was like when kids played street baseball and kick the can, before they ran the 105 freeway through his old neighborhood.

What young people do not ask about, but should, is how Bob came to have the sort of middle-class American career that so few of their parents have had. How he landed a good-paying job with union protections that helped keep him employed even when contracts were canceled and plants closed. How he saved up, bought a house, and retired with enough money to live comfortably and treat his grandkids to ice cream on Mondays, when he drives north to Altadena for what they all call "Pappy Days." And how he did it all on the back of a high school education, working mostly with his hands, with no need for college loans or advanced technical training.

So much of what ails the United States today is contained in the story of what cities like Downey lost when their factories closed, and how they've tried and failed to bring that all back, and what's happened to workers in the meantime. It is a tale that is told so often, by politicians and journalists and even economists, that you could very well think you know it and understand it and could recite it as easily as Neil Armstrong's famous first line when he stepped onto the Sea of Tranquility.

Neil Armstrong is a son of Ohio. But the story of the town that sent him and his fellow astronauts to the moon helps us see how the industrial Midwest does not hold a special claim on the American middle class. The middle class sprawls across the country, in big cities, small towns, and sleepy little suburbs. You are more likely to find a large middle class today in the Mountain West or along the coasts of Florida than in the sash of the heartland that includes Ohio, Michigan, and Wisconsin, according to an exhaustive mapping of middle-class concentration from researchers at the Brookings Institution.

The Midwest does not even enjoy a monopoly within the hallowed subset of middle-class jobs that deal in the hard daily work of making things. Pennsylvania steelworkers didn't build the great postwar manufacturing industry by themselves. You know California for Silicon Valley and Hollywood, but it is also the state with the most factory jobs in the country. The fastest percentage growth in factory jobs in Donald Trump's first three years in office did not come in Ohio or Michigan. It came in Nevada, thanks in large part to a mammoth Tesla plant that builds electric cars.

I went to Downey for the first time near the start of Barack Obama's second term, when the economy was still sputtering to make up the ground lost in the Great Recession and American workers were still waiting to see any signs of "recovery" in their paychecks. Downey embodied the decline of America's blue-collar, middle-class jobs base, in a corner of the country that most people don't picture when they think about factory closures. It was also—like the state of Ohio—a case study in how political leaders have so often erred in their attempts to bring back jobs over decades of trying.

The middle-class dream of the fifties and sixties and seventies in Southern California was strikingly similar to the one in Toledo or Steubenville: a house of your own, a car in the driveway. A more comfortable life for you than your parents had enjoyed, and the promise of an even better one for your children when they grew up. And at the center of it, a job that paid well, that offered protection against economic distress and security in retirement, which you could get without spending four or more years of your life earning a college degree.

In a very simplified way, the disappearance of that job—the straight-from-high-school, secure, upwardly mobile, middle-class job—is a wellspring of America's social, political, and economic turmoil today. Particularly for white workers.

Over the last several decades, the economy has roughed up workers who graduated from high school and did not go on to pursue further education. From 1979 to 2018, according to calculations by the Congressional Research Service, wages rose by 14.4 percent for a typical American college graduate with a bachelor's degree, after adjusting for inflation. For workers who earned no higher than a high school diploma, wages *fell*, by 12.3 percent. The gap between wages for a typical college grad and a typical high school grad, which economists call the "higher-education wage premium," nearly doubled.

Some of those losses came in the early years of the twenty-first century, at a time when the economy was growing but leaving many workers in the dust. Even before the financial crisis swept Wall Street and knocked the country into deep recession, the 2000s were on pace to be the worst decade for American job creation in the history of modern economic statistics, dating back to World War II. It ultimately took a decade and a half for the typical household's income, adjusted for inflation, to return to the heights it had reached in 2000. For some workers, the damage was even worse. In 2011, the Pew Research Center examined how the 2000s, which it dubbed a "lost decade" for the middle class, had treated people across ages, gender, race, and educational attainment. Pew identified a few so-called winners, the people whose income status went up between 2001 and 2011. They included senior citizens, white Americans as a whole, and adults who were married. The groups who had lost the most were adults who had never married and, at the very bottom of the list, men and women with a high school diploma only.

Pew also ran the comparison over forty years, from 1971 to 2011. Again, it found that the group that lost the most economic status was Americans with a high school diploma and no further degrees.

We are talking about a huge group, even amid our national obsession over sending children to college. About one in three American workers today did not complete more education after high school, according to Labor Department statistics. That's forty-six million people. Those workers earn far less on average than workers with college degrees. They also work less. In the late 1960s, nearly every working-age man in America who did not go to college either had a job or was looking for one, as measured by what economists call the "prime-age labor-force participation rate." By 2016, according to calculations from researchers at the Brookings Institution, that rate had fallen by more than 10 percentage points, which means that millions of men with high school diplomas who were in their working prime simply gave up on trying to get a job. For men who did not finish high school, the decline has been even sharper.

Explanations abound for why so many potential workers have quit on the American labor market, and why those who've stayed are faring so poorly in it relative to their more-educated countrymen. Downey illustrates one of the simplest and most powerful of them: so many of the good jobs that once nurtured those workers have gone away for good.

Bob Thompson's life story today sounds like something from an old movie. He was nine months old when his parents left the Midwest for the coast, on a delayed Steinbeckian search for jobs at the height of World War II. Francis and Erma Jean Thompson had met in Wisconsin, she a farmer's daughter, he the son of German immigrants who had settled in Chicago. (Francis's mother, Bob's grandmother, was born on the ship to America.) The Thompsons first found a trailer in North Long Beach, but in short order they settled in Downey. They were one of the earliest families to buy a newly built two-bedroom with an attached garage in a tract on the south end of town off Arrowhead Avenue. Erma Jean did not work outside the home. Francis was an electrician who contracted polio as a child. It weakened his muscles and made it difficult for him to play with other children. So he stayed inside, tinkering and teaching himself, and built a radio by the time he was twelve years old. The lingering effects of polio limited his ability to work strenuous jobs, but he caught on for a time doing electrical work at the Douglas Aircraft Company, which was building the B-17 Flying Fortress in Long Beach. He also did under-the-table work on the side, repairing radios and other devices for folks he met on the job. One of them, a military guy, paid Francis in pork: a ham and a square of bacon. He was carrying both slabs of meat in the car when he and his wife went to look at the model home in Downey.

Bob swears this next part is true. The salesman at the model home was so eager to get the young couple into one of his units that, having spied the food in the back of their car, he suggested a deal. They would give him the ham and the bacon. He would consider it a down payment on a $3,200 house. (In today's dollars, that would be around $50,000.) The Thompsons accepted. They agreed to make payments of $57 a month, they parted with the pork, and they had themselves a home.

Bob grew up in town, climbed through the public schools, and played his street baseball. The city built a school on a lot nearby, where Bob had often fished for crawdads with a line and a hook baited with bacon. In grade school, he would ride his bike home for lunch and eat tomato soup and a peanut butter sandwich with his mother. He watched an interstellar industry grow up around him. There was the Douglas plant in Long Beach, which was transitioning to rockets after supplying airplanes to the war machine with a workforce that was nearly half women. Howard Hughes was building missile systems in Glendale. Large-tract subdivisions were sprouting around the metro area to house factory workers and their families. The state had about 660,000 manufacturing workers in 1947, just after the war ended, according to the Public Policy Institute of California. By the mid-1970s, it had added a million more.

It was, as the great Joan Didion wrote in a 1993 *New Yorker* article about the city of Lakewood, which lay just down the road from Downey, "the perfect synergy of time and place, the seamless confluence of the Second World War and the Korean War and the G.I. Bill and the defense contracts that began to flood Southern California as the Cold War set in. Here on this raw acreage on the floodplain between the Los

Angeles and San Gabriel Rivers was where two powerfully conceived national interests, that of keeping the economic engine running and that
of creating an enlarged middle class, could be seen to converge."

The engine churned out a lot of middle-class houses in Downey, big
adobe split-levels with lush green lawns. Folks say the easiest way to tell
where the factory workers lived and where there managers lived was to
watch the driveways. Everyone got new cars, often Cadillacs. You could
tell the managers because they swapped theirs out for newer models more
frequently.

California's population was booming, and its middle class was growing
fast. It counted nine million residents in 1945. Within twenty years that
number had doubled. The typical family's income grew from $3,600 in
1950 to just under $11,000 in 1970—a near-doubling, after adjusting for
inflation.

The Thompsons weren't rich. But on a high-school-educated electrician's salary, they could afford to buy a home in a neighborhood where
today, even in the shadow of the freeway that smashed straight through
their little green lawn, houses sell for about $500,000 each. Paying for
one of those houses on an average worker's salary is unfathomable now.
Today, if a typical two-worker family in Los Angeles County saved
10 percent of its pretax income every year, it would need to wait fifteen
years to afford the down payment on a two-bedroom house on Air-
point Avenue like the one the Thompsons bought when they moved
to Downey. (There's no chance the bank would accept bacon.) Paying
the mortgage and property taxes would consume nearly half the family's
income. Food, health insurance, and taxes would take most of the rest.

Bob remembers days when there wasn't much to eat in the house, so
his mother would walk out to the family garden, uproot a potato or two,
and prepare a soup using the tuber and milk. He doesn't recall his father
talking much with him about his career or future when he was a boy, but
he could tell when he'd strayed off course in his old man's eyes. When
he was thirteen years old and trying desperately to be cool, Bob let a
neighbor, who was sixteen, give him a tattoo. The boy took a hot sewing
needle, wrapped thread around it, dipped it in blue ink, and wrote the

letters "B O B" between the knuckles of his left hand. Bob's father saw the marks that night and told his son to wash his hands. A few nights later he saw them again, and he realized what his son had done. His father hated it. School principals hated it. A future commanding officer would hate it, and so would the fathers of girls Bob took out on dates. High school students today ask him to tell the story of the tattoo when they visit the historical society. He always obliges. He has long since forgotten what the pain of the needle felt like. But he remembers his father's fury.

When Bob graduated high school in 1959, he had a diploma in one hand and those blue-ink letters on the other. He had no real marketable skills to speak of, and he knew it. "I kind of had little part-time jobs and so on," he told me, "and I could see that I wasn't really going anywhere." A representative for a certified public accounting school had encouraged him to enroll after he graduated high school. Bob's father was all for it—his own father, in Chicago, had been an accountant. Bob told him, "Nah, I don't want to go to school. I just want to . . . relax." He was washing dishes, going to parties, living at home, and paying his father seven dollars a week in rent. "I was spinning my wheels," he told me. So he joined the army, which got him to Germany and then to Fort Hamilton in New York, where he was discharged at the end of a three-year tour. He wasn't sure what to do next. He hadn't been to college or learned a trade. Only one place was home, and he went back to it, and his reward was what seems in America today like a bygone career path. A launchpad to the middle class.

By the time Bob returned to Downey after leaving the army, there was one place in town where everyone wanted to work. It was a company named North American Aviation, which a former Douglas engineer had taken over before the war and moved to Southern California from Maryland. North American built its Downey plant during the Truman administration. Workers at the plant built fighter planes for the war in Korea, helped develop California's first nuclear reactor, and designed guidance systems for ballistic missiles. An author named Russ Murray once called the plant "the Space Age's equivalent of Orville and Wilbur's bicycle shop." Shortly before Bob was discharged from the army, North American company officials turned their eyes, and their extensive experience bidding for government spending, to space. They won the Apollo program contract in 1961 and soon after ramped up to twenty-five thousand workers, including production grunts and engineers.

It took some time for Bob to catch on there, but he still remembers the day that he did. He was hired on August 4, 1965, in a union slot, for $2.59 an hour, which would be about $21 an hour today. The company would merge and grow and change names over the years, and Bob never left its orbit. His rise tracked with the plant's, which tracked with the California aerospace industry and the great American middle class. He could see it all coming, the day he landed that job. "I thought I was a king," he told me.

Bob had gotten married not long before he landed that job. He and his wife rented an apartment in Downey, and on some nights his mother-in-law and his father-in-law would come by to watch bullfights on their little black-and-white VHF television set. Bob decided he wanted to up-grade to the first color TV of his life. Something fit for a man in his new job. For a king.

"I went down to a place, that I know a guy I went to school with worked there, and told him, 'Sam, I want to buy a TV,'" Bob recalled. "I looked around and I bought one. I had to get it on credit of course. And so he said, 'Well, it'll take about two weeks to clear,' and all that. And I said okay." But then Bob mentioned, offhand, more than a little bit boastfully, "I am so glad I got my job at North American."

"You work there?" the clerk said.

"Oh yeah," Bob said.

"I'll bring it tonight," the man said, and suddenly the bullfights were coming through in color.

That's it? I asked, when Bob told me the story amidst the museum relics of the historical society. You didn't need to pass a credit check? Why?

"Well, because it was North American Aviation," Bob said. "You know, that was a big deal in town and, you know, with Apollo being built and so on. People in Downey were happy, you know, during those times."

At the time of the moon landing, the company had renamed itself North American Rockwell, following a merger, and it was hurtling toward more cosmic success. In 1972, Rockwell won the contract to start building a space shuttle. Downey was euphoric. One of the top engineers at the company celebrated by handing the keys to his pickup truck to a younger colleague, to whom he gave strict instructions: fill the truck bed with champagne and ice. He grabbed a second colleague and told him to call a nearby restaurant that was a favorite watering hole for workers at the factory. Tell them, he said, that Rockwell is taking over your place for the next twenty-four hours, at least.

The economy hiccuped a few times in the course of the next couple of decades, but the middle-class workers at the Downey plant never had to worry too much. They had a union, Local 87 of the United Auto Workers, which gave them a formalized version of what was essentially the corporate-worker contract of the postwar boom era. The deal was, sometimes contracts fell through or economic growth stalled out, and the company needed to lay off workers. But the layoffs never lasted. The union would find new slots for as many workers as possible. If your job vanished in Downey, maybe you ended up at the plant in Palmdale or Anaheim. The company would hire back anyone still out of a job, just as soon as the money came rolling back in.

Bob stuck with the company for more than forty years. In the beginning he ran blueprints and other deliveries from one end of the factory to the other, a job known as power trucker. Then he put in for a higher-paying gig, as a plastics fabricator. He didn't actually know anything about plastics, but he was interested, and the company was willing to train him. He got the job. When it died out, they made him a janitor. Later he was a stock clerk. Sometimes he'd have a long-enough spell of layoffs that he'd paint houses or factories to get by, but he was still able to save up and afford a house, just like his parents had. Always he ended up back in a North American plant. He sprayed foam on the Apollo capsule, and also on a space shuttle, his own small steps to help humans reach the stars.

When he retired in 2007, Bob was making what would be about thirty-three dollars an hour today, which is almost exactly the median income for Downey, California. He had accumulated a real, honest-to-God pension, which is such a foreign concept to young people now that none of the members of the high school history club ever think to ask him about it.

In the thick of his career, Bob was living a widely shared, middle-class California Dream. At the end, he was an outlier. A lucky one.

The aerospace industry peaked in Los Angeles County around 1990, when it employed nearly two hundred thousand people. The median household income in the county had more than doubled from 1950, after adjusting for inflation. Then the Berlin Wall fell, and so did the rocket suburbs. America cut back on defense spending. More than a hundred thousand Los Angeles County aerospace workers lost their jobs. Median income dove and did not recover. The plant that cradled Bob's career bled workers and was bought by a rival. It closed in 1999. "It was a sad day," Bob told me. "I mean a lot of people were angry, angry, angry because the jobs were gone. And there was no real other place to go."

When the jobs left, civic leaders in Downey made a bad bet. Politicians were making similar miscalculations all across the country, in city halls and state capitals, all the way up to the White House. Everyone thought they could bring an equal number of good factory jobs back. The city manager vowed not to let just any business take over the land that the abandoned North American plant sat on. Downey, he said, would hold out for a company that would create good middle-class jobs, on par with what the factory workers had earned. Those jobs were worth waiting for. And that is exactly what city officials did: they waited, and waited, and waited, to no avail, but in good company.

In the years after the factory closed, leaving vacant a seventy-seven-acre dirt plot where once stood the home of tens of thousands of blue-collar jobs, American manufacturing employment plummeted. The first half of the opening decade of the twenty-first century saw the nation lose three million factory jobs, battering workers like Bob from coast to coast. President Trump touts the creation of manufacturing jobs on his watch before the pandemic, but at the start of his fourth year in office, the share of Americans employed in factories had not budged. It remained at its lowest level, as recorded by modern economic statistics.

Factory workers had plenty of company in their misery. Millions of administrative assistants, customer service representatives, and other Americans who once held what economists call "middle-skill" positions saw their jobs disappear in the rush to a globalized, digitized economy, in which investment flowed more freely across borders and so many American workers found their services no longer needed.

Middle-skill jobs require technique and training, and they pay better than the jobs that economists often call "low skill," like janitorial work. (It is a standing feature of our economy, and of capitalism in general, that many of the jobs that are paid the least, and are regarded least highly by society, are in fact some of the most difficult to perform on a daily basis.) In the recoveries from the recessions of 1991, 2001, and 2008, and even across many of the periods of economic expansion between those recessions, the American economy shed millions of middle-skill jobs. It failed to create the millions more that history had suggested it would.

This was the trend that David Autor, an economist at the Massachusetts Institute of Technology, would come to call the "hollowing out" of middle-skill employment. It was not unique to factory workers, nor to the United States. It is a feature of an increasingly interconnected economy, across Europe, Japan, and other rich nations, a byproduct of expanded trade with poorer developing countries and improved technology that made American factories and office buildings more efficient. It is almost exactly what economic theory predicted would happen, though its swiftness and severity has managed to take a lot of politicians, and even some economists, by surprise over the last forty years.

The loss of those jobs was a driving factor in the wage declines for large portions of the American workforce, particularly men without college degrees, and in the stagnation of income for the typical American family over the course of more than a decade. It gutted factory towns like Steubenville and Toledo, of course, as well as Downey. It left millions of Americans—and wide swaths of land in the United States—void of economic opportunity.

That sort of disruption has happened before, but with very different aftershocks. At other points in American history, most notably the great wave of industrialization that drove workers from farms to factories at the turn of the twentieth century, technology and other forces have wiped entire occupations off the face of the economy. Workers were displaced, but they recovered. New jobs appeared to employ them—and often they paid better and made better use of the workers' talents. What has been different this time, in the great letdown after the great postwar boom, is that better jobs have largely not appeared.

So why is that? Why hasn't anyone found a better, more productive use for the talents of so many middle-skill workers?

The answer is not "Government didn't try." Politicians at every level have thrown incentives at companies, in an expensive and largely failed effort to attract the next wave of middle-class jobs. Their race to the bottom has hurt worker pay. There aren't just millions fewer factory jobs now than there used to be; the remaining factory jobs have migrated. They're much less likely to be union jobs now, and they no longer pay better, as a whole, than service-sector jobs. The drive to please companies has drained workers of bargaining power. Strong economic growth and low unemployment in the years before COVID-19 yielded much weaker wage growth than America saw during a comparable time in the late 1990s.

The endless wait for new and better jobs, for the workers who lost them, has been particularly torturous in Downey.

City leaders tried and failed, again and again, to attract companies that paid well to the site of the old Rockwell plant. There was going to be an electric golf cart manufacturer, but that plan fell through. There was a movie studio, which actually did set up shop for a time and even filmed a couple of blockbusters, but it didn't employ many locals, and it folded fairly quickly. They thought about building houses on the site, but they didn't. They carved out part of the block for a new Kaiser hospital, and another part for some shops. But they still held out hope for the main building of the old plant. A few years after Bob retired from North American, the only people left working at the shuttered Downey factory were a couple of historians, cataloguing its aerospace past. Like a family inventorying its home with a video camera for insurance purposes right before a big storm hits.

There was a glimmer of hope in 2010. Late in May, the city council called a special afternoon meeting. They had reached what they thought was a deal in principle with Tesla and its president, Elon Musk, to start cranking out electric roadsters in the old space factory. They'd drafted a 143-page lease and landed a multimillion-dollar federal loan to modernize the facilities, with a goal of being the world's lowest-emission car factory. They were planning a press conference. They thought it would bring a couple thousand jobs. It wasn't on the same scale as the North American plant, but it was something.

They'd been played by a savvy tech company, which cut a better deal behind Downey's back. A reporter delivered the news in a call from Sacramento. Tesla was planning a news conference later that day to announce that it was going to open a factory in the Bay Area. Wages were going to start at sixteen dollars an hour, plus benefits. Downey was furious. And it was completely out of options.

City officials decided they couldn't wait any more. They knocked down the factory and leased the land to a developer. The long wait for good new jobs ended, in the most modern American way imaginable, with another shopping center. In Downey today, "We have a lot of restaurants," Bob told me, when the project was just getting underway. "There's a lot of minimum wage. People take those jobs."

Minimum wage in California, in 2019, was twelve dollars an hour. In the stores that now sit on the graves of moon landers, young men and women have to work nearly twice as long to earn as much as Bob did fifty years ago. I drove through the shopping center in the spring of 2019 before meeting up with Bob for another interview. It had sprouted every chain retailer and restaurant you could imagine: Walmart, Home Goods, Five Guys, Panera. My visit there occurred a few months before the fiftieth anniversary of the moon landing, and along a road named Apollo Way, on a fence that appeared to shield cars from the sight of ongoing construction, signs proclaimed a set of cheesy, space-themed slogans, apparently for condominiums. "Walk-in space" and "closet space" and "we have liftoff."

There were also, in the booths of the restaurants and the aisles of the stores, signs of a middle class that had grown up organically in Downey, without government planning or a large industrial employer in place of the Rockwell plant. An example of what politicians and radio hosts and powerful white men usually leave out when they tell middle-class fables: a thriving, professional class of Latino workers. Downey's population is now almost three-quarters Hispanic or Latino, according to the Census Bureau. Its median income is higher than the nation's. Many of those residents work in service industries, and they have quietly worked their way into the middle class.

In the classic white telling of the birth of the great American middle class, the heroes were usually white and usually men. They were usually hearty midwesterners. They worked with their hands in factories when the factories still existed. As the politicians like to say, they worked hard and they played by the rules, until some people changed the rules and rigged the game against them.

The rule changers, the villains of those old tales, were frequently not white and often not American. Japanese carmakers, Mexican poultry pluckers, Chinese factories churning out shoes and toys and televisions. They all conspired to gut the heartland and kick away the ladder that Bob and so many white men like him climbed into the middle class.

This is a lie, and it has helped scorch the middle class—a lie that projects working America as white and male and under siege from outsiders. A lie sold by powerful men, in order to keep their hold on the nation's economy and government.

For many Americans, their collective national memory has narrowed the middle-class story, left big parts out, clung to a limited picture of who and what built the economy that lifted so many people, through hard work, to a comfortable life with a fulfilling job. Critical players are minimized or left out entirely. The true villains—to the extent they exist—rarely make an appearance. The maps are off, the battle lines are wrong.

Left uncorrected, that story can turn corrosive, dehumanizing, and dangerous.

Understanding what happened to the middle class, and where to find the trailhead for the route to reviving it, requires spending what might seem like an uncomfortable amount of time with this thought: the middle class is broader and more diverse than many Americans have been led to believe.

It requires spending time in the tobacco country of North Carolina, with a black worker clinging to the middle class that his parents helped build.

5

Winston-Salem, 2013

WORKING HARDER, FALLING BEHIND

Ed Green was ambling through the concourse on the last day of the season as the North Carolina sun dropped behind home plate. It was a warm night in what was once called tobacco and textile country, cooling off from the mid-eighties high of a clear day. Ed was in short sleeves, a purple polo with a white T-shirt peeking out from underneath. It was the final breath of August, a Friday evening, and I had driven more than three hundred miles to watch minor-league baseball with a boy who had just turned seven years old. We were there for the game, but we were mostly there to see Ed. He made his way toward us, six-foot-four and slightly balding, twelve hours into his work-day with a few still to go. He shook our hands. Within a few minutes he was telling my son why it's so hard to scrub spilled Pepsi off concrete.

A few innings earlier, we had watched Ed walk from the grandstand at BB&T Stadium, the fifty-five-hundred-seat home of the Winston-Salem

Dash, to the green sweep of the playing field below. Ed ran the janitorial crew at the stadium. He had just finished sweeping peanut shells and was on his way up to the luxury boxes to empty the trash. Fans in the boxes paid as much as forty-two dollars each for a seat and all the hot dogs, nachos, and beer they could put away—for a game in which almost none of the players would find their way to the Major League. On his way up, Ed had been diverted. A radio crackled from his utility belt, and the voice of his boss floated over it. It was the middle of the game, and Ed was needed down on the field. He didn't hesitate or complain. He headed straight there. We watched him step onto the grass.

The team had a surprise waiting for him along the first-base line. As players warmed up for the bottom half of the fifth inning, one of the Dash executives presented Ed with an award: Employee of the Year. He was there every night, scrubbing soda from the concourse, picking up peanuts and hamburger wrappers—keeping the park, which had been open for only three years, shining like it was new. And as his reward at season's end, Ed earned a brief ovation from the sellout crowd, a handshake from the team president, and a fifty dollar gift card from the bank that the ballpark was named for. When I heard that from the stands— only fifty dollars!—I nearly spit up my microbrew. But Ed just thanked the man, and then he walked back upstairs. The game was tied 2–2. In the luxury boxes, the trash was still piling up.

Cleaning up for baseball fans wasn't even Ed's primary job—that was on a highway crew for the state of North Carolina. This was his second job. Actually, one of several second jobs, which rotated through the year as the sports seasons changed. Baseball janitor in the spring and summer. Wake Forest football usher in the fall, basketball usher in the winter. Church handyman all year round. That's a lot of work, I said to him, when we shook hands on the concourse, after he'd won the award and dumped the luxury-suite garbage. His smile just grew. "Gotta pay the bills," he said.

Ed Green used to work a middle-class, union job in a big city. When I met him, he was hanging on to a middle-class life—by working two jobs, full-time, all week. Ed never slacked off or got himself fired; like millions of other American workers who share his plight, he never did anything wrong. He worked really hard. He played by the rules. He still does.

It's the American economy that broke the rules—or at least broke its compact with workers like Ed. He was less than twenty years younger than Bob Thompson, but that generation gap was a chasm.

Ed told us his story on the walkway behind first base, between innings. He would fill it in later, in progressively longer conversations, but we could hear, even in the first summary, just how swiftly the American economy had stuck its knives in Ed. One day he was driving a bus for the public transit authority in New York City, earning nearly $70,000 a year, which would be six figures in today's dollars. Then his mom got sick with cancer, and he moved back to her ancestral home, in North Carolina, where she had relocated years earlier, to care for her. When he first moved, he looked for driving jobs. It was what he knew—what he was good at. He tried a bunch of different ones, none of which paid anything close to what he had left behind in New York. Finally, he caught on with the state, driving trucks and fixing roads. "I figured after twenty years driving a bus," he told me, "I could try something new. I was young enough to try something new. It's physically demanding, but, you know, I'm used to working hard. So it's not that hard for me."

In order to make ends meet and send his six children to college, Ed began logging nearly eighty hours a week on the job. He became a pronounced example of a decades-long trend in the United States. Today, middle-class American families work harder but earn less money than they did in 1973. Some politicians and economists—like Michael R. Strain of the American Enterprise Institute, the author of *The American Dream Is Not Dead*—will tell you that the crisis of the American worker is largely a myth. That's wrong from every possible angle, starting with this one: those folks, the ones who deny the struggles of the middle class, never tell you that families have to work longer and harder now just to earn less than their parents did.

Before meeting Ed, I had been talking to economists about trends for American workers—how much they earned, how much they worked—and honing a description of what I have come to see as the "devaluing" of millions of Americans over the course of the last quarter century. I had met a lot of workers who embodied that trend, but I was hoping to find one in the South, away from the familiar stories of the industrial Midwest. I made a connection that led me to the ball club in Winston-Salem. I've got a guy, the man at the Dash told me. I made plans to drive down and see Ed.

It was the summer of 2013, the early days of Barack Obama's second term as president and several years into what remained an anemic recovery from the country's worst recession since the breadlines and Hoovervilles of the Great Depression. The typical American worker was still earning less than she or he had in the late 1980s.

The brutality of the financial crisis and its aftermath has obscured, in retrospect, just how lousy the preceding decade was for American workers. Even before the crisis hit, the 2000s had produced the slowest job growth, in percentage terms, of any decade since the 1930s. From January 2000 through the eve of the crisis, in late 2007, the country shed a fifth of its manufacturing jobs—more than 3.5 million of them. North Carolina lost nearly a third of its factory jobs in that time. The recession made it worse: by the summer of 2013, there were almost 400,000 fewer North Carolinians working in factories than there had been two decades before. The share of the state's workers who held manufacturing jobs had been cut in half.

Factory jobs had long been a route to the middle class in North Carolina, as they were in Ohio, California, and across the country. They didn't pay as well as the more heavily unionized manufacturing jobs of the industrial Midwest, but they still paid well above the state's minimum wage. Their disappearance practically overnight eroded the state's middle class. So did the loss of other middle-skill jobs—the ones the economist David Autor pinpointed in his research on the "hollowing out" of the American labor market—like clerical work and handling customer complaints in large call centers. North Carolina's median income, which is the amount that a typical household earns in a year, fell by 10 percent in the 2000s, after adjusting for inflation. In Forsyth County, which includes Winston-Salem, it fell by 20 percent.

The hollowing out was especially devastating for workers like Ed Green who never graduated from college. Autor unpacked that phenomenon in 2019, in a lecture to the largest and most prestigious annual gathering of economists in the United States, using somewhat technical terms that were nevertheless blunt for an economist. "In broad strokes," he wrote, in a copy of the speech that was published later that year, "the work performed by college adults has changed little over four decades. While they perform fewer middle-skill jobs than four decades earlier, this contraction has been modest, and it has been substantially offset by their upward movement in the occupational hierarchy. Among non-college workers, conversely, *polarization has exerted pressure almost exclusively downward*: Almost all occupational change among non-college workers reflects a movement from the middle toward the bottom of the occupational distribution." (The italics are mine.) Autor concluded the thought by saying that changes in the economy have not just been transformational; they've been "deskilling," which is to say devaluing. These changes have reduced the number and type of jobs that are the best fit for less-educated workers, which means those workers are now earning less than they would have.

Here is what that devaluing looked like for Ed Green. When he moved to North Carolina, he had a reasonable expectation of being able to find a job that made good use of his skills as a worker, whether that was driving or lifting heavy things or working with his hands. He arrived just as the state's manufacturing sector was falling off a cliff. Every day, more laid-off factory workers competed for the few job openings left in the industry. He caught on in a battery plant, making twelve dollars an hour, which was a little more than a third of what he made driving the New York City bus. "It didn't pay enough," he explained in our first interview at the ballpark, which lasted no more than a full inning, because he had too much work to finish to chat for very long. So he moved on to the state transportation department, earning a slight raise to thirteen dollars an hour. And he started looking for more work. Soon, he was stacking extra jobs onto his day job. He knew that if no single job would pay him a middle-class wage, he would need to work extraordinary hours to compensate. "I feel comfortable working," he said. "That's the way my parents raised me—work hard."

We had left Northern Virginia midmorning, in order to hit Winston-Salem in time for the evening game. By the time my son climbed into the car, Ed had been working almost half a typical workday on the highway crew, starting at six thirty in the morning. When that shift ended, he changed uniforms in the transportation department locker room, then drove over to the ballpark. He wouldn't finish until nearly midnight, well after my son had fallen asleep on the short drive to our motel.

Ed was born in Manhattan in 1960, at the tail end of the baby boom generation. Raised in Queens, a Mets fan. ("Somebody has to be," he said.) His father always worked two jobs. Ed and his sister worked, too, from an early age. After high school he'd gone to a technical college for a couple of years, seeking a computer degree, but like so many men of his generation, he'd fallen out before he graduated. "My plan was to go back to school," he said, "but then I started having kids."

He had three of his own, marrying and divorcing twice in the process. His third wife, Kimberly, also had three children. He called all six of them his kids, and he helped to put them through college. When we first talked, he was still paying some of the tuition for his youngest, who was finishing up at a state university down the road. His wife worked full-time as a social worker, in a job that was relatively low paying. Between the two of them, he estimated, they probably worked 110 to 120 hours a week.

Ed works more than almost anyone I know; statistically, he works much more than the typical American. But his family's experience, of picking up more hours just to tread water economically, mirrors what's happened for families across the American workforce in recent decades.

Let's step back for a moment. I need to tell you about one of the more infuriating and pedantic debates in economic policy over the last decade: the middle-class stagnation wars.

Populist American politicians have long appealed to working-class voters by telling them they aren't being paid enough, particularly in comparison with the rich (or, in the case of a certain brand of populist, when compared with "undeserving" poor people). It is in many ways an impossible argument to refute: so long as some workers earn more than others, politicians will be able to tell the lower-paid group that they're being shortchanged. And yet, polling suggests that very few Americans agree with the idea that everyone should earn exactly the same wage in the United States. So we are left, in every political era, to debate a simple but powder-keg question: Which workers are being shortchanged, and by how much?

As long as we have good economic data—reliable, reportable evidence of who's earning what in the American economy—we should also be able to construct a pretty good answer to that question. We have a lot of it, stretching back decades and, in some cases, more than a century. Tax records tell us how much income individuals reported to the government in a particular year. Census records pinpoint what a typical person earned, or a typical family, or a typical group of people who choose to live together, which statisticians call a "household." Other government surveys show us what companies paid in wages, or how much they paid for worker benefits like health insurance coverage. We can trace tax rates, revenue collections, and the value of what economists call "transfer payments," including health benefits like Medicare, retirement payments like Social Security, and aid to the poor like food stamps.

There are so many data points that almost anyone with a facility for numbers can shape them to construct whatever story they'd like to tell about who earns what in America and how fair that is. Since the turn of the century, as the economy sputtered for working people and policymakers struggled to explain why, a cottage industry has sprung up in telling stories with numbers about the middle class. There are people who will tell you it is dead, and there are people who will tell you it has never been better off, and they all come in wielding stats and charts to support their arguments. They argue about the best ways to measure changes in price levels over time. They argue about the right group to track if you're measuring middle-class health, whether to adjust for how many children a typical worker has, and even about what really counts as "income." (Should we count just what shows up in your paycheck? What about taxes? Or Social Security payments? Or a market value of the health care benefits you may or may not ever use?)

I'm going to spare you the intricacies of the arguments. Broadly speaking, there are two things you need to know. The first is that in many cases, the competing sides are stacking the numbers not as an effort to learn what's really happening to workers, but instead to justify the economic policies they would like to see government officials adopt. People who want to make it easier to form and join labor unions tend to favor the numbers that show middle-class incomes stagnating as union membership fell. People who want to keep tax rates low for businesses, investors, and high-earning individuals tend to favor the numbers that show that the middle class, after a lot of adjustments, is healthier today than it ever has been. You can see why the first group would highlight the numbers that show the worst performance for the middle class over the last several decades—for example, the finding by the French economists Emmanuel Saez and Thomas Piketty that, from 1979 to 2014, middle-class incomes in the United States did not grow at all, after accounting for inflation. You can also see why the second group would highlight numbers that look much better, such as a recent study showing that middle-class incomes actually rose by 40 percent from 1979 to 2014. (That study, mind-blowingly enough, was also by Saez and Piketty, along with another French economist, Gabriel Zucman. They used an entirely different data source than they had used in their previous study. You see how this can be confusing.)

But the second and far more important thing to know about these debates is that nearly every serious study, regardless of methodology, confirms a devastating story about the middle class since the 1970s. Which is to say, they all show the American economy delivering far less for middle-class workers than it used to, and far less than those workers had grown to expect in the years after World War II. None of them show the middle class bringing home a fair share of the economy's growth in that time.

Whether you count just worker salaries, or salaries plus benefits, or salaries plus benefits minus taxes plus aid from the government, the story remains the same: working-class Americans haven't seen their earnings grow like they used to, and they haven't seen them grow in proportion with the more-than-doubling of the United States economy.

The disappointment has become particularly acute since the turn of the century. The late 1990s were, briefly and gloriously, a driver of middle-class prosperity that rivaled the postwar boom. Median household income was soaring—and then the tech bubble burst, and America fell into recession. Afterward, incomes started to grow again, but slower than they had before. They fell again during the financial crisis and kept slipping for the early years of the recovery, before finally revving up again—but still, at the end of 2019, not growing nearly as fast as they had in the nineties or the Golden Era after World War II. Then COVID-19 hit.

It all came at a huge cost to the middle class. If incomes had just kept rising throughout the twenty-first century at the same pace as they did in the 1990s, a typical American household would have earned 50 percent more in 2018 than it actually did.

By our Game of Life metric, the trend looks even worse. Compared with the economy in 1999, millions fewer Americans today can afford the middle-class security blanket of a house, car, health insurance, college for their kids, and saving for retirement. For example, there were three million fewer homeowners of prime working age in 2019 than there would have been if America had maintained its 1999 levels of homeownership, according to the Census Bureau. This shift is partly obscured by inflation statistics, which capture changes in all the prices across the economy, not just the essentials of middle-class security. In the last few decades, overall inflation has been relatively tame compared to its rapid growth in the 1970s. That's the product of two big price trends canceling each other out. Housing, education, and health care have all grown much more expensive. Electronics and clothing have become much less expensive.

In effect, the economy gave middle-class Americans a trade. They got cheaper consumer goods. They got more access to entertainment and personal communication (a fact some researchers in the workers-are-fine crowd love to tout—*if things are so bad, how do poor people have smart phones and flat screen TVs?*). They got a better variety of seasonal produce in the grocery store and no real need to ever mend their own socks. And in exchange, it got harder for them to buy a house, see a doctor, and send their children to college, even as the economy increasingly demanded a college degree in order to earn a living wage.

Which brings us back to Ed Green and the inescapable truth for the crowd that tries to argue that the middle class is doing just fine: any income gains middle-class parents have enjoyed in recent decades are the product not of rising pay but of more work. Researchers at the Brookings Institution laid it out in 2011, in a chart I had in the back of my mind as I drove down to meet Ed for the second time. Median earnings for a two-parent family were up 23 percent over the last thirty-five years, the researchers wrote. But median hours were up even more—26 percent. In three and a half decades, American families had cranked up their time on the job, and their reward was earning less for every hour they worked.

My second trip to Winston-Salem took place in early December, when Ed's second job had changed from baseball to Wake Forest football and then basketball. A colleague and I met Ed on a bleak morning to tag along with his highway crew on a day that was too cold for paving work. Assignments change day to day this time of year, he told us. On that Tuesday, the workers were slowly canvassing Interstate 40 as it ran toward Winston-Salem from the east. They grabbed branches and brush from the side of the road and fed them into a wood chipper. Sometimes they sliced up large chunks with chainsaws. They cleared the branches and loaded the chipper and didn't stop to watch the sawdust pile up.

The work was plodding and dangerous and loud. Ed told us his ears rang at the end of each day. He and his colleagues watched each other's backs as they bent to lift debris into the chipper. They listened for the sound of brakes squealing on the highway or tires crunching along the rough edges at the side of the road. If you hear those things, he told us, you don't look back to see what's coming. You run as fast as you can for the trees.

Ed left the house at six thirty a.m. to arrive on time for his seven a.m. shift. He packed a peanut-butter-and-jelly sandwich to eat on his half-hour lunch break. By the time the shift ended at three p.m., he was beat. He said summers were worse, fighting the ninety-degree heat radiating off the pavement and trying to stay hydrated. At least, he joked, the grind kept him in shape. "Doing this type of work, you don't have to go to the gym very often."

After work he showered and discarded his jeans, work boots, orange vest, and ski cap. He changed into dark slacks, high-top dress shoes, a polo shirt, and a gold windbreaker with the logo of Wake Forest, an elite private college that plays in one of the top basketball conferences in the country. He was on tap to usher at the game that night and the next night, a Wednesday. He helped people find their seats and kept the court secure from any overzealous students who might try to rush it. Thursday night, he was scheduled to spend two or three hours cleaning rooms at his church. Friday, he said, he only had his day job for a change. He counted his hours for the week, and they came to about seventy, all jobs included.

He was needed at the arena by five thirty for a game that started at seven. He walked around, chatting with staff and fans, a headset connecting him to his colleagues in security. A while before tip-off he was able to take a quick break, to sit in a chair for the first time in Lord knows how long.

He told us about how he got by even though he earned so much less in his main job than he had driving the bus in New York. He said that when you're looking for a job that pays twenty-five dollars an hour, and you can find only one that pays thirteen dollars, well, an eight-dollar-per-hour supplement can help to close the gap. "This is normal for this area," he said. "You just have to learn to cut back a lot, eat a lot of peanut butter and jelly." He said the factory jobs that still existed in the area came with a catch: variable hours. "A lot of those jobs are seasonal—you get laid off a lot. If you just want to constantly work, you have to take a lower-paying job. I could take a job in a factory making twenty dollars an hour, but if it dries up I get laid off half the year. So you have to pick your poison."

He told us there was, in his view, "no more middle class" in America. Either you have a lot of money, he said, "or you're scraping by. The middle class used to be higher double figures. But now, if you're not mak-ing $100,000 or $200,000 a year—that's what's considered middle class."

Other workers on the highway crew had it worse than he did, he said. "Leaving out all my day jobs, I'm not even the oldest. We have people that retired from good jobs, and had good incomes, that still have to work to make it. We have guys well into their sixties who still need to work. That's just how times are now."

Are you tired?

"It's a lot," he said, "but I'm just used to it."

How do you spend your leisure time?

"I don't have too much leisure time."

He told us about his health problems: type-2 diabetes, high blood pressure, cataracts, a stroke, a heart stent. Twice he'd had to go to urgent care from the baseball stadium. He'd had prostate cancer, and for that he underwent radiation five times a week for four months. Throughout the course of treatment, he never missed a day of work. In all the time I've since spent with Ed, he's never once complained about his health or about how much he works. Years after that interview in the arena, Ed's son, Jordan, told me that his father had not mentioned at the time of his treatment that he had been diagnosed with cancer.

Near the end of our visit with him that December, I asked Ed about the first day I'd met him, at the ballpark, when he'd won Employee of the Year. He told me about walking upstairs to dump the trash right after shaking his boss's hand on the field. I asked him what he'd done with the fifty dollar gift card. He told me he'd used it to buy gas for his car so he could take his grandkids to the beach for a weekend.

He asked how my son, Max, was doing. I thanked him again for let-ting a seven-year-old tag along for the interview. It was a bonding trip, at a time when my son's mother and I were splitting up, when he was still at an age when it was exciting to see his dad work. I told Ed how much Max had loved the experience of the park—the red and yellow lights of a car-ousel in center field, the glee of running the bases with other kids after the game had ended. He'd ordered a "Superman" ice cream—a wild mix of blue, red, and yellow served in a black helmet for a cup. "Write that in the story," my son had said. He grinned, a rainbow of sugar dripping from his lower lip to his chin. "I like this stadium," he said. "Who are we cheering for?"

By the end of the night, which finished in a loss for the home team, we were both cheering for Ed. My son reminded me not to spill soda, because Ed had said it was so hard to scrub from the concrete. There was a fireworks show to celebrate the end of the season, and though it was well past Max's bedtime, we stayed for it, our bodies shaking in the thunder blasts of the display, as though a battalion of sprites were shelling the stadium. Ed later told me he'd paused to watch the fireworks, too. Then he'd walked into the outfield, leaned over, and begun picking spent shells out of the grass. The lights dimmed in the outfield, and the night fell around us—a white man and his son leaving the stadium, and a black man lingering behind to clean up after them.

6

Winston-Salem to Queens, 1960

TORCHING THE BLOCKADES

There is great and dangerous power in narrative storytelling, in deciding what *not* to show to your audience. What you leave out of a story can matter more than what you leave in. Some of those omissions are deliberate, the act of a writer building drama and driving the reader to a conclusion. Some are reflexive, almost involuntary habits built by decades of following other writers who were themselves meeting the expectations that readers had been trained to bring to every story. It can be jarring when a writer breaks with those conventions. Usually, for example, news outlets don't tell you when a person who appears in a story is white; it's just a sort of default setting. It shouldn't be, especially not in stories about the economy. Because in the full story of the American middle class, it is impossible to separate economics and race.

To understand the full story, the real cause of what's gone wrong for workers in the twenty-first century—men and women, black and white, native born or immigrant, anyone who has seen the promises of the American economy float further and further out of reach—you have to start hundreds of years before the Golden Era of the middle class. You start in the cotton fields of the South, and then you work your way forward in time and north in latitude. Eventually you will meet a young woman who is leaving the tobacco town that had both nurtured and poisoned her family, to seek her fortune in a city that is beginning to torch the blockades that had always kept people like her from getting ahead.

For centuries, stretching back to the settling of the colonies that would become the United States, men of color and women of all races and ethnicities were shut out of the greatest opportunities of the American labor market. Through colonization and revolution, civil war and its segregated aftermath, the most lucrative economic prospects were mostly limited to white men.

Black workers were enslaved and then were penned into sharecropping, handing the fruits of their toil to a white landowner. Women worked in the fields or in the home or both, almost always underpaid, if they were paid at all. Some jobs in growing, industrializing America were too brutal or dirty or dangerous for almost any native-born workers to take. So in crowded eastern cities and across the vast open West, when work needed doing and there weren't enough willing native-born workers, immigrants stepped in. Those immigrants were lured by opportunity but often confined, through generations of prejudice, to lower-skilled work.

After emancipation, black workers followed a faint trail of middle-class possibility. They migrated and muscled their way into the most hazardous corners of the industrializing North, only to find themselves underpaid and overworked. Wherever they went their children were denied access to the schools, skills, and social acceptance that would allow them to compete for the best jobs America had to offer.

You could smell that injustice upon entering Winston-Salem in the early 1940s. Two scents greeted visitors in the fast-growing city. One, which wafted from the curing sheds and great factories downtown, was of the sweet leaf of tobacco baking in the heat. The other rose from the slums where Winston-Salem housed its black workers. As Lorraine Ahearn, a writer for the *Greensboro News and Record*, would put it, "It was the stench of neglect: sludge and raw sewage running down dirt streets and under the shotgun houses in what was disparagingly called 'Monkey Bottom'—the black section where the lowest-paid R.J. Reynolds Tobacco workers lived."

Those were the smells of Vandelia Correll's childhood.

She was born in a tobacco county, Forsyth, to tobacco-worker parents. She grew up in conditions that today we would call squalor but at the time were a generational improvement for a black family in the South.

Vandelia's mother and father both worked at the Reynolds plant, which churned out Camels in pocket-sized boxes with cellophane wrap. Her father fixed machines, her mother worked in packaging. The timing of their careers means they almost certainly overlapped at the factory with Theodosia Simpson and the sit-down strikers of 1943. They squeezed their growing family into a one-bedroom house on the north side of town, on a street called Tobacco Road, with no bathroom inside and an outhouse in the back.

Their situation was the product of a deliberate devaluing of black men—and women of all races—in American history. Across generations and all around the country, black men and women were systematically denied access to schools, jobs, and entire occupational classes. White women were educated far less than white men. Even the most educated women were, for most of the nation's history, funneled into a narrow set of occupations and strongly encouraged to stay out of the workforce entirely while focusing on raising their children. Progress for black workers, and women of all races, has come in fits and starts. Their greatest advancements have typically occurred in wartime or its immediate aftermath. Almost always, though, when opportunities have opened and black and female workers have seized them, groups of white men have found ways to slow, stop, or even reverse the progress. This is a repeated theme of the American story: economic necessity widens the lanes for talent to flow upward, and then soon after, threatened white men find new ways to throttle it.

Slavery was the ultimate devaluation. It devalued enslaved workers as human beings. It also prevented them from achieving their full potential and reaping the greatest possible rewards from a nascent North American economy. Its damage did not cease when the Southern defenders of slavery lost their war for secession and the reunited nation abolished the institution. The damage lingered and festered, and it haunts the country and the economy to this day. Its legacy is worth volumes on its own. It has been the subject of groundbreaking work in recent years, including Ta-Nehisi Coates's landmark article in *The Atlantic* magazine, "The Case for Reparations," and "The 1619 Project," produced by Nikole Hannah-Jones and a large group of writers for the *New York Times Magazine*.

Most Americans see that legacy every day, whether they realize it or not. It was impossible to miss in Winston-Salem when Vandelia Correll was born in 1933, to a mother and father whose only path to economic improvement ran through a factory that was slowly killing them.

The story of Winston-Salem and its black population is a vivid example of economic and social devaluation, though far from the most egregious one in the nation's history. It is filled with the fits and starts that characterized black advancement in America. You can see it plainly in several written histories of the city and its surrounding region, including *Forsyth: A County on the March*, published by Adelaide L. Fries and a long list of coauthors in 1949; *From Frontier to Factory: An Architectural History of Forsyth County*, published in 1981 by Gwynne Stephens Taylor; and the most recent edition of *Forsyth County's Agricultural Heritage*, published in 2012 by Heather Fearnbach. The brief history outlined in this chapter draws from their accounts.

The first white settlers of the land that would come to be called Forsyth County were members of the Moravian Church, a Protestant denomination whose members bought land in the British colonies. The settlers spoke German. It would remain the official language in Salem, which later would merge with nearby Winston to form the area's largest city, until not long before the Civil War. Some historians depict the Moravians as reluctant converts to the concept of slave ownership. Taylor, for example, wrote in her 1981 architectural history of the area that the Moravians had in 1763 "*hired* a Negro woman to serve as maid in the Tavern," a development so notable that she italicized "hired." She notes that it was a momentous occasion for the Moravians to baptize a black man, named Samuel, a few years later. But, she goes on to say, within a few years the Moravians were becoming more aware of how other North Carolina residents treated the black men and women in their midst and were "feeling more pressure to conform to the Negro-White relations practiced by outsiders." Fearnbach is more blunt. From nearly the start of the settlement, she wrote in 2012, labor from enslaved Africans and African Americans was "crucial" to the area. That included Samuel, the baptized man, who she makes clear was enslaved. In 1790, she reports, the county's population included 13 free black workers—and 787 enslaved ones.

The histories are filled with examples of the Moravians denying opportunity to African American workers, sometimes because they were forced to but usually because they chose to. In 1814 they banned black men and women from Salem, with an exception for the tavern, which was having a hard time finding white workers to wait on the clientele; they were, in other words, willing to hire black workers only for a job that whites refused to do. In 1827, missionary women in the settlement started a "Sunday School for Negroes" that taught black women and men how to read and write. Those lessons were shut down three years later by a new law from the state General Assembly that prevented teaching enslaved workers to read. "The law did not prohibit education for free Negroes in North Carolina," Taylor wrote, "but lack of funds and opportunity had the same effect."

Within a few years, Salem's residents had buried their lingering Christian misgivings against buying and selling human beings. A leading Moravian man forced enslaved workers to build a factory in town. The town abandoned its last restrictions on slaveholding.

The Civil War ended slavery, but in its immediate aftermath few opportunities opened for former slaves in and around Salem. Black Americans mostly worked as sharecroppers, farming on someone else's land and handing a large portion of their harvest to the landowner. The United States government had very briefly promised each enslaved worker who had been freed up to forty acres of land, to have and own and till and profit from. The land was appropriated from Southern farmers who had rebelled against the government. But the promise was quickly canceled and the land returned to the white men.

Outside of agriculture, there was hardly any other work a black person could aspire to, especially in the South. Most histories of the area seem untroubled by this fact. In Salem during Reconstruction, Fries wrote in her history of Forsyth County, which was published in 1949, "Most of the former slaves continued to serve the families that had *been kind to them before the war*" (italics mine).

The 1870s brought one of those brief fits of progress. You could attribute it to Reconstruction or to the political clout that black men had realized when they won the right to vote. You could also just chalk it up to tobacco—and a factory in Winston opened by a man named Richard Joshua Reynolds. It was the first plant in what would be an empire, powered in large part by black workers, including, more than a half century later, the Correll family.

Reynolds needed a lot of people to run his factory, for sorting, wrapping, and packaging tobacco and also for a particularly grueling task called "stemming"—removing the tobacco leaves from their thick stems, by hand, over and over and over again. White workers took some of those jobs. Black workers took the worst of them. More specifically, black women began to dominate the stemming ranks in Reynolds's plants. It was hard work, and it did not pay well, but it paid better than the alternatives in the fields or in white people's homes. Black workers flocked to the chance to earn more, moving to Winston and Salem from nearby rural areas and from farther away in the South. In this way, Forsyth County was a pioneer: it opened the window of opportunity just a crack more for black workers, and it boomed economically when those workers came pouring through in search of even a marginally better life.

Other cities and industries followed suit. There was a moment in the late 1800s when black men in particular were beginning to gain access to higher-skilled, higher-paid jobs in the South. It did not survive to the twentieth century. Aggrieved white men slammed shut the doors of opportunity, disenfranchising black men at the ballot box and sometimes seizing their land and businesses with violence.

Reporters often ask interview subjects a certain type of question when they are piecing together what are called "tick-tocks," short, narrative histories of, say, the final passage of a tax bill, or a decision to go to war in the Middle East. The question is a version of "Do you remember your 'aha' moment?" What single piece of information made you decide to go ahead with the vote? What one thought made you green-light the bomb? Most of the time the subject will tell you, "Sorry, there wasn't one." Life isn't a movie script; change rarely appears in such tidy fashion.

For black workers in North Carolina, though, there really was such a moment. A single, bloody day that unfolded on the state's southeastern coast in November of 1898 turned the economic fortunes of an entire race of Americans. In the port city of Wilmington, prior to that day, African Americans had been flocking through the opening doors of Reconstruction-era opportunity. A state commission would report more than a century later that black men and women in the town were employed as "professionals, skilled artisans, government employees, maritime crew members" and other types of skilled workers. The events that came next slammed the doors shut. They were the reason for the formation of the state commission, which finally, in 2006, reported on the true horrors of that day.

In what was effectively a coup d'état by white nationalists, a mob of white men stormed through Wilmington on November 10, 1898. They burned a black-owned newspaper office and destroyed other black residents' homes. Many black residents were killed, though there was no official count. The white Democrats who seized control of the town banished several black leaders, businessmen, and their white political allies. Other black residents fled the city by the thousands in the aftermath.

Black workers and business owners, the state commission reported, suffered losses "in terms of job status, income, and access to capital."

For a long time North Carolina called those events a race riot, but the commission rejected that description. It was a premeditated attack, lethal economic robbery committed by white residents against their black neighbors.

State and federal officials stood idly by. Emboldened, white Democrats passed state laws that blocked black residents from voting, discriminated against them in the workplaces, and denied them equal access to amenities enjoyed by whites in the public square. They underfunded black schools, drove down the literacy rates of blacks compared with whites, and hindered black students' pursuit of the skills that could have opened up a new array of higher-paying occupations. In Winston, those laws helped to ensure that the economic ladder for African American workers effectively ended at the most difficult jobs in the R.J. Reynolds plant.

Other states passed similar laws. Other communities saw similar white attacks on blacks. Less than a half century after slavery ended, most of America's black workers found themselves stuck, once again, in an economic system that offered very little room for advancement.

Black workers kept knocking on doors, looking for any opportunities that might open to them. Those opportunities, they discovered, lay to the north. Millions of African Americans in the early twentieth century took huge risks, packed their bags, and moved to colder climes. The phenomenon was called the Great Migration, but you might think of it as a parade of workers marching ever so slowly toward a better use of their talents.

What those workers found in the North was a slightly more open job market, which was still undeniably stacked against them. Take Detroit, a city that provided some of the most lucrative jobs for black workers in the years before and after World War I. In Detroit, black workers found a willing employer in Henry Ford, whose automotive factories at one time employed just over half the black men who worked in the Detroit metropolitan area. Ford's practices, and their effect on black workers, were the subject of an entire study by the economists Thomas N. Maloney and

Warren C. Whatley, which was published in 1995 in the *Journal of Economic History*. They paint a grim portrait of what black workers endured to get ahead.

Ford's plants, known as "man-killing places," left workers so exhausted at the end of every shift that they slept on streetcars going home and in cars on the way to church on Sunday. Ford paid well, but most white men, particularly married white men, moved on to less-demanding factories. Married black men who needed to keep food on the table for their families had fewer options, because other plants were less willing to hire black workers, and so they were stuck bleeding themselves for Ford. They were, once again, doing the jobs that whites would not do.

In North Carolina, Vandelia Correll's parents bled themselves in a factory too. Vance and Beatrice Correll took the best jobs available to them at the time, in the R.J. Reynolds plant. Getting hired there was nepotistic—if you knew someone, or better yet, were related to them, and you could usually get yourself a job. It paid enough to support the Corrells' sixteen children. And it killed them all, Vandelia's son would conclude. Both the Correll parents, and all their children, would eventually die of cancer.

Vandelia was the third oldest. Like her seven most immediate siblings, she was tasked by her parents with raising one of the younger children. Many of her sisters and brothers would go on to work for Reynolds or in other factories. She would not. The world was changing in the wake of a second great war, and Vandelia Correll was dreaming bigger than her mother or grandmother could ever have dared to.

America was entering another fit of progress, for black workers and especially for women, and Vandelia was ready to lead the way. Soon she was heading north herself, chasing opportunity. She was also in love.

The man's last name was Green.

They met through a mutual friend, a young man who knew one of her sisters. Edward Junior Green—that was his middle name, "Junior"—had been orphaned at a young age. His mother had come to Winston-Salem from South Carolina, his father from West Virginia, both drawn by the

jobs for black workers that had appeared there at the turn of the twentieth century in the shadow of the R.J. Reynolds tobacco plant.

When that mutual friend introduced Edward to Vandelia Correll, the
war in Europe and the Pacific had ended. The union at the Reynolds
plant had struck for better wages and won them. Vandelia was seventeen
years old. Edward was sixteen. And Winston-Salem, though it offered
marginally better jobs for black workers than many other towns and cities across the South, was still heavily, debilitatingly segregated. It would
be a full decade before a young black man named Carl Wesley Matthews
planted himself at a whites-only lunch counter in a Kress department
store, touching off a 107-day protest, which would begin to crack the segregation regime. The formal regime, anyway.

Vandelia and Edward would not wait around to see those first cracks
form.

"I guess," their son would tell me on a break from one of his multiple
jobs, nearly seventy years after his parents made their escape, "they were
in the generation that wanted to get away from the South."

Edward was the first to leave Winston-Salem. He had finished high
school and joined the Marines, who sent him to Morocco. By the time
he was discharged, Vandelia had also left North Carolina. She, too, had
graduated high school, which, in 1950, was something that only fifteen
out of every one hundred black women in the United States had done.
That number was rising fast. There had been a proliferation of public
high schools across America over the previous several decades, and they
were steadily churning out more and more graduates, women and men,
white and black. Young Americans across the board were increasingly
completing a high school education, though in the deep shadow of discrimination, black Americans were still far less educated than whites.
Still, black women like Vandelia had seen schoolhouse doors flung open
before them over the course of a half century. In 1900, according to federal education statistics, roughly one-third of black girls aged five to nine-
teen were enrolled in school. By 1950, three-quarters of them were.

Vandelia did not stop with high school. She earned a degree from
Russell Business College, a two-year secretarial school that primarily

served black women and was run out of the basement of a church. This was pioneering. In 1950, only six out of every one hundred black women in America had completed even a year of college. Women overall were still less likely than men to pursue advanced education. But more of them were heading to college or trade school every year. Soon enough, they would outnumber men on campus.

In 1957, with a degree in hand and the man she loved serving his country overseas, Vandelia Correll moved in with a cousin in New York City. And she went to work.

Vandelia, and women like her, are glaring omissions in the Rockwellian middle-class story that white America tells itself about the fifties, sixties, and seventies—a story about the greatest proliferation of the middle class in the history of American capitalism. In the quarter century following World War II, the typical family's income more than doubled, after adjusting for inflation. Homeownership climbed by 50 percent. Economic growth routinely topped 5 percent a year. It was the definition of what Americans have come to call an economic "boom," and whether you lived through it or not, you at least know what it looked like on television or in the movies. New Chevys in the driveway, green grass under the grill, men—white men, if we're being honest about the pop-culture canon here—wearing crisp suits to their office jobs or carrying lunch pails to their factories. There is a lot of truth in that picture. The postwar boom was real, and so were the factory jobs and the soda fountains and the suburban lawns. The middle class really did balloon after the war as the United States claimed its place as the globe's economic superpower. American factories really did crank out a lot of cars and a lot of steel. Men on Madison Avenue sold a lot of cigarettes and cola.

Notably missing from that picture are the workers who proved the difference in making the postwar economy hum: black men, and women of all races.

I want to be careful with how I describe what happened in those decades to Vandelia and the man she would marry, and to the children they would have, and to the vibrant middle class they helped build. I could tell you the story in a way that sounds triumphant: racism conquered, barriers to opportunity falling like the walls of Jericho. That's the way many white Americans today see the civil rights movement and the way many men see the women's liberation movement. As breakthroughs, as leveling agents, as one-time fixes that delivered equality across racial and gender lines.

It would be wonderful if those stories were true. But they aren't—even though a lot of Americans, particularly conservatives, believe them to be. (We'll talk about this more later, when we get back to the populism story and the state of America's sclerotic middle-class economy today, but it is worth noting that just over fifty years after the assassination of the Rev. Martin Luther King Jr., polls showed that Republicans were *less* likely to believe that discrimination against black people was a "serious" problem than to believe there was a serious problem with discrimination against *white* people. Vast arrays of economic data show that's wrong.)

I could also tell you the story in a way that emphasizes the struggles of women and black Americans, even in places like New York, because those struggles were immense. Here, for example, is a paragraph from an essay published by the Schomburg Center for Research in Black Culture, a division of the New York Public Library, in an online exhibit on the black experience in the city: "Between 1940 and 1950, 211,153 southerners settled in New York City. But there, as in other cities, segregation and discrimination created an explosive situation. The resentment over discrimination in jobs and housing, police brutality, and humiliations of all sorts culminated in major riots in 1943, from Detroit to New York. The Second Great Migration resulted in the 'ghettoization' of the African-American population, with long-ranging social, political, and cultural consequences."

That story is devastatingly true, but it's not complete. The full story—as so often is the case for marginalized groups in America—reveals bursts of advancement, spasms of backlash, and some fits of progress that proved more durable than others. Women and black Americans faced persistent barriers to advancement at the start of the middle-class boom. By the end, those barriers had fallen, and the fortunes of those groups had improved. But discrimination was still going strong—weaker, but still strong.

In 1950, only a third of American women worked outside the home. By 1980, half of them did. The increase largely reflected a surge of white women into the workforce; black women had been working outside the home at high rates, but for low pay, since the early 1900s. In the postwar era, black women found that better, higher-paying jobs were opening up to them more frequently; the same was true for black men and white women. It was partly the product of economic necessity. During World War II, with millions of working-aged men deployed in Europe or the Pacific, the United States called on previously underutilized workers to keep its war machine humming and its economy on the rails. When those new workers thrived in their formerly off-limits jobs, employers adjusted somewhat and after the war made more of those positions available to workers who weren't white and male. They remained, on average, lower paying and less prestigious than the jobs white men could get. But they were better than working at the R.J. Reynolds plant, and that was enough to draw Vandelia Correll north.

So what does the full picture of the American middle-class heyday look like, the one that includes those workers that the Rockwell paintings and the pandering politicians often leave out? It looks like the New York City borough of Queens in the mid-sixties. It's an economy not unlike the rocket suburbs in California or the steel towns of Ohio, viewed through the eyes of a young black family working extraordinarily hard to overcome obstacles that never should have existed in the first place.

The Green family settled in Queens after hopping around the city, solo and then together. Vandelia moved in with her cousin and got a job with the telephone company—in the collections department, her son recalls. Edward was discharged from the Marines and moved up north to be with her. They were married in the city and lived briefly on the Lower East Side of Manhattan. They had a son and named him Edward Junior Green II. Everyone called him Eddie Jr.; today he works a highway crew in North Carolina and goes by Ed.

Soon after Ed was born, Vandelia's father, one of the Reynolds plant workers, died young. Vandelia kept working at the phone company. The couple kept saving money. Four years later they had a daughter, and they used their savings to buy a house in Queens—first a starter home and then a larger one, in a neighborhood where Count Basie and James Brown and a burgeoning class of black professionals also lived. A black middle class was growing in the New York boroughs, thanks to women and men who worked as hard as the Greens.

Vandelia's husband, Edward, drove a bus in the city, on a split shift, working the morning and evening rushes. In the five or six hours between driving shifts, he ran a plumbing business, snaking and fixing pipes. His son remembers how as a young boy he helped his dad clean the grime off the equipment after especially tough days.

Edward wasn't the only one in his family to work multiple jobs. Vandelia had earned a realtor's license. Their son Eddie had two paper routes, pedaling around the neighborhood on his Stingray bicycle to deliver both a morning paper and the evening *Long Island Press*. In the early seventies, when her son was in junior high school, Vandelia opened a laundromat. Eddie would come home from school, finish his homework, deliver his papers, and then relieve his mother among the washing machines. He would make change, sell soap, and clean floors. At home, his mother would make dinner, which his father would eat. Then the older Edward would head down to the laundromat, send his son home, and close up shop for the night.

Vandelia and Edward never sat their son and daughter down and told them about the importance of working hard, at least not that their son recalls. Ed told me, "It was kind of just, this is what we do." The family work ethic never changed. Ed Green took on multiple jobs after the turn of the twenty-first century, when he returned to Winston-Salem to care for his ailing mother, who had retired there years before.

What changed was the reward the American economy offered for that work. In the middle-class heyday, Vandelia and Edward could afford almost all of the Game of Life set of middle-class security blankets with the money they earned. They owned a house. They had a car. They saved for retirement, and they could afford to send their children to the doctor. That would not be true for their son.

The Greens were able to build that middle-class life in spite of the barricades, both long-standing and shiny new, that policymakers threw in their way. After World War II, federal housing officials worked to deny home loans to black buyers, thereby exacerbating residential segregation, through a process known as redlining. The postwar growth of the sub-urbs largely excluded black families; one of the reasons the Greens could afford to buy a home in Queens was that white families were moving to new developments farther out on Long Island, which black families were largely unable to buy into. (In 2019, an investigation by the reporters at *Newsday* uncovered substantial evidence that Long Island realtors were *still* discriminating against nonwhite homebuyers.)

Black soldiers coming back from the war or from future campaigns found it much harder than whites to access the benefits of the GI Bill. The war had opened more jobs to women and African Americans, but not nearly as many as they were qualified for. Federal antidiscrimina-tion efforts proved only mildly effective. As the Schomburg Center essay notes, in 1946, "The National Urban League reported that there were only twenty-two licensed black electricians in New York City and only six had been admitted to the International Brotherhood of Electrical Workers; only six black men were in the plumbers' local; and only two belonged to the plasterers' union."

Progress was also impeded for women, no matter their race. Until the war, working women in the United States had followed the path through the beginning and middle stages of what the Harvard University econ-omist Claudia Goldin has shown to be a worldwide pattern as countries grow richer over time. When countries are poor, Goldin has written, women work in farms and fields—sometimes for pay, often for nothing. As incomes rise and countries mechanize their production, women tend to leave the workforce and focus on so-called home production, like rais-ing children, in part because of social stigmas against women working in factory jobs. The richer a country gets, the more education it tends to provide to its people, first to men, and then, usually much later, to women.

When women finally catch up to men in schooling, Goldin wrote, they flock back to the workforce, creating over time a labor-force participation rate that appears on a graph as a U shape. Along the way, they must evade occupational, social, and civic restrictions placed on them by men.

That was basically the story of America's working white women, who farmed in the nation's infancy, left the workforce as the economy matured, and were widely denied the same access to education and careers that their brothers were given. In the twentieth century, they slowly began to crack the workforce open, teaching school, taking notes in shorthand, supporting the growing white-collar sector. But even by midcentury, entire professions remained closed to them, as four economists would note in a landmark 2019 academic paper that showed just how important women have been to America's postwar economy. When a rancher's daughter named Sandra Day graduated third in her class from Stanford Law School in 1952, the economists wrote, the only job immediately available to her was as a legal secretary. (She would later become the first woman on the Supreme Court of the United States.) In 1960, nearly three in five white women were employed as nurses, teachers, salesclerks, secretaries, or food preparers. As Goldin, who is herself a female pioneer in a high-skilled field—economics—noted in her history of women in the workforce, in those days, "interviews for first jobs, even those of women with college degrees, often began with the straightforward question: 'How well do you type?'"

A wide range of economic research has catalogued the barriers women and minorities faced in gaining access to the best jobs in America. One illustrative example was published in the late 1990s, by the economists William A. Darity Jr. (then of the University of North Carolina) and Patrick L. Mason (of the University of Notre Dame). It was called "Evidence on Discrimination in Employment." Among its many damning data points, it excerpted help-wanted advertisements that appeared in 1960 in top newspapers from large cities—including the *Chicago Tribune*, the *Los Angeles Times*, and the *New York Times*. There were separate ads for men and women, and each category contained overt requests for white or "negro" applicants. On January 3, 1960, the *Washington Post* ran an ad seeking truck drivers, "colored, for trash routes." Another ad asked for "AMBITIOUS MEN (WHITE)" to work in an executive's library department.

The Darity and Mason paper was descriptive—its main purpose was to show, through a variety of measures, that discrimination against women and African Americans was, in fact, *a real thing.* The paper was published in 1998, an embarrassingly late moment for the economics profession to still be debating whether disadvantaged groups actually experienced discrimination in the United States or whether the free market had magically erased any traces of it. Darity and Mason made clear that it had not. "Competitive market forces certainly did not eliminate these discriminatory practices in the decades leading up to the 1960s," they wrote. "They remained until the federal adoption of antidiscrimination laws."

The law that Darity and Mason most credit for reducing racial and gender discrimination, which stands as arguably the most significant piece of legislation in supercharging the American middle class, was the Civil Rights Act of 1964. It banned state and local laws—and company policies—that barred women or nonwhites from certain jobs. (Textile mills in South Carolina, for example, discriminated systematically against blacks workers before the act was passed.) It strengthened antidiscrimination enforcement by federal agencies and forced open government and contracting jobs to workers who weren't white men. It helped America win the space race by pushing factories like the Rockwell plant in Downey, California, cradle of the Apollo module, to hire highly skilled black and female workers who might otherwise have been consigned to sweeping its floors.

The opportunity boost that the Civil Rights Act gave women and minorities in America was relatively short in the context of the nation's history. Darity says it probably lasted a decade for black workers, two decades for women. *Fits and starts.* But it was hugely important to the growth of the middle class—and not just for the workers it lifted up, but for everyone, across the economy.

The Greens, in this story, are not simply the avatars of a black middle class that blossomed, even amid the thorns of discrimination, in the postwar era. They are the engines of the great middle-class boom. They built a middle-class life, and their life and work helped other people rise into the middle class. They did this by adding value to an economy that previously denied them the chance to.

It's more valuable to you if you hire a plumber who knows exactly what he's doing when he snakes your pipes. It's valuable to have an affordable place nearby to wash your shirts. It's valuable for a company to have workers who can efficiently collect its bills. It is *incredibly valuable* to have generations of girls and boys growing up to believe that they can do whatever job they dream of, if they work and study hard enough. It is better for those workers, for those children, and for the country as a whole.

This, then, is the true story of the Golden Era of the middle class.

In the decades surrounding World War II, women and black men and other long-devalued workers began to gain access to occupations they had been previously denied. America finally started allowing the majority of its people to put their full talents to work.

Unlocking the potential of those workers made the economy grow faster.

That growth lifted all workers in America, not just women and minorities. It lifted white men too. It fueled the most lucrative decades for the common worker in the history of capitalism.

But that success was fleeting. The economy today once again devalues large groups of workers. Their talents are being held back, which in turn holds back the middle class.

You can see it all around you. And thanks to a quartet of economists who started thinking about discrimination, workers, and talent more than a decade ago, you can see how much it has cost the nation.

7

Aggregate Consequences

A STORY IN NUMBERS

Millions of American families have middle-class stories like the Greens'. Math shows us how those stories fit together. It gives us the statistical power to prove how the fortunes of workers so frequently pitted against each other by the powerful are actually interlocked.

Here is what the numbers tell us about the advancement of men of color and women of all races to better jobs during and after World War II, and how it affected the overall economy and the white men who had up to that point been its primary workers.

Numbers tell us that twenty-seven million women entered the American labor force between 1950 and 1980, nearly a 150 percent increase.

Millions more nonwhite men joined as well. The share of prime-aged white men who were working or looking for work fell slightly—though it was still around 95 percent in the late 1970s—but economists have generally attributed the decline to men leaving work in order to collect disability benefits from Social Security, not to displacement by women. During that forty-year period, America gained millions more workers without knocking working-age white men out of the labor force.

The numbers also tell us that a rapidly expanding workforce generated swift and sustained economic growth. In the 1950s, the economy grew on average by 4.2 percent a year after adjusting for inflation. In the 1960s, that accelerated to 4.5 percent. In the 1970s, it was 3.2 percent. Those averages include multiple (and typically short) recessions. They also include twelve years when growth topped 5 percent, seven when it topped 6 percent, and two when it topped 8 percent. Those levels are unheard of in the United States today, politicians' promises notwithstanding. There has been exactly one year since 1980 with annual growth exceeding 5 percent. It was 1984.

Most of the rapid growth came at a time when American companies were, oddly enough, having a relatively tough time finding workers. From 1950 to 1975, the unemployment rate rarely popped above 6 percent. When it did, it fell quickly. It enjoyed a three-year stretch—from 1966 to 1969, in the immediate aftermath of the Civil Rights Act becoming law—of continuous readings under 4 percent. From an economist's point of view, for most of the postwar expansion the economy was at or near what is called "full employment," which basically means that everyone who wants to work can find a job in a reasonable amount of time.

That was great news for workers. All workers. Wages rose faster than inflation throughout this period, for workers at all rungs of the economic ladder. They rose for women. They rose for black men. They rose for immigrants. And they rose, at a pace rarely seen since, for white men without a college degree. If there is a magic formula for widespread wage growth in America, this was a great example of it: a fast-growing economy with a low unemployment rate, which kept businesses hungry for workers and gave workers the power to demand higher pay.

More work and fatter wages vaulted millions of Americans into the middle class over those decades. The exact number depends on your definition, of course, but the trend is unmistakable. It shows women and black men climbing from poverty into the middle class, and white men climbing alongside them. In 2001, the National Academy of Sciences published a retrospective on race and the American economy, including research by a wide-ranging group of top economists. In one chapter of the two-volume work, the report uses an income-based calculation of "who is middle class" to tally how many Americans moved into it during the postwar era. From 1940 to 1970, it found, the share of American white men who were in the middle class jumped from 38 percent to 65 percent. The share of black men tripled, from 22 percent to 68 percent. The share of black women in the middle class rose by 25 points from 1962 to 1973 alone.

Not one of those measures shows black workers or women prospering at the expense of white men. To the contrary: they show that for white men who were in the middle class or working their way toward it, their best years went *hand in hand* with the best years for women and minorities.

It sure looks like there's a relationship there, right? Especially when I tell you that in the late 1970s, when the economy worsened, and black, Hispanic, and other minority workers started to fall out of the middle class, white men did too. To researchers, the fortunes of all those groups appeared to be connected.

A fun thing about academic economists is they're never satisfied if things appear to be connected. Some political economists—the hired guns whose job it is to make every tax cut or spending program look like a smashing success for the candidate who won an election campaigning on it—are happy to stop at relationships that kind of, sort of look linked. Serious economists go further. They run sophisticated analyses and sometimes build theoretical models of how the economy functions in order to tease out whether certain events are connected or coincidence. It helps them discern whether statistical trends are related. And it helps them find relationships that you would never see with your naked eye.

One of those serious research projects, which was first posted online in 2012, reexamined the postwar era for clues to what had really fueled America's rise to global economic dominance. What it found revolutionized the way I thought about workers, American history, and the middle class.

The paper had four authors: an Asian-American economist named Chang-Tai Hsieh, from the University of Chicago, and three white male economists, Erik Hurst, of the University of Chicago, and Charles I. Jones and Peter J. Klenow, both of Stanford University. It had a dry title, "The Allocation of Talent and U.S. Economic Growth," which hid a complex and important story.

"In 1960," it began, in the summary at the top of the first version the economists posted online, "94 percent of doctors were white men."

You're by now quite familiar with the narrative that came next: it's the Green family's story. The paper recounted all the ways that the United States economy, before and immediately after the Second World War, had shut women and nonwhite men out of its highest-skilled, highest-paying jobs. More than half of black men in 1960, it said, were employed as janitors, freight handlers, and other similar jobs. Only 2 percent of women and black men worked in so-called high-skilled occupations, as architects, engineers, scientists, doctors, lawyers, and such. It noted how many women were funneled into those "How well do you type?" jobs as secretaries or clerks.

The authors called the skewed distribution what it was: evidence of discrimination, which hurt the people being discriminated against. It's easy to see why. Women and black men were all too frequently unable to get hired into the jobs that would make the best possible use of their skills—the ones that allow them, in economist-speak, to maximize their "comparative advantage" over other workers. Two sets of barriers held them back. One, an inequality of access to and quality of schooling, kept women and minorities from the same educational opportunities and skill development that white men enjoyed. The other, overt discrimination in the marketplace kept well-qualified women and minorities from ever making it past a hiring manager. Even the paper's footnotes are devastating in their casual roundup of previous research on the forces that held American citizens back for generations.

"Karabel (2005) documents that Harvard, Princeton and Yale systematically discriminated against blacks, women, and Jews in admissions until the late 1960s," one of the notes begins. "Card and Krueger (1992) documents that public schools for blacks in the U.S. South in the 1950s were underfunded relative to schools for white children."

Many other economists had noted the nation's entrenched discrimination and its damage to the workers who were discriminated against. An exhaustive literature describes the gaps between black and white Americans, and between men and women, in earnings, opportunity, and accumulated wealth. What this paper did that others had not done was spell out how that discrimination hurt the entire American economy. It also added up the costs.

The paper took the radically intuitive position that the distribution of workers in 1960 was inefficient—because workforce talent is not disproportionately concentrated in white men. There were explanations for why in 1950 almost every doctor or lawyer was a white guy. But they were explanations of culture, discrimination, and path dependence. They were not a reflection of who in America was best qualified to be a doctor—or, more importantly, who had the *best potential* to be a doctor—if only they could gain access to the education, training, credentialing, and hiring necessary to pursue that career. By keeping talented people out of lucrative jobs, the economists reasoned, the people perpetuating discrimination were actually hurting themselves.

In dry economist fashion, Hsieh, Hurst, Jones, and Klenow called those means of discrimination "frictions," defined as trends that hurt workers by preventing them from maximizing their talents in the economy. A simple way of thinking about how an economy operates most efficiently in a capitalist system is that we want every worker doing the job she or he is best at, compared to other workers. For example, a woman whose comparative advantage is rocket science should, in fact, work as a rocket scientist. If for some reason the economy consigns her to a job where she cannot add as much value, the whole economy loses out. You don't want would-be rocket scientists answering phones in the lab. You don't want skilled mechanics plunging toilets in the shop. There is value and dignity in the work of answering phones and plunging toilets, but if a worker can add more value elsewhere, we want her in the job that maximizes value. (Value to the economy and also value to her personally; fulfillment from work matters in this equation, as we'll see later.)

Hsieh, Hurst, Jones, and Klenow surveyed the economy as it had existed in 1960 and saw a lot of talented people unable to do what they would be best at because of discrimination and unbalanced access to education. "The change in the occupational distribution since 1960," they wrote, "suggests that a substantial pool of innately talented women and black men in 1960 were not pursuing their comparative advantage. The resulting (mis)allocation of talent could potentially have important aggregate consequences."

That last sentence is the hammer. The phrase "aggregate consequences" means that discrimination did not hurt just the workers who were discriminated against. Discrimination hurt the whole economy, including the white men who were practicing discrimination. The authors measured the size of that pain by estimating how much the economy was helped when Americans accelerated their efforts to chip away at discrimination.

In the fits and starts of gender and racial progress in the United States, the postwar period was a brief, luminescent period. Barriers that had kept women and minorities out of entire fields were falling. Not as fully or as quickly as they should have, but they fell. And the distribution of talent changed when they did. By 2010, the share of lawyers and doctors who were white men had declined from nearly 95 percent to about 60 percent. That's still not proportionate, if you believe, as you should, that talent and potential are evenly distributed across races and genders. But it was enough progress to dramatically alter the course of the economy, the Chicago and Stanford economists found.

The paper has been revised and updated several times, most recently in 2019, ahead of being published in the peer-reviewed journal *Econometrics*. In its first draft, it presented a striking finding: that nearly one-fifth of all economic growth per worker in the United States since 1960 was the product of knocking down the barriers that kept women and black men from doing the work they were best at. Those workers account for nearly all the rise in labor-force participation in that time.

It seemed initially like a staggering finding. Twenty percent of all growth! Just from reducing discrimination across the economy!

And it turns out to have been wildly off.

In the most recent draft of the paper, the one published in a peer-reviewed journal, the economists updated their staggering finding with improved data and modeling. The new statistic was twice as powerful as their first estimate. They now report that *more than two-fifths* of economic growth per worker in the United States since 1960 came from tapping the talents of the women and minorities whom white men had shut out of opportunities for centuries. Forty percent! That's the difference between a red-hot economy and a lukewarm one. It strongly suggests that expanding opportunity for women and minority workers kept the economy growing fast enough to generate the wage gains that lifted all those workers, male and female, white and black and otherwise, into the middle class during the great postwar boom. Even after the boom fizzled, the upward flow buoyed an often slumping economy. Without those workers, America's middle class would be even smaller today. Its distressed areas would be in even worse shape. Its white male workers would likely be much angrier.

That upward flow of talent, loosed on the economy, swelled the ranks of the middle class and made everyone in the country better off.

Once more to the numbers: in the postwar era, America reduced its discrimination against women and minorities, which generated faster economic growth that lifted all workers. In the fifties, sixties, and seventies, that growth helped drive down the unemployment rate, even as millions of new workers sought and found jobs. The ensuing competition for workers helped lift wages. More Americans were making full use of their talents. Women and black workers were not displacing more qualified white men in professional positions. If they had been, the economists would have found a drag on economic growth. They didn't. Their findings suggest that white men, whether they realized it or not, were helped by the influences of workforce equality.

Too many Americans never learned that lesson of what looms, in our national memory, as the Golden Era of our economy. For too long, our leaders told stories about civil rights and gender equity that were far too narrow. They sounded like victories for one group—not victories for all groups. Too many Americans have not been taught that their stories are everyone's stories, their victories are everyone's victories. It is a strange idea—that the liberation of the oppressed actually helps the longtime oppressor—but the evidence is clear, in the people and in the math. But when you don't hear that idea repeated to you, when it's not drilled into you in school or over the airwaves or on the campaign trail, you fall vulnerable to an easily told, easily grasped lie about the economy: the idea that progress for one group necessarily brings down another. And if you believe that lie, you blind yourself to what's really afflicting the economy—and what we really need to do to get it back on track.

I never met Vandelia Correll—I only learned about her through her son and grandchildren—but she was a face of that upward flow. The flow both for black workers and for women of all races.

Taken together, the advancements of those long-oppressed workers powered the great American middle-class expansion of the postwar era. The reason the middle class has stagnated in recent decades is that women and men of color are not getting ahead like Vandelia and her husband did.

The upward flow of talent has clogged.

That clogging is an American tragedy. It was foreseeable. It was preventable. It continues to hold workers back. Barriers new and old are blocking women and nonwhite workers from economic opportunity, from doing what they are best at. Sadly, those workers now have more company. New barriers, raised by tectonic shifts in the global economy, have hindered another group of workers from putting their full talents to use.

This true story of America's great middle-class expansion is a hopeful one. It's not naive or unrealistic. It is a real-life, historically documented success story that boils down to empowering people to make the best use of their God-given talents. It is a reason to believe in the power of a market-based, democratically governed economy to seed and nurture a growing, thriving middle class. But for many Americans, that hope is long gone. It vanished when the Golden Era ended and a middle-class malaise set in.

Something broke in the American economy around 1978. It stopped functioning as well as it had for working-class people over the previous several decades. The great middle-class expansion was ending. A middle-class shrinkage was starting. At the center of it all was a divergence. An economy that had been delivering for everyone—at the top, the bottom, and the middle of the income ladder—was beginning to pick winners and losers in the American workforce. That was not in and of itself a new development. The American economy had to varying degrees selected winners and losers from the beginning. What was new was the fault line dividing the haves and the have-nots in the 1980s economy. It did not always cut neatly across racial and gender lines. The new divide was over education. It left a lot of white men on the wrong side of the split.

The divide was opened by technological progress and an accompanying economic evolution that shifted the business of the United States away from building or fixing things with your hands and toward helping people or solving puzzles with your brain. In a world where machines get better every year at doing work previously handled by humans, some of that evolution was inevitable. The pace and the scope of the change were not. They were stoked by policymakers, usually in Washington, and cheered on by the titans of commerce who just so happened to reap the rewards more than anyone else.

Policymakers sped up the loss of factory jobs in horrific bursts by amplifying automation trends that were already at work. They popped the regulatory restraining bolts off the financial industry, allowing it to double in size and set up vulnerable populations for a spectacular crash by selling them hard on dreams and loans that were too good to be true. (The 2008 financial crisis was the most visible failure of that bipartisan stampede to appease Wall Street, but as we'll see later the less visible failures have been just as devastating for American communities; they are a large reason why the economy has been slow to create better jobs to replace the good ones that policymakers helped kill through the 1980s, 1990s, and 2000s.) And policymakers permitted—and in part facilitated—the flooding of prescription painkillers into small towns and inner cities across wide swaths of the country, creating the deadliest drug epidemic in American history.

In all those cases, the victims of bad policy were disproportionately the same working-class people who struggled to keep up with the economy's organic transition from physical work to service work.

The consequence of the changes was that the great middle-class expansion sputtered in the early 1970s, kicked back on briefly, then died before the decade was out. From 1964, the year that President Lyndon Johnson signed the Civil Rights Act into law, through the end of 1978, the average hourly earnings of an American worker rose nearly 20 percent, after adjusting for inflation. It was a sustained period of strong income gains, mitigated only by an early-1970s recession that saw worker pay decline then partly rebound. The next decade and a half was very different.

From 1979 to the middle of the 1990s, average earnings fell by nearly 7 percent. They did not return to their 1978 levels until 1999, nearing the end of the first dot-com boom. I was born in January 1978. Average hourly earnings crested at the end of that year. I made it to legal drinking age before the typical American worker got another raise that went beyond the cost of living.

Buried in those averages are several overlapping stories of workers whose fortunes no longer always rose and fell together, as they had after the war. It's easiest to see them if we break the postwar American economy into a few distinct periods. First came the Golden Era of the middle class, roughly from the end of the Second World War to the middle of the 1970s. Next came a decade and a half of middle class decline, before the tech boom of the late 1990s.

Let's talk about that period—the Gordon Gecko, "greed is good," fall-of-communism 1980s. The Dodgers won the World Series (twice). I watched a lot of *He-Man* and *Care Bears* and regularly played a computer game on our Apple IIc called *Lemonade Stand*. Its graphics were crude. Its problems were basic. It simulated a summer of youthful entrepreneurship, telling you the weather report every day, asking how many ingredients you wanted to order and what price you wanted to charge. You made choices. Then it told you your sales. It was a cartoonish lesson in supply and demand—an economics tutorial masquerading as video gaming for kids who did not own an Atari system. I spent hours on it. I was a really fun kid.

For the grown-ups who spent the decade actually working, as opposed to pretending to on a computer, the 1980s were a mixed bag. They were great for the most educated Americans; the rewards of wage growth accrued almost entirely to workers with college degrees. With one glaring exception—and we'll get to that in a moment—the rule for the decade was: If you had a college degree, your income went up. If you didn't, it either flatlined or, more likely, fell.

That was a particularly good development for a lot of American women, who were fast catching up with men on educational attainment. At the start of the 1980s, women in the United States between the ages of twenty-five and twenty-nine were just as likely to have graduated high school as men of the same age, and female high school graduates were suddenly *more* likely to go on to college than men. By the end of the decade, women in their late twenties were nearly as likely as men to have obtained a bachelor's degree. Their earnings rose accordingly. As Claudia Goldin, the pioneering Harvard economist, has shown, the educational gains women made between the 1950s and 1980s did not meaningfully narrow the gap between a typical woman's pay and a typical man's pay. But in the 1980s, powered by educational gains and social shifts, including a trend toward women putting off marriage until after they had established careers after college, women made huge strides. At the start of the 1980s, as Goldin has documented, women earned about sixty cents for every dollar that men earned. By the end of the decade, that had grown to seventy cents.

The gains were greater for white women than for black or Hispanic women. When the 1980s began, the typical white and black female college graduates earned about the same amount of money each week. The typical Hispanic female college graduate earned slightly less. All three groups of women saw their incomes rise and their ranks grow; they were all studying more, learning more, and claiming their place in more lucrative occupations. Their salaries rose faster than the cost of living. But pay rose even faster for white women. At decade's end, college-educated white women had opened a meaningful pay gap of their own—over college-educated women of color.

Their advantage also grew over women who graduated from high school but not college. That group still made up the majority of women in the workforce, and in the 1980s their earnings stagnated, ending the decade where they began it, after the cost of living was factored in. It may not have seemed so, but comparatively speaking the stagnation represented a certain kind of progress. It in part reflected the tumbling of a few more occupational barriers for women, even women with only a high school diploma. As a group they got better jobs. But their pay didn't budge.

How is that progress, by any definition? Because their male counterparts were falling backward, fast.

For men who stopped their education after high school or dropped out before they graduated, the fifteen years starting in 1980 brought steep and constant decline. These were the guys I watched leave school in McMinnville and the other towns of Yamhill County to chase the fading fortunes of timber work. Their good jobs were vanishing. The jobs they could find were paying less. And the advantages they had long enjoyed over other workers were gone, like a DeLorean hitting eighty-eight miles per hour. By the time *Back to the Future* arrived in theaters in 1985, the typical man with only a high school diploma was earning less per week than the typical woman who had graduated college, a first in American history. By the start of the Gulf War in 1991, that man was earning less than a typical college-educated black woman.

You could see the talent story again at work in all those experiences of the 1980s. It was more complicated, and it was changing, but it was there—and it was not always a happy story. The flow of talent was continuing to rush upward for women. They were blazing new trails to campuses, professional offices, and the occasional executive suite. They were still realizing their full potential as workers, and the economy continued to encourage them to. Those flows were helping the economy grow faster.

You could also see, for the first time since the war, the talent pipeline becoming clogged and workers being pushed backward. Some of that resulted from the shifting structure of the economy. In the moment, that shift looked like a lot of other periods in American history. It was a time when the economy began demanding less of a certain set of skills and more of another. That happens fairly often in capitalist economies, and when it does, the people with the suddenly less desirable skills are out of luck. Economists like to talk about the craftsmen who made buggy whips for use on horse carriages whose services were no longer needed after the automobile came along. The economy didn't value buggy-whip making anymore. It valued car making. So the people who knew how to make cars on an assembly line could command more money than the whip makers, who had lost the market for their product. If you were one of the couple million Americans to lose a factory job in the 1980s, or you were laid off by your timber company in the recession at the start of the decade, there was a chance you never found another gig that took advantage of your particular skill. The economy was coldly and rudely moving on from you.

It's tempting to look at that data and say that what broke in the 1980s was the nation's educational pipeline. After all, there was plenty of growth to go around. The economy expanded at an average rate of 3.1 percent a year, just a tick below the average for the 1970s. The Federal Reserve whipped inflation with high interest rates, then unleashed growth by slashing them. President Reagan cut taxes several times, and he won reelection in 1984 by a landslide, asking voters, "Are you better off today than you were four years ago?" The economy was more than 20 percent larger, per person, at the end of the 1980s than it was at the start. You could look at those numbers and look back at that distribution of who benefitted from the growth, and you could talk yourself into a very simple assessment of the decade: the workers who didn't go to college should have.

Economists have a wonky name for that argument, which is "skill-biased technical change." A debate has raged in the field for years about how much it explains the middle-class stagnation of the last few decades. The theory works like this: Advancing technology, like computing power in the 1980s, gives an advantage to workers whose primary talent is brainpower as opposed to muscle power or salesmanship or the ability to repair an engine. Some of that brainpower talent is built in college, so the workers who stayed in school longer were the ones who profited when technological progress sped up. This absolutely explains *some* of what happened to workers after the great middle-class boom ended. It does not explain all of it.

For starters, it doesn't explain why men continued to outearn comparably educated women in the 1980s, no matter how much school they'd completed. Men who dropped out of high school saw their average hourly earnings fall in the 1980s, but they kept earning more than women who dropped out. The same was true for high school graduates and college grads. It wasn't because men were smarter or did better in school. As Claudia Goldin noted, in a prestigious lecture to the American Economic Association in 2006, "In the 1970s and 1980s, girls began to take more college preparation courses in high school and narrowed the gap between girls and boys in science and math courses. Relative to boys, girls increased their aptitude scores in math and reading." They increased those scores, she wrote, to such a degree that in 1992, "girls who were high school seniors were just slightly behind boys in math and considerably ahead in reading." The gains women were making in closing the pay gap with men were the product of their commitment to education and the fact that more and more women were earning college degrees. They were not a sign that companies were willing to pay a woman as much as a similarly educated man if they both held the same position. Discrimination had not gone away.

There was also the continuing inequality of outcomes by race. White workers consistently outearned their similarly educated black and Hispanic peers. That was true for white men compared with nonwhite men and for white women compared with nonwhite women. The smallest racial gap in the 1980s was at the very bottom of the income distribution, between white and black women who had dropped out of high school; they earned very little, and the advantage white women enjoyed was minuscule. The largest gap was at the top: a widening chasm between black and white male college graduates. White men with college degrees captured more gains from the 1980s economy than any similar group—even more than college-educated women. Black men were the opposite: a college degree did nothing to insulate them from income losses. They were the only group of college-educated workers to actually lose ground during the decade. They were the exception to the skills-pay connection.

That's all compelling evidence that the 1980s breakage was about more than a shift to knowledge jobs. Yes, it was better for workers if they had more education. But a lot more was working against less-educated workers than a growing bias toward certain skills. Economists have pieced together a long list of important factors. Union representation declined across the private sector, which reduced the power that workers got from bargaining collectively with an employer. The federal minimum wage did not budge for a decade, which meant it lost value as prices increased. Slammed by recessions—which always hit factory workers hard and fast in America—and a strong dollar that made it easier for American consumers to buy imported products, domestic manufacturers shed jobs that had mostly paid good wages to workers who didn't need to go to college.

Those changes hurt less-educated workers regardless of race or gender. A different set of changes hit black workers but not whites: a reemergence of some of the discrimination that civil rights legislation had seemed to drive away. The legislation, protests, and political shifts of the 1960s had failed to vanquish discrimination. They had simply beaten it back—not completely, and not for very long. The great upward rush of black talent, set free by civil rights laws, barely lasted a decade before it slowed and in some cases reversed.

The reversal wasn't an accident of history or the result of a natural social drift toward racial division. It was, as always, a policy decision. Discrimination against black Americans and other disempowered groups had been enshrined by America's leaders from the founding of the nation. It was eroded by economic events, like the mobilization for war in Europe and Japan. And at the higher points of the nation's history, it was broken down by other, deliberate policy decisions. But in the 1970s and 1980s, American politicians made a series of policy decisions that had the effect of bringing some of the discrimination back.

Many of those policy changes were pursued by a president who had, ten years before taking office, disclosed in a phone call that he did not see black people as a fountain of talent to be tapped. He saw them as savages. "To see those monkeys from those African countries, damn them," Ronald Reagan had said, in a conversation with President Richard Nixon in 1971. Reagan, then the governor of California, had called the Oval Office to complain about a victory and celebration by an African delegation at the United Nations, which had come at the expense of the United States. He was furious at the Africans. "They are still uncomfortable wearing shoes," he said. Nixon laughed heartily.

The American public did not hear those words from Reagan until the summer of 2019. They had been withheld by the National Archives from a set of recordings of Nixon until a historian named Timothy Naftali, a former director of the Nixon Library, demanded the tapes be released in full. But Americans had certainly heard plenty of insinuation from Reagan about white people unfairly subsidizing black people and how antidiscrimination laws were hurting whites. Reagan had built his national profile in 1976 in part by promoting the story of a black woman in Illinois who had defrauded the government welfare system, a focus that helped to build a "welfare queen" stereotype of black women in the eyes of the white public. He launched his 1980 general election campaign with a racially coded appeal to white voters in the town of Philadelphia, Mississippi, where white supremacists had murdered three civil rights activists who were attempting to help African Americans register to vote.

Reagan was neither the first nor the last politician who saw that votes could be had by downplaying the idea that discrimination was holding back black Americans and exploiting voters' fears that racial progress was disruptive and damaging to predominantly white cities and neighborhoods. He said publicly that he favored empowering black Americans through a program that relied more on markets and less on government to deliver positive outcomes for them. And he did, for example, reduce tax rates for all workers as part of his sweeping tax cuts early in his first term—though white workers benefited much more from the cuts, which were targeted at high earners, who were predominantly white. Reagan also swung the great apparatus of the federal government to dent or demolish some antidiscrimination efforts by, for example, having his administration argue before the Supreme Court against a system of race-based preferences known as affirmative action. He presided over a federal "war" on drugs and crime that resulted in what many economists believe to have been the single greatest barrier to economic advancement for black Americans of the last forty years: the mass incarceration of millions of young black men, which both pulled them from the labor force and hurt their ability to work once they were released from prison.

You do not have to believe that those efforts were malicious or even deliberate to acknowledge that, while they were in place, black men moved backward in the economy. The current of the American labor market pushed against large groups of workers. Simply choosing not to paddle forward toward more equal opportunity, as the country had done during the civil rights decade, appears to have damaged workers whose improved access to better jobs helped build the middle class. A wide literature of economic research now recognizes this. "Just as focused government policy can improve the relative position of blacks in the labor market," Katharine L. Bradbury, an economist at the Federal Reserve Bank of Boston, wrote in an exhaustive study of the interplay between race, gender, and education in the Reagan and Clinton eras of America, "its absence can allow discriminatory patterns to reemerge."

Discrimination has not left the American economy. To varying degrees, it still hinders women, black men, Hispanics, and others. It even hinders—in areas like admissions to elite universities—Asian Americans, who by and large have attained the highest levels of education and income of any nonwhite group in the country, but who remain underrepresented in top schools as judged by standardized test scores. Breaking down that discrimination is the closest thing we have to a video-game cheat code to revitalize the middle class.

Restraining the advancement of nonwhite workers has not helped the economy, and it has not helped the white workers whose education stopped after high school. There is no evidence—not from the postwar boom times, or from the 1980s, or from the decades that followed—that white male workers with high school diplomas have lost jobs and income to similarly educated women and minorities. Those workers suffered together in the 1980s and into the mid-1990s. In the late 1990s—when growth ran hot, the unemployment rate sunk low, and wage growth sped up—all those groups got raises.

The late 1990s were a brief, budget-balancing throwback to the Golden Era, like a summer breeze in the middle of October, and a good reminder that the best medicine for ailing workers is a tight labor market. But do you know who did best, by far, in the late 1990s? White men who went to college. They rode the end of that skill-biased-technical-change wave. The internet had modemed its way into American homes. Stanford classmates of mine were graduating straight into Silicon Valley, snatched up by venture-capital-fueled start-ups with nebulous business models, at best. One of my good friends from the student newspaper, who is white, took a job for a tech company. It paid him, among other things, to produce a business-to-business newsletter that included a recurring column on the "search for the perfect martini," which had something to do with the company's name. I still have no idea what he, or the company, actually did. The bubble burst before his one-year anniversary, the company folded, and he was left to maximize his talents in another field.

The tech bubble gave a final boost to the "college premium"—the difference between wages earned by college graduates and those earned by non-college-educated workers. If you look at the average hourly earnings data for the 1990s, it's impossible to miss the huge gains made by white male college graduates. They're right at the top of the chart, looming above everyone else and rising fast. And then . . . poof. The bubble burst, and the college premium stopped growing. It's basically the same today as it was twenty years ago. That timing involved a real element of luck for certain graduates, like me (class of 2000). I caught the tail end of the tech boom, a break of the calendar that has unquestionably lifted my lifetime earnings. If I'd taken a year off from school and graduated in 2001, I would have entered the job market in the midst of a recession, with significantly worse job prospects and almost certainly a lower starting salary once I found work.

David Autor also hit the job market at just the right time, in 1999. It was ten years since he had earned his bachelor's degree from Tufts University in Boston, after dropping out of Columbia University earlier in the decade. Autor was a psychology major, and he once thought he was headed for a doctoral program in that field. But by graduation he was sure it was the wrong fit, dwelling too narrowly, and not rigorously enough, in issues of individual well-being. "I liked the questions," he told me in an interview, "but wasn't satisfied with the answers. . . . I wanted to go bigger."

Autor was interested in technology, and in people, and so in 1989 he had moved across the country and taken a job running a computer learning center at a black Methodist church in San Francisco, California. He stayed three years. He left convinced that technological advancements were leaving already disadvantaged communities further and further behind. Computers demanded more problem solving and critical thinking. The people he was trying to help learn them were living in the middle of a crack cocaine epidemic. Many of them were recovering addicts, or children of addicts. They were less equipped than the city's wealthier children, who did not have to navigate drugs or violence or hunger at home to focus on the skills that computers demanded from them. "I could see," Autor said, "how disequalizing that was."

His next job took him to South Africa, where he worked for a trade union, helping underemployed workers improve their fortunes by introducing them to better sets of tools. Again, he saw a chasm between education and opportunity for the black people he helped and the same things for the wealthier, white people around them. He did not forget those observations when he left South Africa and San Francisco behind and returned to Boston to enroll in a public-policy graduate program at Harvard's Kennedy School.

As often is the case with economists, Autor held on to his personal experiences, to the big questions they had raised about fairness and justice and opportunity. They became the scaffolding for one of the most important bodies of economic research in the coming century.

The first economics course of Autor's life came in graduate school. He was instantly hooked. "It was the questions I cared about," he said, "with the rigor that satisfied me." His master's thesis was titled "Charting the Impacts of the Computer Revolution: New Evidence from the Current Population Survey," and his doctoral dissertation was called "Essays on the Changing Labor Market: Computerization, Inequality, and the Development of the Contingent Work Force." They helped earn him a public-policy doctorate, but they were functionally economics papers— and impressive enough to land him a job in 1999 as an assistant professor in one of the country's top economics departments, at the Massachusetts Institute of Technology.

The job was tenure-track, which means it gave Autor the opportunity to earn what is typically a lifetime appointment to do research and to teach. For economists, the key to securing tenure is to publish as many research papers as possible in prestigious, peer-reviewed academic journals. The process rewards the prolific. Autor was prolific. His early papers built on his interest in the impact of computers on the labor force, pushing the economics profession into new levels of understanding about how rapid technological change had pried open the gap between college-educated workers and everyone else in the 1980s and 1990s.

With two colleagues, he set out to answer a question. What it is that computers do—or what it is that people do with computers—that causes educated workers to be relatively more in demand? The answer, they showed, was that computers did very different things for different workers, depending on what sort of tasks the workers were engaged in.

Computers at the end of the twentieth century were good at following rules. They were easily programmed to calculate sums, route phone calls, or generate imaginary weather reports for kids running virtual lemonade stands. A lot of American workers at the time had jobs that also largely consisted of following rules, with either their minds or their muscles. That made them highly vulnerable to being replaced by computers. Autor and his coauthors cite several examples: bookkeepers, telephone operators, the men who monitored temperatures on steel-finishing lines or lifted windshields into place on automobile assembly lines. Those jobs did not usually require college degrees, and the workers did not usually have them. For those workers, computers were a substitute. Companies could invest in a machine to replace them, and often they did.

But for another group of workers, computers were complementary: they helped the workers do more at their jobs in the same amount of time. Those workers were primarily engaged in tasks that did not follow rules. They involved solving problems, or thinking creatively, or communicating in ways far more complex than computers were capable of. Computers could not do most of those tasks on their own. They could not devise a marketing plan or manage the egos of a sales team. What they could do was help people perform those tasks. A computer could quickly pull up sales figures to show a manager which employees on her team were underperforming. It could search case law to help a lawyer build a closing argument for trial, or medical journals to help a physician make a diagnosis. The workers who were helped in this way by computers usually had college degrees. Computers did not replace them. Computers made them more valuable to their employers. Instead of losing their jobs to a machine, workers used the machine to earn more money. Autor's paper estimated that the divide between tasks that were *replaceable* by computers and those that were *complemented* by computers explained three-fifths of the economy's tilt toward college-educated workers from 1970 to 1998. He thought the paper would sum up an interesting period of the American economy, and he thought that period was probably over and that "the world would move on" to other interesting economic topics.

The world was not moving on. Autor's most important work was still to come.

In the early years of a new century, the nation's economic polarization was intensifying. American manufacturing employment was in free fall. The labor market was not churning like it once had. Even before the financial crisis crippled the economy, the economy of the 2000s under President George W. Bush was delivering effectively no wage growth for the typical worker without a college degree. Communities in Ohio, North Carolina, and other traditional manufacturing states were watching jobs fly out of town. Policymakers were fueling their flight. Autor was showing how.

In one series of papers, Autor examined a rise in companies laying off workers in the United States and hiring workers in low-wage countries overseas, like India, to do the tasks those workers had performed. Autor linked the rise to the American judicial system. Rulings from judges across the United States had made it effectively more difficult for companies to fire workers; the unintended consequence was that companies in those states appeared to have been much more likely to have given up on American employees and shipped their jobs overseas. That dovetailed with Autor's work on polarization due to automation. In a later paper, Autor and two colleagues showed how such trends had "hollowed out" the American labor market by eliminating millions of middle-skill jobs that dealt primarily in tasks that were replaceable with machines. What was left was an economy split between low-wage service jobs that were more difficult to automate, like fast-food cooks, and higher-wage jobs that more and more required computer skills.

There was also disruption from trade. In the 1980s and 1990s, politicians had blamed a series of international trade agreements for lost jobs in the industrial Midwest and elsewhere. Democrats like Sherrod Brown of Ohio—one of the politicians I had followed around the state— hammered the North American Free Trade Agreement, which President Bill Clinton signed into law in 1993, as a community-destroying giveaway to big corporations. Economists had generally dismissed those

arguments. Their studies showed that deals like NAFTA actually created more jobs than they displaced by opening new export markets for
American products and otherwise making the American economy run
more efficiently. They also lowered the cost of consumer goods that could
be manufactured abroad, like televisions, which economists called a win
for Americans. The gains from lower prices were widespread across the
economy, but the people who lost jobs—and there were many of them,
even though new jobs were created—were concentrated in that same
group of less-educated workers that was being socked by computerization.
Quite conveniently for Americans with college degrees, the trade agreements rarely threatened their jobs or their wages. By making it easier to
buy and sell manufactured goods across borders, the agreements forced
American factory workers to compete with foreign workers in countries
where wages were dramatically lower. Doctors, lawyers, and other professionals, whose livelihoods were protected by America's professional
licensing structure, faced no such competition injection.

The economics profession had reached a consensus of sorts on trade
and how it had not been an overall harm to workers. Then, as Autor
told me, "the facts changed." Specifically, policymakers changed the
facts by extending their trade push to the world's most rapidly advancing
economy.

In a last bit of legacy building for the Bill Clinton presidency, Congress
voted in 2000 to grant permanent normal trading-relations status to
China, a distinction that gave businesses certainty that tariffs would remain low on Chinese imports—and cemented the Chinese ascent to the
world trade stage. Republicans supplied most of the votes in the House.
The Senate vote was bipartisan and lopsided. The next president, George
W. Bush, embraced the opening of trade to China. Again, populist politicians howled. Over the course of several ensuing years, Autor and his
colleagues examined their complaints for any sign of validity. Was this
time different? Could trade with China be hurting American workers,
on balance? They found a way to test the question by looking at manufacturing communities that had been immediately subjected to increased

competition from China when permanent normal trading relations were established.

"We were astonished by what we found," Autor told me.

The research, spelled out over a series of papers, showed that what the economists called "the China shock" was responsible for the loss of as many as 2.4 million American jobs. The losses were concentrated in factory states that produced goods that were particularly vulnerable to competition from Chinese imports, like Ohio and North Carolina. That finding alone challenged standard economic theory. But there was more. Autor and his coauthors, along with a growing number of economists in other top university departments and in the Federal Reserve, found that the China shock hit harder and lingered longer than economic models would have predicted. It did not kill just manufacturing jobs. In places where the shock hit hardest, employment was reduced in service sectors as well. Models had predicted that workers whose jobs were swept away by the shock would find new and better jobs, either locally or by moving to the parts of the country where new opportunities were springing up. But the better jobs did not appear, and the workers, by and large, did not move. Cities like Downey waited and waited for industries that did not arrive. Workers like Ed Green watched factory jobs fade away in areas like Winston-Salem, and they were stuck in lower-paying jobs if they could find work at all.

Autor and his contemporaries had discovered, years after the fact, that the American economy broke again in 2000, and not from any Y2K computer meltdown. It broke because of another structural shift that pushed millions more out of the middle class, and which enriched an even more select group of the wealthiest Americans in the process. Once again, the pain of the breakage fell disproportionately on workers without college degrees. Economists had predicted that those workers might have a tough transition to new careers, but there had been widespread belief that, after they had made their way into new jobs in different industries, they would be better off. A full decade after the China shock hit, Autor saw little evidence that this was the case. "There was never another oasis of jobs to swim over to," he told me.

This is all to say that when the financial system plunged the American economy into crisis in 2008, millions of workers were already drowning in a disaster that had inundated an entire generation.

Middle-class workers had tried to bridge their way through the stagnation of the 1980s and early 1990s as though it were a temporary condition. They remembered the golden years. The late 1990s had reminded them that the economy had delivered for them before. They expected it to do so again, on a continuous basis. When the China shock struck in the 2000s, they thought it would be temporary, too. They borrowed their way through it, spending more than they earned. Policymakers were happy to help them by making it easier for Wall Street to steer workers into riskier bets on their financial futures.

Deregulation of the financial industry under Reagan, Clinton, and Bush enabled the rise of the subprime mortgage industry and the complex, interconnected, and deceptively fragile mortgage-backed securities market. It helped inflate a housing bubble in the mid-2000s. The modest gains of the 2000s were illusory—inflated by the housing bubble—and they disappeared when it popped.

A financial crisis that began in the trading houses of Wall Street—on the computer screens of college graduates whose salaries had soared with the advent of new technology—dragged the entire country into recession. It was the deepest economic pain the nation had felt since the 1930s. Factories laid off millions more workers without college degrees. Bipartisan majorities backed a plan by the Bush administration, which would also be implemented by Barack Obama's administration, to bail out large financial institutions. Obama pushed an $800 billion stimulus bill through Congress shortly after taking office. It did not prove nearly as effective as his advisers had hoped; the consensus now among Keynesian economists is that it was far too small for the crisis at hand. Obama's administration brushed aside calls from some outside economists to aggressively intervene in the mortgage market by forcing financial institutions to write down or forgive loans that had gone bad. Such a move would have spared millions of Americans the pain and difficulty of losing their homes, albeit at a high political cost. Many economists say it would have shortened the nation's hangover from recession by shoring up family balance sheets and revitalizing consumer spending much faster. Instead, the administration pursued a more limited homeowner aid package, and the recovery was slow. Not until late in Obama's second term would the typical American household finally see its income rise faster than inflation.

As Obama's presidency wore on, the lingering damage of the recession—piled on top of decades of middle-class disappointment—plagued Americans of nearly all walks of life. It plagued women and black people and immigrants and white families in the Midwest.

I watched that plague spread in the run-up to the 2012 election, as I reported from hard-hit communities around the country. I did not entirely understand at the time what those trips—and the numbers—were showing me. I realize now it was a warning.

What I could see in the moment was an America united in anxiety, but divided in how it coped.

What the 2008 recession wrought was more than just job loss and foreclosure and a winnowing of the middle class. It also helped to cleave American workers and pit them against one another, to accelerate a racial fissure that complicated the task of bringing the county together to restore the upward talent flow that built and sustained the middle-class expansion.

More than a decade would pass before another recession rocked American workers, but the country did not make productive use of the intervening years. Instead, one group of white workers—one politically crucial group—buckled under the weight of its anxieties. It lost hope and grew angry.

Then it rebelled.

8

Chicago, 2011

FORWARD PROGRESS, LOST

Ambar Gonzalez slumped in the passenger side of a compact rental car, a gray hooded sweatshirt zipped over a sweater insulating her from the chill wind blowing in from Lake Michigan. We were driving through the Pilsen neighborhood, an epicenter of Chicago's Latino community, on a tour of her life, her dreams, and her heartbreak.

She pointed out her grammar school, the church where she had been baptized, the coal plant she said had given her asthma. It was nearly fall in 2011. A real estate mogul and reality television host, Donald Trump, had recently ruled out a campaign for president, after several weeks of whipping the country into a frenzy with allegations that the first black president of the United States had not been born in America. I was reporting a curious story that had begun to play out in opinion polls soon after the Great Recession ended. It was about a divergence of optimism among working-class Americans that was opening along racial lines. Some workers were rapidly losing their hope for the future. But they were not the workers who had fared the worst in the recession and recovery. Those were the workers like Ambar, and their hope still burned bright.

Ambar was twenty-five years old. She was directing the car through the neighborhood that had cradled her from birth, toward the house that was until very recently the only home she had ever known.

We drove past it twice, spying it first on a corner, then circling the block to pass it. It was yellow brick, dulled by the punishing snow, ice, and sleet of Chicago winters, with awnings of red and white. The backyard was large enough to host extended-family barbecues every weekend. The inside had been remodeled only a few years before, when Ambar's mother had installed a basement guest apartment, complete with a kitchen. It was a confident decision. A bet on her future, a gift to herself and her family. It had all gone wrong.

Ambar's freckles tightened around her light brown eyes. She had avoided this house, this street, ever since the American economy had driven her family out of it. Do you ever think, I asked her, as she stared out the window, about buying it back? "Yes," she said, without hesitation. "Even if I don't live there, I want it to be my house."

Like millions of other middle-class Americans, Ambar had ample reason to be angry after the Great Recession of 2008. Shortly before it began, with no indication that the bottom was about to fall out of the national housing market or that years of reckless bets were about to drive Wall Street and the global financial system into crisis, Ambar's mother, an immigrant from Mexico, had made a bet on the house and her future. She took out a second mortgage and used the money to refurbish the basement and to spruce up the hair salon she owned and operated nearby. She then watched, her distress growing every day, as the cratering economy sucked away customers. The bills mounted. The double mortgage payments were too much. Ambar's mother, Marcia Soto Rochel, ignored her daughter's offers to help and sold the home that Ambar had assumed she would someday bring her own children to visit. That dream was, if not gone, now very much deferred.

Like Ambar, millions of Americans lost their homes during the recession. Many of them were angry. Ambar was not.

She was determined. She was hopeful. She had been knocked back in the pursuit of her dreams, but she was already up and running toward them again. She had exactly the sort of optimism and grit that white Americans had long said you need to climb the ladder of opportunity into the middle class and beyond—the optimism that many white workers were now losing.

Ambar was emblematic of the nation's racial and ethnic minorities who were scarred by the recession but undeterred in their faith that they could work their way to a better future. And she exemplified a stark contrast to America's angriest group of distressed workers—white workers without college degrees—who were fast losing hope of regaining the middle-class lifestyles their families had built and two decades of policy decisions had crushed.

I had flown to Chicago carrying a backpack stuffed with polling data. It was two years after the end of the recession, which had bloodied workers of all colors but had hurt blacks and Latinos the most. And yet, the polling showed, the resentment and anxiety that festered in its aftermath was decidedly white.

Today, nearly a decade later, Ambar's determination and optimism remain some of the most remarkable displays of economic resilience that I have seen as a reporter. But the passage of time has lent an eerie glint to her story and its contrast with the fading hope of white workers. It was prescient. A divergence that hinted at the electoral conflagration just a few years down the road.

When America's housing bubble popped at the tail end of George W. Bush's administration, and its financial markets began to melt down, the faces on the news were overwhelmingly white: the traders panicking or packing their desks, the Federal Reserve and cabinet officials struggling to bail out the banks. Barack Obama won the presidency in part because he projected a measure of calm and competence amid the downward spiral of an economy that lost more than seven hundred thousand jobs in the month he was elected, what was then its biggest drop in nearly sixty years. He had been on the job less than a month when a white man—a CNBC analyst—whipped up a frenzy on the floor of the Chicago Board of Trade in a backlash to government efforts to assist homeowners who were falling into foreclosure and repossession. "President Obama," he said, in the rant that launched the Tea Party movement, "are you listening?"

The recession hit white Americans hard. Plunging home and stock prices lopped 20 percent off a typical white family's net worth between 2007 and 2010. But the damage was worse for minorities. Incomes fell faster for black Americans and Latinos during the crisis than they did for whites, even though whites earned more, on average, to begin with. Black and Latino families also lost 20 percent of their net worth from 2007 to 2010. But unlike whites, who stabilized in the next few years, minorities kept losing wealth through 2013. Their recession was longer and deeper than it was for whites—and they entered it with far less wealth in the first place, thanks to the racial wealth gap that has haunted America from its founding. Even after gaining some ground in recent years, the typical black family had a net worth of just $17,000 in 2016—one-tenth of the typical white family's.

At the start of 2020, a black worker still earned about sixty cents for every dollar a white worker earned. The black unemployment rate was several percentage points higher than the rate for whites. That inequality isn't just about wages or savings or finding a job. Republican economists on the congressional Joint Economic Committee recently developed a measure of "social capital," which gauges community ties, family support, and other ingredients of lasting economic success for Americans. A leading predictor of a community's social capital was the percentage of its residents who were white; whiteness was a ticket to a high score.

Working-class whites have found little comfort in those statistics. In the poll I took with me to Chicago, a plurality of white voters said they believed that their children would have less opportunity to get ahead in the future than they had at the time. Majorities of black and Latino voters said the opposite: they expected their children to have more opportunity. The nonwhite voters were also much more likely than white voters to report that their own economic opportunities were greater than the ones their parents had enjoyed. Whites were far more likely than other groups to say they expected the economy to worsen over the next year (it would improve, though quite sluggishly) and to report that they were "significantly worse off" from Obama's economic policies. A plurality of whites said they expected that actions taken by the Obama administration would "decrease opportunity for people like [me] to get ahead." Only a small fraction of nonwhite voters agreed.

There is a reason for that divergence, which fuses the anxieties of race, class, and economic status. But it is important to understand, before we unpack those fears, that a collapse in economic optimism was not the automatic, baseline worker response to an event as cataclysmic as the Great Recession. Plenty of Americans were walloped by the economy in the late 2000s, absorbed the damage, and went right back to their dreams. Before we get to the despair of the white working class, it's important to understand why, and how, other workers held on to their optimism.

Start with Ambar and her mother, Marcia, who told me their stories in September of 2011. Marcia moved to the Pilsen neighborhood as a young woman from Durango, Mexico; she was engaged to be married to a Mexican American man from Chicago. When she was a girl, her village was so small that it had only a single store, and she studied at a boarding school in a larger town. She was not fleeing her tiny village when she moved to America; at first, she did not want to leave her simple life at all. But she had agreed to marry the man, even though the thought—leaving her home, losing her independence—saddened her so much that she cried while walking down the aisle at her wedding. The marriage did not last, unsurprisingly, though the couple had two sons. She left her husband, took her boys, and lived for a summer under the canopy of a pickup truck along with a much younger sister. She regained her independence in the same way that so many immigrants, women, and other marginalized groups have moved ahead in America: by working hard and studying.

Marcia juggled waitressing, beauty school, and a long commute, leaving her children with a relative when she was in class or at work. She saved her wages and opened her own salon in Pilsen. Eventually she remarried, and she had a daughter, Ambar, who grew up bilingual and fearless. They bought the house with the yellow bricks, which was located not far from a Catholic cathedral. Their neighborhood had been built by German immigrants, and for years it welcomed other immigrants from a changing array of countries, including Italy, Poland, and, eventually, Mexico. Ambar learned to toggle freely between English and Spanish. Her mother wanted more for her. She wanted her to study, to earn degrees, to win her independence. She made Ambar take a bus, a train, then another bus to attend a private school in the suburbs. When Ambar began to forget her homework, her mother made her pack up her entire desk every afternoon and carry it home from school.

"She was always there, pushing me, telling me I could do whatever I wanted," Ambar told me when I first met her, at breakfast at a Pilsen mainstay called Nuevo Léon Restaurant. "She always told me that I had to go to college, but I could be whatever I wanted to be."

Ambar believed her. She enrolled at DePaul University after high school. She graduated with a degree in political science in 2009 with visions of becoming a lawyer, just as the customers were disappearing from her mother's shop. Marcia had borrowed against their home in 2007, a $127,000 loan from JPMorgan Chase with a variable interest rate that started at 8.25 percent. Ambar was living there as she studied for the LSAT exam, worked at a nonprofit that helped immigrants, and prepared to apply to law school. Family members were always coming to Chicago for stays, and Marcia's house always welcomed them. There were cookouts nearly every weekend. Marcia wanted her guests to be more comfortable, and she wanted to spruce up her hair salon with new wood floors and bright coats of paint, and so she took out the loan. But when the remodeling was done, her clients only trickled back.

At first Marcia did not understand. She had invested in her business; where was the return? She phoned some former customers to ask where they had gone. In their replies, she heard the free fall of the American economy. Some had lost their jobs, or their husbands had lost jobs. Others had moved, looking for new employment. Time and again, her once loyal clients told her they simply couldn't afford hairstyling any more.

Her income was depressed, her payments on two mortgages were higher, and Marcia fell behind on the second loan.

JPMorgan filed to foreclose on Marcia in the Cook County Circuit Court in May of 2010. Ambar begged her mother to allow her to take over the payments. Her mother refused. She would be fine, she said. But if Ambar saddled herself with a mortgage now, she would never make it to law school. She would stop climbing that ladder of opportunity. Marcia would not allow it. She put the house on the market. It sold in September of 2011 for $175,000, avoiding foreclosure. Three years later, it would sell again, for nearly a third more, as a new wave of gentrification brought eager young professionals, many of them white, into Pilsen.

When I met Marcia later that September, she and Ambar had only recently unpacked from their move to a new apartment. It was a few blocks from the home they'd sold, perched above Marcia's salon on a wide main street called West Cermak Road. Their cookout-sized backyard had been replaced by a deck that was just large enough to hold a grill. The walls of their bedrooms wrapped tightly around their beds and dressers. Ambar had cleaned out twenty-five years of mementos, jamming Barbie dolls into a duffel bag, and she had made an effort to avoid her old street before she directed me past it on our drive through the neighborhood.

The day after that drive, Marcia's sister Paula cooked lunch for Marcia, Ambar, and me in the apartment above the salon. We ate Spanish rice, warm and fresh tortillas, and chicken cooked in mole sauce, which blends dark chocolate and chiles. While I sopped up mole with tortillas, the women argued gently about the house. Ambar was still upset that her mother had not let her take on the payments. "I thought I would walk out of there married," she told Marcia. "I thought I would visit it with my children. I always saw it in my future."

Marcia, too, was thinking about the future. "Education is more important than one house," she told Ambar, who had recently aced the LSAT, landed a new job with an immigration law firm downtown, and was preparing her law school applications. "With education, you can buy many houses." Keeping her focus on the future was how Marcia stayed upbeat. She told me she did not trust the government or the big banks, and that she was worried that American manufacturing was in decline. But she said she blamed no one for her financial struggles. She told me—in 2011, a month after she had been forced to give up her home—that too many Americans were angry. Too many feared losing what they had gained. "When you are afraid, I can do with you what I want," Marcia said. "And I am not afraid."

Lunch lingered through the afternoon, ending around four p.m. Ambar, whose legal ambitions were already inspiring her nieces, nephews, and cousins to dream of becoming lawyers themselves, helped her mother wash the dishes. She had told me about her dreams after law school, of moving back to the neighborhood and starting her own firm. Marcia and her sister, Paula, gave me a jar of their homemade mole to take home and share with my son. Paula told me something in Spanish, which Ambar translated. "She says, 'You came to interview the richest ladies on Cermak Road.'"

I was thinking about those ladies a few years later, shortly after American voters used the 2014 midterm elections to deliver a final message to Obama, who was term limited and was still presiding over an economy that was not working for most working people. Obama was not personally on the ballot in those midterms, but his party was, in contested elections for the House and the Senate. Democrats lost the House in 2010, in the first Tea Party revolt against Obama's policy agenda. In 2014, they lost the Senate too. I wanted to know how economic attitudes had influenced those results. That's how I ended up on the phone with Patrick.

He was from New Jersey, self-employed, white. He didn't want his last name printed in the newspaper. In his business he had to hustle to attract customers, and he did not want to risk relationships by offending anyone's politics. His wife had been out of work for a year and a half after losing her job. His salary alone did not feel sufficient to buy the middle-class security package, particularly health insurance for his children. So he had dialed back his work hours to keep his salary low enough to qualify for free government-provided insurance. He was angry at Obama, whom he had voted for in 2008 but not in 2012. He had backed a Republican for the House in that week's election and, like a third of the Republicans who turned out in the midterms, he took a view of the economy that had mostly been espoused by Democratic candidates for federal office. The system, he said, was rigged to favor the rich.

"All I know is that I look around and when I go to diners, or when I talk to people when I go out to breakfast, and everyone feels the same way," Patrick told me. "We don't have a shot. You want to move up? Why should I work harder if you're going to tax me more? Why should I work harder and get above the poverty line and have my kids lose health insurance?"

It was late evening, and he had wandered away from a hockey game on television. "It really sucks," he said. "I like working. You have a sense of accomplishment. I like doing it." He said he felt like he could not chase the American Dream anymore. He was not even asking for the chance to scale the economic ladder and become rich himself. He would have been fine, he said, just doing a little better than he was. "I don't even want to get ahead right now," he said. "I just want to survive."

I don't know if Patrick ended up voting for Donald Trump two years later. But rereading his words, I see the seeds of Trump's outsider, populist appeal. Patrick voiced those sentiments near the end of our chat, when I asked him who he would like to see take over from Obama, and he offered a bleak assessment of the choices. "I don't know who's left," he said. "I look at the political stage right now, and all I see is a bunch of hacks who want to make their $5 million when they leave."

He believed that Obama had failed to revive the economy. He also believed that under the right leader, the system could be unrigged and the economy could start working for people like him again. "It would take an act of Congress," he said. "It would take an act of the president of the United States actually giving a shit."

As America raced toward the 2016 election, the despair of the white working class continued to build, polls would show. So did a white hostility and resentment toward black people and immigrants—Americans of color, like the ladies of Cermak Road, who had held on to their hope through everything.

In some ways the trend seems counterintuitive. Black, Latino, and other nonwhite workers were not surging ahead of similarly educated white workers before, during, or after the recession. Whites had actually started to recover sooner than minorities. So why were whites angrier? Why were nonwhite workers so much more hopeful for the future?

The difference is expectations. Many workers of color never saw themselves or their families as having fully attained the American Dream. Many of their families were recent arrivals from much more impoverished nations. Many of their ancestors had fought for generations to attain something that even mildly resembled the economic opportunity that white families enjoyed. Marcia owned a home and a business but did not see herself anywhere near the end of an upward economic journey. She saw her daughter, the future lawyer, climbing further still. She kept that faith through good times and bad. She had seen poverty and she had seen hardship, and her dream had always remained in front of her; no recession was going to change that.

White working-class families didn't see their journey that way. So many white men without college degrees have told me how, at one point, they felt like they had made it—not all the way to the top, certainly, but to a comfortable perch that matched their aspirations. And now, they felt that perch being threatened. They worried for their kids because they saw the economy pushing them, and guys like them, down the ladder.

Another poll, from the Pew Economic Mobility Project, conducted in the spring of 2011, drove home that point. It showed that white Americans who earned incomes that would qualify them for the broad middle class were more than twice as likely as black Americans with similar incomes to say that they had already achieved the American Dream. They were nearly twice as likely to say that as Latinos. Income figures still showed similarly educated white families outearning their nonwhite counterparts and holding more wealth. But white Americans no longer saw themselves as climbing. They were just trying to hold on to what they had. Nonwhite workers, no matter how hard the economy pushed them back, still held out hope that they would climb the ladder someday.

Economists have documented this phenomenon. People don't just look at their place in the economy and ask, Am I better off today than

I was four years ago? They look back in time and ask if they're better off than their parents were when they were growing up. They look around and ask, Am I keeping up with other workers? Am I getting ahead as fast as they are? Because they are humans, and prone to all sorts of biases, they often make those judgments based on information that is incomplete. Sometimes the information is flawed or flat-out incorrect. Sometimes it is prejudiced. Sometimes it is a deliberate lie, sold to them by someone trying to elicit a response and profit off it.

What we have seen time and again across American history is workers, particularly white workers, assessing their future prospects based on this relative view of their current status. The important variables in the equation of "Will my children have a better life than I do?" include "Do I have a better life than my parents?" and "Is my life improving as fast as, or faster than, the lives of people around me?" I'd argue that a third variable has proven particularly important in this century, when the 1990s tech boom gave way to a prolonged stretch of middle-class stagnation and the declines of the Great Recession. It's this: "Am I getting ahead as fast as I expect to, given how things have worked out for me in the past?" If you compare this century so far with the 1990s, the answer to that question for working people is "absolutely not."

A Harvard economist named Benjamin M. Friedman offered an early warning about how workers' souring assessments of their *relative* economic status could lead a country dangerously astray. He published a book in 2005 called *The Moral Consequences of Economic Growth*, which argued that even rich nations face political and economic peril if growth no longer lifts the incomes of their citizens. He expounded on the themes in a 2006 lecture to the American Economic Association (at the same annual meeting where Claudia Goldin laid out her case on how and why women had narrowed the income gap with men in recent decades). Near the beginning of his remarks, Friedman, who is white, asked his audience of economists what might have seemed to be a rhetorical question: "For those of us who are blessed to live in a society where the average standard of living is far beyond anything our ancestors historically could have imagined," he said, "the question remains: Why should we, and why do we, care about rising incomes?"

We care, he said, because rising incomes lead people to treat one another better. When incomes rise for everyone, people discriminate less based on race or religion. They exhibit more generosity to the less fortunate and more support for opening opportunity to all. And, he said, they "strengthen democratic political institutions"—the necessary gears of government by the people.

Vast economic evidence, Friedman said, shows that people's sense of well-being "depends both on how they live compared to how they have lived in the past and on how they live compared to others around them." He suggested that those assessments were substitutes: people who saw themselves getting ahead worried less about comparisons with people around them. And he pointed out that any country, no matter how rich it might get, could see "its basic values at risk whenever the majority of its citizens lose their sense of forward progress."

Midway through the second decade of the twenty-first century, the typical white worker with a high school diploma was earning less than she or he had at the end of the 1990s. That worker could look back and see not just a lack of progress but a backslide. The same was true for a similarly educated Hispanic worker. A similarly educated black worker had seen her or his income fall even more. An entire class of economic thinkers in Washington kept churning out research papers about how, actually, those workers were doing just fine. They had PlayStations! Their incomes were nearly as high as they had ever been in American history! Still, workers of all races had a right to be frustrated. They really were falling behind their parents.

A massive study, first released in early 2017, confirmed that fact. It came from a University of Minnesota economist named Fatih Guvenen and other researchers from the University of Chicago, the Social Security Administration, and Princeton University. Using government records, it painstakingly constructed estimates of how much money individual workers earned over the course of their lifetimes. It concluded that the typical American who entered the labor force in 1983 went on to earn *less* than one who entered it in 1967. The size of the decline varied depending on which inflation adjustment the researchers used and whether they included the value of employer-provided health benefits in the calculation, but the trend remained constant in every case: downward.

In the spring of 2018 I visited one of the authors of that paper, Greg Kaplan, in his office at the University of Chicago. I was there to talk about a different research project of his, which helped illuminate another source of anger for working-class white men in America. Greg, who is Australian, builds models of the economy that start with actual people and work their way out to an entire labor market. One day he was walking to work while listening to the podcast *Planet Money* on his headphones, and he heard the hosts talking about John Maynard Keynes. Along with founding an entire branch of economics in the early twentieth century—called Keynesianism, appropriately enough—Keynes famously predicted in 1930 that his grandchildren would only work fifteen hours a week. Technology would advance, production would require far less time and effort, and so, he reasoned, the work week would shrink and everyone would have more leisure time. The podcast episode was about how, and why, Keynes had been so wrong about that.

Kaplan had a theory about why people have kept working far more than Keynes predicted, even though, indeed, economic output has grown dramatically more efficient. His theory was simply that people like work. "Maybe we're just thinking about leisure wrong," he told me, his accent rhyming "leisure" with "pleasure," as Australians do, "because work was very different back when Keynes was writing than it is today." He had started to think about his own job, as an economist in one of the world's premier universities for economics. How much would he work if he didn't get paid? The answer, he reasoned, was less than he works now. But it wasn't "Not at all." He gets paid, he confessed, to come to work every day and sit and think about things he finds interesting. "Maybe," he said, "I should think of the time I spend at work as time I actually enjoy. Maybe what's gone on is we are consuming more leisure than we were in the past—much more leisure. It's just hidden inside the jobs that we do."

It was a provocative idea for a research paper. He decided to test it by looking at how much satisfaction workers reported feeling in their jobs, dating back to that Golden Era of the American middle class. There was one small problem: the government only recently began collecting the detailed data on worker satisfaction that Kaplan wanted to track. So how could he map its change over time? He and a coauthor, a Federal Reserve of Chicago economist named Sam Schulhofer-Wohl, devised a work-around. They looked at how worker satisfaction varied based on occupation—the job the worker was paid to do. They traced the shifting composition of American occupations back over time; since the 1950s, those occupations have become far more concentrated in the service sector and other so-called knowledge jobs, and far less in manufacturing and other jobs that require physical skills like strong backs or deft hands. The economists broke workers into groups based on gender, race, and education level and looked at how each group reported feeling about various occupations in recent years. They assumed that individual occupations gave workers the same satisfaction in the 1950s that they give workers now. So a shifting set of occupations could plausibly engineer shifting satisfaction among types of workers, from jobs they liked a certain amount to jobs they now like more—or less.

Their calculations identified one group that, unlike what Kaplan theorized, did not see a rise in fulfillment on the job. Those workers had experienced a sharp decrease in what they called "meaning" from work, over the course of several decades. That group was men without college degrees.

Non-college-educated male workers endure less pain and other physical distress from their jobs today than they did from the more physical jobs they used to have. But they also derive less meaning from their new jobs. "There's a bunch of things that men report as being kind of low stress and happy and positive emotional responses, and they're doing less of them now, and they're moving into what people call these pink-collar jobs, which require you to put a smile on every day and be nice to people," Kaplan told me. "And for some people that's extremely stressful. They'd much rather be doing something that's physical. And they're doing less of that."

He said it was hard to tell if the loss of fulfillment flowed from the actual shift in tasks—doing service work when you'd rather be in a factory—or if there was what he called a "social-capital" aspect to it. Which is to say, maybe working-class men weren't just less fulfilled by the duties they were now being asked to perform at work. Maybe they had lost the cachet of doing work that was more celebrated by society. Work that *felt important.* Either way, it was more evidence of moving backward—of losing a sense of meaning that you, or your father, once brought home every night from the job. I would add that such a loss stings especially painfully in America, a country where work and identity have long been wrapped tightly together. There may be no more common icebreaker, when you meet someone new at a party or a cookout or a back-to-school night in the United States, than asking, "What do you do?"

While I was on campus that day, I stopped in to see another Chicago economist: the lead author of the talent-allocation study, Chang-Tai Hsieh. It had been seven years since I'd first read his evidence that reducing occupational barriers for women and minorities had fueled a surge in American growth after 1960. I wanted to know if he had found anything, in his latest update to the paper, that changed how he thought about the flow of talent and its role in the stagnation of middle-class American workers in recent decades.

In fact, he had found two things.

"There's been a bit of a reversal in the last ten or twenty years," Hsieh told me. "Most of the changes took place in the sixties and seventies. So I think of that paper as really about documenting the economic effect of, let's say, the social revolution that took place in the United States."

"Reversal?" I said. "Like you mean we've moved backwards?"

"We've moved backwards a bit," he said, "primarily in terms of what's been happening to African Americans." Women, he said, have seen their progress slow since the 1960s and 1970s. Black workers, particularly men, have actually been shoved backward. Discrimination, reasserting itself.

There was something else. "The other part which we don't document, but I think is there, but we just don't have an easy way of trying to get an empirical handle on," he said, "is a story of what's happening to a subgroup of white males."

Which was to say, white men without college degrees.

In particular, Hsieh was talking about white men concentrated in distressed parts of states like West Virginia, Ohio, or Michigan—the working-class white guys whose incomes and fulfillment from work had begun to fall long before the Great Recession and its feeble initial recovery. The reversal, he said, was in the opportunities that were available to those men. He did not have the full data to show it—it was hard to tease out the group of men he was discussing from a talent-allocation standpoint—but he had a conjecture.

"The situation of that subgroup of white men, I think," he said, "is like the situation of women in the 1960s." Except the men were headed toward less opportunity in the future, not more.

This is a new truth about the American middle class that is uncomfortable to deal with for almost everyone.

The truth is that the economic playing field is not just tilted against women and men of color anymore. It is now tilted against some white men too. Shifts in the structure of the economy, in the 1980s, 1990s, and especially the full course of the twenty-first century, have dramatically changed the fortunes of white workers without college degrees. Those white men still enjoy some advantages over similarly educated black and Latino workers, and even over white women. They do not face discrimination based on their race or gender. But they are increasingly blocked in the workforce from doing what they are best at. The economy has begun to hit them with the sort of barriers to talent deployment that women and minorities have faced for centuries.

It is ironic, tragic, and, historically speaking, predictable: the anger stirred in white men without college degrees when they fell into the ranks of the economically disadvantaged led them to a presidential candidate who made other disadvantaged workers a central villain in his fables about the battered middle class. In 2016 they turned toward a politician who bashed immigrants and away from the workers of color who could be their natural allies against an economic system that was now holding all of them back.

Before I left his office, Hsieh told me how he and his coauthors had dreamed up the talent study in the first place. He had been talking with

Peter Klenow, one of the Stanford economists who would join him in writing the paper, about the caste system in India, which effectively bars children born to certain parents from ever climbing out of the occupational class to which they are assigned at birth. "There's a caste in India called the rat-catchers caste," Hsieh said. "And it's exactly what you imagine. Basically you grew up in the rat-catchers caste—and guess what kids that grew up in the caste are supposed to do with their lives? They're supposed to catch rats. They catch rats. It's not a law, it's just a custom. So people know what your caste is, and then when you apply for a job they figure out what your caste is, so that all the other opportunities are closed off to you." Hsieh and Klenow had wanted to study the effects of those occupational barriers, but a law in India prevents the government from collecting data on castes. If they wanted to study the effects of blocking talent, they would need to look somewhere else.

It struck them that the next-best analogue to an ingrained caste system was the modern American economy.

I thought frequently about Hsieh and his new theory, and about Ambar Gonzalez and her optimism, and about Patrick and his front-porch angst, when I reread Ben Friedman's 2006 speech to the American Economic Association warning of the risks of income stagnation in a democracy. The speech came two years before the trough of the Great Recession and a full year before almost anyone started worrying about a downturn. The economy had grown 3.5 percent in 2005, after adjusting for inflation.

But in his speech, Friedman noted that for several years running, the typical American's income had not kept pace with rising prices. "If we continue along our current trajectory," he said, "many of the pathologies that we have seen in the past in periods of economic stagnation will once again emerge."

He went on to list the "pathologies" he was thinking of. He started with a brief but exhaustive history of Americans turning, sometimes violently, against immigrants in times of economic malaise. He went on to list racial, gender, and religious discrimination, and the undermining of democratic foundations like the right to vote. And he warned of a coming chaos in American politics.

"It would be foolish to pretend that every twist in this 150 years of American attitudes toward immigrants was driven, in a tightly deterministic way, by the ebb and flow of economic prosperity and stagnation," Friedman said. "But it would be even more foolish to pretend that the underlying economics had nothing to do with it." He continued, "As we now enter what may well become the seventh consecutive year of declining incomes for the majority of America's citizens, this is indeed a sobering thought."

If you put that all together—the polling, the warnings, the rising white anger, and the divergence of optimism between white and nonwhite workers—it becomes clear very fast that the question American political leaders should have entertained after the Great Recession was not *whether* someone running a campaign like Donald Trump's could rocket toward the White House.

The only question was when he'd show up.

9

Washington, D.C., 2016

A LIE IS SOLD

The *Washington Post* newsroom was unusually crowded and quiet as the clock ticked past midnight on November 8, 2016. Election returns were still trickling in, but in the totals on our screens, and in the shocked faces of the pundits on the televisions hanging near our desks, the result was becoming clear: Donald Trump was going to win. Sometime in the early morning hours, from my desk in the *Post*'s Business section, I tapped out a few hundred words—drawing on all the interviews I'd done and the polls I'd dissected in the preceding years—that attempted to explain why, and how, he'd pulled it off. It ended up drawing more page views than almost any other story I wrote in my time at the newspaper.

The headline read, "How Trump Won: The Revenge of Working-Class Whites."

What I wrote was correct. In retrospect, it was also dangerous. It fed a false narrative about workers that the national press, myself included, had inadvertently built in the course of the campaign. It gave one group of workers the impression that their struggles were unique—that workers who did not look like them had somehow stolen the prosperity they had come to expect the American economy to deliver.

We whitewashed the middle class, and in the process, we legitimized a lie.

In the analysis of the national exit polls, I saw the theme I had been exploring, episodically, ever since Trump rode his campaign-opening attack on Mexican immigrants to the top of the Republican primary polls. Trump had blown out Hillary Clinton with white voters without a college degree. They were the foundation of his hair-thin victories in the swing states of the industrial Midwest. They had responded to his appeals on the economy, on immigrants, on gender and race and Washington elites. Black and Latino voters had not—not at all. (I devoted a single line in the election-night story to that fact.) But there were just enough motivated working-class whites in Pennsylvania, Michigan, and Wisconsin to deliver the White House to the New York real estate mogul.

There is a prevailing myth that the media "missed" the possibility of a Trump election because it did not understand his appeal to voters, especially white voters without college degrees. Reporters and political strategists repeated it back and forth to one another so many times in the wake of the election that it quickly passed into the realm of conventional wisdom: Americans by and large were surprised by Trump's victory because the news media did not show them a full enough picture of the support he was generating in the industrial Midwest, the Sun Belt retirement communities, and the rest of the electoral battlegrounds where whites without college degrees have long provided the votes that swing elections.

As the myth goes, reporters had not spent nearly enough time talking to those working-class white voters. They did not understand the ways in which those voters felt abandoned by the structural shifts of the globalized economy, embittered by the slow recovery from the recession and the Obama administration's failure to improve it more for people like them, and alienated by cultural shifts that threatened their white working-class values—whether those values held that marriage should be reserved for the union of one man and one woman, or that the English language should be spoken at all times around them.

One of the best editors I have ever had, my friend and mentor Mike Tackett, who hired me to come to Washington, likes to say that elections are about the country. They tell us who we are. Who we've become since the last time we voted.

The myth that took root after Trump's election was that we as a country had changed profoundly, and that the news media had missed it.

Every part of that myth is wrong.

The country didn't change dramatically in the four years between Barack Obama's reelection and Donald Trump's victory to succeed him. And the news media absolutely did not overlook the voters who turned out in force to help Trump win.

We did overlook a critical group of voters, and in doing so we abetted a lie about American workers.

It's true that most pundits and many polling models predicted a Clinton victory. It is also true that many writers ignored or downplayed the possibility that the vote could be swung by white working-class voters in Ohio or Wisconsin, writing them off as a shrinking coalition that was lashing out as it lost electoral power. But the idea that reporters did not see the victory coming because they had not invested the time in finding and talking with the people who might power that victory? That's wrong. More than wrong; it's backward.

The news media—me very much included—lavished attention on Trump's perceived "base" voters in the white working class. We elevated them because they were so visibly angry, both about economics and about racialized issues like immigration, but mostly because they were swing voters. They piled into Trump's camp to deliver him the Republican nomination and then the White House, and along the way reporters made them the subject of endless diner interviews, television focus groups, and national best-selling books. When the election was over, white workers had spoken, and reporters had been there to catch every word—whether they regarded the speakers as an electoral force to be reckoned with or not.

In the process, we, the news media, missed a critical story about the struggles and concerns of working-class voters who were not midwestern, or from manufacturing towns, or, you know, *white men*. We did not adequately convey the anxieties of those workers, or how policy changes under the next president could affect them.

More importantly, we fueled a dangerous, self-perpetuating, and false narrative: the idea that the anxieties of the white working class were more pronounced, more damaging, and more significant than those of workers of color. By focusing almost exclusively on distressed white guys, we gave them the false idea that their trials were unique. That their problems demanded a special set of solutions, that their fates were not shared with other workers. We unwittingly reinforced the claims that those "others"—the other workers—were an impediment to the renewal of the white working class.

A raft of statistics shows just how lopsided our focus was. For reasons that seemed understandable and defensible in the moment, national news reporters showered attention throughout the 2016 campaign on working-class whites in the heartland. They largely ignored every other type of American worker who was struggling to recover from decades of middle-class stagnation, to the detriment of their audience and the general electorate—because that focus perpetuated a damaging divide between groups of workers whose fates are intertwined.

Allow me to illustrate by picking on a single reporter at a large national news outlet: myself. Scanning through the stories I wrote in the years leading up to Trump's election, I'm struck by how many unsettled white workers I quoted, even when I wasn't writing about presidential politics or looking for anything about Trump. And I'm struck by how similar they all sounded, in their frustrations and their pessimism—and, often but not always, in their search to blame outsiders for what was happening to them.

In the spring of 2015, I'd driven from Oklahoma, where I was talking to white workers who had recently lost high-paying jobs in the oil industry, to Tennessee. The expansion from recession was more than half a decade old, and across the oil patch, as prices fell and investment and hiring collapsed, thousands more Americans had seen their tickets to the middle class canceled. "I see people who are being evicted. I see people who are homeless," an Oklahoma social worker named Earlene told me. Foreclosures were up, and so were missed child-support payments. "People think the money's going to flow forever," she said, "and of course it does not."

Rain spat down for much of the drive to Tennessee. Behind me on the road, tornadoes spun up and slashed through the Oklahoma City area. I put Merle Haggard on the car stereo and called my dad from just outside Muskogee. By lunchtime the rain had stopped and I was eating barbecue in what appeared to be a converted old gas station in Memphis, surrounded by black and white men in suits eating pork sandwiches and baked beans on plaid tablecloths, sitting alone, lost in their sauce.

In the cooling orange glow of late afternoon, my rental car carried me into Decaturville. The road dipped between flat stretches and deep hollows. The downtown was a quiet few blocks. The Tennessee River loomed to the east. The town had about a thousand residents. The county surrounding it had twelve thousand. An air of temperance lingered in town; it was hard to find a mini mart that would sell you beer.

In the waning years of the 1980s, there had been a thrumming textile industry here. A plant called Decaturville Sportswear had employed as many as fifteen hundred local workers. It closed in 1991, and a year later a presidential candidate named Bill Clinton put its laid-off employees in a campaign advertisement. It ran during the World Series, and it blamed the incumbent president, George H. W. Bush, for trade policies that encouraged the factory's owners to essentially ship the Tennessee jobs overseas. Clinton promised hope; the ad said he was ready to invest in America. I drove to Decaturville because Clinton had never delivered on his promise. The town's textile industry never recovered. Its economy remained depressed in the spring of 2015. White men in town told me that Clinton had betrayed them by signing NAFTA instead of fighting for their jobs. Now another Clinton—Hillary Rodham Clinton—was running for president, leading the Democratic field. No one expected her to carry Tennessee like her husband had, but even in the spring of 2015 it was already clear that white workers who had experienced Decaturvi-lle-like decades of distress could prove critical to her chances of winning states like Ohio or North Carolina.

I spent much of my stay in the area driving around with the head of the county's chamber of commerce, a kind, soft-spoken, silver-haired white man named Charles Taylor who had moved to Decatur County to make a home on the river. "The working class," he told me, as we toured the green hills and abandoned storefronts of the county, "has gotten to the point where they don't trust anybody." The experiences of towns like Decaturville and Downey, California, suggested they were right not to.

This slice of the electorate was not hidden from news consumers or from the politicians who aspired to harness their frustration at the ballot box. In February of 2015, the man who was considered the front-runner for the Republican presidential nomination was former Florida governor Jeb Bush, son of one former president and brother to another. He flew to Detroit to give the first major policy speech of his campaign. Bush wanted to make a case that he was the candidate best equipped to win the struggling industrial Midwest, and so he launched his policy conversation with Americans there, using words he hoped would resonate with the disaffected working-class whites who played such a pivotal role in the states' elections. He told his audience in Detroit that the "opportunity gap"—the difference between who could get ahead and who could not in America—was "the defining issue of our time." He lamented that the American Dream had become a "mirage" for too many workers. "If Americans are working harder than ever, earning less than they once did," Bush said, "our government, our leaders, should step up, fix what went wrong, or step aside."

One line of Bush's sounded as though it could have come straight from Bill Clinton's old commercials. "Today, Americans across the country are frustrated," Bush said. "They see only a small portion of the population riding the economy's up escalator."

Then came the man on the down escalator.

Donald Trump had toyed with presidential runs before. The brash real estate mogul considered a third-party campaign in 2000, after years of warning about the rise of Japan as an economic rival to the United States and complaints about bad trade deals selling out American workers. He ultimately decided not to run. In 2011, he made noise about running for the Republican nod. He passed again, but not before he briefly commanded the nation's attention with a racist conspiracy theory. In March of that year, Trump, who already had a wide television platform due to his hit reality show *The Apprentice*, began to spring up all over cable news. He wondered aloud if America's first black president, who was born in Hawaii, had actually been born outside the United States. Trump had no proof for his allegations. Despite his promises to investigate them, he never followed up. But cable bookers could not resist giving airtime to his conspiracies, which sought to undermine Barack Obama's legitimacy as president. Trump elaborated on them on the social media platform Twitter, where he routinely mocked Obama and claimed without evidence that unemployment statistics were rigged.

When Trump rode the escalator down into the Trump Tower lobby in Manhattan on June 16, 2015, he carried with him a campaign kick-off speech that seamlessly wove together the racial and economic grievances that he had honed for decades and which had endeared him to a growing band of white workers without college degrees. That group was primed to receive his message. Those workers had helped elect and reelect Obama. But in the course of Obama's presidency, they had turned against him and, increasingly, against nonwhite Americans and immigrants. Opinion polls and political science research showed a rise in the measure of what analysts call racial animus among white Americans. Trump played to those resentments in the remarks he had prepared for delivery that June—the ones he and his advisers had written down for him to read in his speech. And then he went off script, and the resentments veered into unbridled contempt.

"Our country is in serious trouble," Trump said, shortly after his speech began.

> We don't have victories anymore. We used to have victories, but we don't have them. When was the last time anybody saw us beating, let's say, China in a trade deal? They kill us. I beat China all the time, all the time. When did we beat Japan at anything? They send their cars over by the millions—and what do we do? When was the last time you saw a Chevrolet in Tokyo? It doesn't exist, folks. They beat us all the time. When do we beat Mexico at the border? They're laughing at us, at our stupidity. And now they're beating us economically. They are not our friend, believe me, but they're killing us economically. The US has become a dumping ground for everybody else's problems.

Someone in the audience cheered.

Trump continued. "It's true. And these aren't the best and the finest. When Mexico sends its people, they're not sending their best. They're not sending you. [He gestured to the crowd.] They are not sending you. [He pointed again.] They're sending people that have lots of problems, and they're bringing those problems [to America]. They're bringing drugs, they're bringing crime, they're rapists, and some, I assume, are good people."

Reporters were shocked. So were a lot of strategists and Republican leaders. Most pundits wrote off Trump's chances—if they ever thought he seriously had them in the first place—from that line in the start of his speech: "They're rapists." They spent less attention on the rest of the speech, which wandered through Trump's you-versus-them framing of white Americans' economic and social ills. It is worth revisiting now.

"Our real unemployment is anywhere from 18 to 20 percent," he told the crowd. (The official figure was just under 6 percent; using the most expansive government definition of unemployment made it about 10 percent.) Don't believe the numbers, Trump said. "A lot of people up there can't get jobs. They can't get jobs, because there are no jobs, because China has our jobs and Mexico has our jobs. They all have jobs."

All those other Republican candidates, the ones reaching out to the dissatisfied middle class? Trump eviscerated them with faint praise. "I like them," he said.

And I hear their speeches. And they don't talk jobs and they don't talk China. When was the last time you heard China is killing us? They're devaluing their currency to a level that you wouldn't believe. It makes it impossible for our companies to compete, impossible. They're killing us. But you don't hear that from anybody else. You don't hear it from anybody else. And I watch the speeches. I watch the speeches of these people, and they say the sun will rise, the moon will set, all sorts of wonderful things will happen. And people are saying, "What's going on? I just want a job. Just get me a job. I don't need the rhetoric. I want a job."

The next day, Trump's campaign released data showing that the speech had captured millions of viewers on social media. A news release claimed he had been the most searched Republican candidate on Google in every state.

Within a month, he was leading national polls for the nomination.

Quite a few journalists and pundits thought Trump wouldn't stay in the lead for long. His numbers were a product of name recognition, they said. His love of roving off script would quickly sink his support. I recall chatting with a prominent political analyst shortly after Trump criticized former Republican presidential nominee John McCain, a war hero who spent years in a prison camp in Vietnam, for his service record. "I like people who weren't captured," Trump said. The analyst said Trump's campaign was over. But his support kept growing.

It grew after Trump laughed off questions from a moderator in the first Republican presidential debate who raised his past statements calling women "fat pigs, dogs, slobs" and suggesting to an *Apprentice* contestant that she'd look good performing oral sex. How, asked the moderator, Megyn Kelly, will you respond to attacks that you are part of a "war on women" in America? "I think a big problem this country has is being politically correct," Trump replied, and the audience cheered. His polling lead soon grew to double digits.

I wanted to know why. Other Republicans had taken positions similar to Trump's, particularly on immigration, an issue on which the party had shifted to a hard line against people who were in the country in violation of American immigration law. Every candidate was appealing to frustrated workers who had been left behind in the recovery. Why was Trump standing out? I figured we should ask his supporters—literally, by interviewing them, and figuratively, by breaking down the polls. Thus began a quest, which persisted and evolved over the course of more than a year, to understand working-class white voters and why Trump's message was capturing their imaginations in a way that other candidates' could not.

In late July, a month after Trump had announced his campaign in New York, I drove to a hilltop home located an hour and a half west of Washington. I had been invited by a group of conservative immigration activists who were delighting in Trump's rise. They all blamed workers who came to America illegally for stealing jobs, suppressing wages, and soaking up taxpayer-funded welfare benefits. They hated traditional Republican elites, who they said had broken promises to secure the country's border with Mexico. They loved Trump for his brashness, for his willingness to denounce immigrants in terms that other politicians would not use, and especially for his open contempt for those elites they also loathed. They felt as though America had been taken advantage of for years by outsiders and insiders alike, and in Trump they had finally found a candidate who shared that assessment.

"The Hispanics have taken over the construction industry," one of the activists, a general contractor named Rick Buchanan, told me. "All my drywall guys are Hispanic. Plumbers, painters, framers, they're at least half Hispanic." He voiced no complaints about the quality of those Latino workers. He was upset about their displacement of white ones. "These people are taking their jobs," he said. "Literally, taking their jobs." Trump, he added, was "hitting a chord with not only the lower-income people. I consider myself middle class, and he's resonating with me, too."

Polls suggested that those men represented what you could call the base of Trump's supporters: white workers without college degrees who saw immigrants as a threat to America's economy and culture. It was an intuitive appeal: I talk to white workers frequently who believe they are locked in an us-against-them economic battle with immigrants. Economic research, as we'll see, shows that that's wrong. Native-born workers aren't losing out to immigrants, even if white Americans think that's the case.

The campaign marched on. Trump held his polling lead, with only one brief interruption, through the early primaries, Super Tuesday, and the winnowing of the Republican field. After he called for the United States to stop accepting refugees from Syria, a *Washington Post* poll showed that nearly three-quarters of Trump's support was coming from Republicans who favored both the following policies: barring Middle Eastern refugees, and deporting immigrants who were here illegally. (That group disproportionately comprised white workers who did not graduate from college.) In January, polls showed that Trump was faring best with "the most economically anxious Republican voters"—the ones who said they feared they could not maintain their standard of living—and, once again, with Republicans who said that immigrants weaken society. (Not immigrants here illegally—all immigrants.) By March, rank-and-file Republicans were increasingly aligning with Trump's critique of foreign trade, a decade and a half after Republicans in Congress had helped Bill Clinton open the spigot of job loss to China. In October, data from the Chicago Council on Global Affairs showed how immigration and economic concerns formed a feedback loop for Trump's core, largely white, working-class supporters. "Those Americans who feel more threatened by immigration, favor deportation, and feel unfavorably toward immigrants believe that the next generation will be economically worse off than adults today," the council's researchers wrote. "Unease with immigration and pessimism about the next generation's economic prospects reinforce each other and have proven to be key factors in support for Donald Trump."

Johnny West was the last working-class white Trump supporter I interviewed before the election. He had answered the phone when a *Post* pollster called to ask about the campaign and how Johnny felt about how the United States economy was treating him and his children. Johnny had given the pollster permission to pass his name on to a reporter. It had come to me in a spreadsheet, which also said he lived in Delaware, a few hours away from my office. I called him, we talked a bit, and then we made plans for me to drive out and visit on a hot September day, almost exactly five years after I had toured the Pilsen neighborhood with Ambar Gonzalez. Johnny was amiable, matter-of-fact, and, best of all for my story, statistically representative. Trump supporters, our polling showed us, were far more pessimistic about America's economy and far more likely to say life had gotten worse for them compared with the workers who came before them. "I'm doing worse than my parents' generation," Johnny told me as we sat on his mother's back porch. "I can't speak my mind. I can't get ahead. They take every dime I make anymore—in taxes, in insurance, whatever." His frustration was visible. The contrast with Ambar, the hopeful young woman I'd interviewed five years before in Chicago, was unmistakable.

The campaign focus and the media focus on white workers were so strong that I specifically raised their struggles with Hillary Clinton when I interviewed her over the phone in June of 2016. "I would be remiss," I said in the final question of the interview, "if I didn't ask you about the anxiety we are seeing among white working-class Americans, particularly men, in this campaign cycle. Where do you think that anxiety is coming from, and how would your policies help those anxious workers?"

Clinton gave me an answer that was nearly six hundred words long. It explicitly rejected Trump's diagnosis for what had gone wrong—the blaming of immigrants—even as she struggled to articulate a catchy summation of her own proposed fixes. This was before she was caught on tape calling some of Trump's supporters "deplorable." In terms that created a lot less news, she tried to sympathize with the anxieties of Trump's most dedicated voters.

"Jim, I think it's real," she said, referring to that anxiety, "and I respect the fear, the anxiety, even the anger that a lot of people are feeling, because the advance of globalization and technology has really replaced or undermined the future for many jobs." She continued:

You don't have to go just to coal country to see that. You can go to a lot of parts of America, where people had good, decent jobs that provided a good middle-class life for them and their kids. That was the American Dream. That's how we used to define it. Now, we've seen so much downward pressure on wages. We've seen the disappearance of a lot of jobs that used to be available. And so I do think globalization and technology have played a role. But I also think decisions made by business leaders and government leaders have also played a role. I just don't think we are as focused as we need to be on trying to rebuild economic opportunity in places that have been hollowed out.

She went on to talk about rebuilding the federal research budget, about investing more in higher education and innovation, about spending more on infrastructure, and, above all, about focusing policy on the overarching goal of creating jobs that paid better so that incomes could grow. Solid plans—but plans many workers had heard about for years.

"What people are feeling is that the economy failed them, their government failed them. They just are looking for somebody who will explain, in a way they will accept, what's happened. So Trump comes along and he blames immigrants and he blames minorities and he blames women, and people are responsive to that because these are hard times that folks are going through," she said. In closing, she added, "I respect the legitimate concerns that so many Americans have, because of what has happened to them. But I am offering a path forward that I think can actually produce results for them."

Clinton did not have a simple message to sell voters on that path. The first time I interviewed her, when she campaigned for Democrats in Ohio's midterm elections in 2006, she had told me the country needed to return to "Clinton economics"—the budget-balancing, trade-opening policies her husband had pursued in the years that produced the last great income burst for the middle class. But now, a decade later, voters were angry about trade with China and Mexico and about the deregulation of Wall Street that Bill Clinton had pursued as president. "Clinton economics" were decidedly out of vogue, even among Democrats.

On Election Night in 2016, voters split on the economic question. Exit polls showed that nationally and in Ohio, voters trusted Trump more to handle the economy. But voters who said the economy was their top concern narrowly preferred Clinton over Trump.

The interview I conducted that most sticks with me from the campaign was not the one with Clinton, or any of the ones with Trump supporters that I ended up writing about in the newspaper. It was one my editors decided was too dangerous to print.

Every journalist's email inbox is barraged daily by press releases, a natural result of the trend in the economy that has seen thousands of newspaper reporters lose their jobs over the last decade while public relations firms have *added* thousands of jobs. Mixed in with the lobbying groups, think tanks, and campaign releases is a steady dose of emails promoting books by self-published authors. In 2016, one of those emails piqued my interest. It advertised a novel written by a man who lived in the logging country of Oregon. The plot touched on job loss, Hispanic immigration, and a rising sense of alienation among white workers, carried to a violent end. Its cover showed a group of migrants as seen through the eye of a rifle scope. "Disenfranchised American voters and Donald Trump supporters," the release proclaimed, "will love this novel." I asked the publicist to send me a copy and set up an interview with the author, whose name was Robert Bennett but who published under the moniker "Skookum Maguire."

The book was a working-class-whites revenge fantasy. Its heroes were aging white men who were good with their hands and their guns, and who were disgusted by what they saw as an invasion of job-stealing, Spanish-speaking immigrants. The villains were Latino, lazy, and corrupt. The crux of the plot was that the white men drove to the Mexican border, where they shot and killed an immigrant attempting to sneak across. It was hard to read—a blend of lovely nature description and ugly cultural stereotypes, building to a climax so disturbing that my editor turned down my pitch to profile the author. He said he didn't want to encourage violence.

Before I made the pitch I called Bennett, the author, for a long chat about Oregon, immigration, and the decline of the timber industry. He told me a story that sounded familiar. He'd been running a small business in a timber town called Grants Pass when the logging economy went bust in the 1980s. He'd moved south to chase work and found himself in California, where, he said, "the whole complexion of the place changed in just a couple years" from an influx of immigrants. He tried to start a contracting business but was undercut by competitors paying immigrant workers half of what a native-born worker typically demanded; the immigrant workers were paid under the table, with no benefits and no payroll taxes paid to the government. He left California and wrote his book, originally publishing it in 2005 then rewriting it and reissuing it in the spring of 2016 as Trump stampeded to the Republican nomination. I questioned the book's portrayal of immigrants as lazy but calculating invaders.

Bennett told me that the characters were drawn from his personal experiences of working with immigrants in California. He said he had enjoyed coworkers who were first-generation immigrants, drawn to the United States by opportunity.

"They were the nicest people you'd want to meet," he said. "You'd see why they were there—they wanted to survive. It was a bad situation. But the second generation, they were a lot more militant. And they were citizens."

If you talked to those children of immigrants, he said, you could begin to see what appeared, to him, as a sort of ethnic replacement plan. "If they come in large enough numbers and have enough children, they could take over one congressional district at a time," he said. "That was their goal."

I asked if he was surprised by Trump's success.

"I'm surprised it didn't happen sooner," he said.

I asked if he was concerned about the violence in his book.

He laughed. "I guess I didn't think about it," he said. "It's how I see the world."

Three years later, a white man shot and killed twenty-two people, many of them immigrants, at a Walmart in El Paso, Texas. He left behind a manifesto, which warned of immigrants invading America. Trump had used similar language—that of invasion—in his rallies. "If Mr. Trump did not originally inspire the gunman," my colleagues Peter Baker and Michael Shear wrote in the *New York Times* after the killings, "he has brought into the mainstream polarizing ideas and people once consigned to the fringes of American society."

Would a story about a self-published author whose books didn't sell many copies have helped prepare the country for the possibility that the sort of rhetoric Trump used to appeal to working-class white voters might encourage violence? It's hard for me to say. But the story might have helped balance the way the news media, me included, reported on the economic aspects of Trump's pitch by showing how that appeal so deftly complemented the racial codes of "invasion" and "replacement" among some working-class whites.

After the election, political scientists and other academic researchers conducted a wide variety of studies to tease apart the motivations of Trump supporters. They tended to find stronger effects from racial animosity and less pronounced, but significant, effects from economic anxiety. It remains difficult to separate the two; it is a fact that racial animosity rose among working-class whites at the same time that their optimism for economic advancement cratered. Polls, interviews, and sophisticated analyses all have shown linkages between the two over time. Racism and hostile sexism have always been a part of America; they were certainly *not* created by the failure of the economy to meet the expectations of middle-class white men over the course of several decades. They also, undeniably, were inflamed in the years before Trump arrived, then harnessed by a candidate who was more willing to play on overt racial division than any of his recent predecessors.

It is also clear, in retrospect, that the news media helped perpetuate a very different sort of linkage between race and economics, one that gave white workers the impression that they struggled uniquely and fed the idea that "others" were to blame for their problems.

We weren't trying to elevate Trump's ideas or to endorse violence; news reporters who cover immigration issues, even tangentially, are routinely chastised by anti-immigration activists for writing unsympathetically about their positions. But if elections are truly about the country, and if it is a critical job of the press to hold up a mirror so that voters can see the country's changes for themselves, then we clearly failed in that responsibility.

It is easy to quantify that failure. An online research tool called the Television Explorer, built by the GDELT Project, has compiled an exhaustive database of the words spoken on cable news networks since 2009. It affords an unparalleled source of insight into the patterns of America's news media and the public discourse they both foster and reflect. The database tracks how frequently particular terms, topics, or people come up on networks like CNN, Fox News, and MSNBC. In the 2016 primaries, I mined its data for stories showing the overwhelming airtime advantage that Donald Trump was getting—for free—over his Republican rivals because cable news was addicted to showing and discussing his campaign rallies. (That addiction remains. Through the first two and a half years of his presidency, Trump had exactly *one day* when he was talked about less often on cable news than Barack Obama was talked about on his most-talked-about day in eight years as president.) Looking back on the campaign, the explorer shows a clear and damning picture of the attention news organizations showered on working-class white Americans, to the exclusion of workers of color.

As the campaign wore on, cable news hosts, reporters, and panelists talked more and more frequently about the "working class," the data shows. They were mostly talking about white workers. From the start of 2016 through the election in November, nearly half of all cable-news mentions of the working class were specifically referring to white workers. Less than 5 percent of the mentions referred specifically to black workers. The remainder were largely focused on a more nebulous "working-class" vote, which, anecdotally, was very often a proxy for the white working class. In the final six months of the campaign, you were fourteen times more likely to see a cable news segment on the white working class than on the black working class.

Print media were no better. The *New York Times* archive shows sixty-eight stories for the calendar year 2016 in which the phrase "working class white" appears. For "working class black," there are four stories, two of which are book reviews. Only one—a late-October report from Philadelphia by Sheryl Gay Stolberg—includes interviews with working-class black voters.

In the run-up to the election, I interviewed far fewer workers of color than I did white workers. Several of those conversations focused on issues like government-provided health care and the level of the federal minimum wage, which Trump and Clinton disagreed sharply over and which were far more likely to affect black and Latino workers than whites. I interviewed several home health-care workers who were black and who supported Clinton. Their quotes would have fit well in any story about anxious workers backing Trump.

"I'm just hoping to be able to survive, and I'm hoping somebody can do something about the wages we earn, because I feel like I'm trapped," Sherleen Bright, a Clinton supporter from Richmond, Virginia, who was earning nine dollars an hour and worrying about her health care, told me. She sounded just like the white workers who were flocking to Trump—but reporters seemed to care a lot less about what she had to say.

Newsrooms, like most American institutions, have long suffered from racial bias, and the coverage choices of the 2016 election were no exception. Those biases were compounded by the news bias toward writing about so-called swing voters—the ones who are the most likely to switch their partisan allegiance between elections. In 2016, the polls showed that large pools of potential swing voters, in toss-up states like Ohio that could decide the Electoral College, were working-class whites. That by itself was a failure of political reporting; just because black voters had largely decided they would not support Trump—as polls consistently showed during the campaign—did not rule them out as swing voters. People don't merely choose between candidates in elections. They choose whether to vote at all. In 2018, two graduate students, Jon Green and Sean McElwee, published a study that showed how the decision between voting and staying home was itself a product of economics in the Trump-Clinton election. "Local economic distress," they wrote, "was strongly associated with non-voting among people of color."

Stolberg had hinted at that possibility near the end of her story on black voters in Philadelphia for the *Times*. "When people here watch Trump rallies, some see imagery that reminds them of their childhoods in the Deep South; some go so far as to wonder if Mr. Trump's supporters have been planted by the Ku Klux Klan," she wrote. "Their feelings about Mrs. Clinton are mixed, but those who are voting for president will vote for her."

Those who are voting for president. In an election in which black turnout declined, including in states like Michigan and Wisconsin where a higher turnout could have pushed Clinton over the top, the relative inattention given to nonwhite workers' economic anxieties seems now to have been a dereliction of political-reporting responsibility. Distressed whites weren't the only swing voters, but they got all the press.

Crucially, that inattention also failed *white working-class voters.* When they heard about the middling economy and how it affected them, they were mostly hearing about it in a vacuum. When they heard about workers of color, they were mostly hearing, from Trump, that those workers were villains. They rarely, if ever, heard about how immigrants and black people and other workers of color had helped deliver the prosperity that white workers now felt had been ripped away.

The autopsies of Clinton's loss in major news outlets largely portrayed her campaign as having faced a binary choice—between courting white working-class voters and trying to energize a coalition built around nonwhite workers—and having chosen incorrectly. Relatively little attention was given to efforts to contextualize the suffering of workers of all colors, men and women, or to remind them that American history suggested they needed one another to get ahead.

There was never much attention given to the idea that Clinton— or Trump—could try to win by uniting distressed white and nonwhite workers against the forces that were holding them back in the modern economy. Both candidates complained about rich elites ripping off workers. But neither of them, and hardly anyone in the mass media, hammered away on the idea that the elites had divided the workers against each other, exploiting fissures of race and gender and culture, in order to keep a grip on power in a time of great unrest. Trump was a political outsider, yes, but he ran and won as so many other presidents have in American history: as a rich white man playing one group of anxious workers against the others.

The news media helped him do it. They ran his immigrant-bashing rallies live on the air. They focused undue attention on working-class whites at the expense of nonwhite workers. In the process, they unwittingly fed Trump's story about what had gone wrong for white workers. They lent credence to his boasts that he, alone, could fix those problems.

Here is what happened next, after Trump won the election and ascended to the White House.

He did not fix what had gone wrong for workers.

Not even close.

10

Manhattan, 2016

THE WHOLE CHESSBOARD

Mariko Mori was not yet thirty years old, a former fashion model fresh off her first photography exhibit in New York, when she completed a work she would call *The Last Departure*. It stretches seven feet tall and twelve feet wide. Its backdrop is a digitally manipulated photograph of an airport terminal in Osaka, Japan; it looks like the bridge of a hulking space cruiser. In the center of the bridge stands Mori herself. In previous works she had appeared as a mermaid, a geisha with silvery Spock ears, and what a reviewer would call "a cross between a samurai waif and a robotic streetwalker." Here, she was a sort of extraterrestrial fairy, in shiny black leggings, tall white leather boots, and a short flared dress with winged shoulders. Her hair was a cropped silver-white wig, piled up like a small beehive, adorned with a tiara. On either side she was flanked by a translucent clone, as if she were her own holographic bodyguard. She held her arms with elbows pointing outward, right palm positioned directly over the left. In between her hands hung a glowing blue orb. It was the focal point of the piece. A crystal ball. A window into a bright and cartoonish future.

The Last Departure hung on the wall of the reception lobby of WL Ross & Co. in late October of 2016. I was staring into the orb—into the future Mori had conjured—when Donald Trump's economic advisers summoned me into a private office to talk about their plan to revive the jobs of the past.

Trump was an improvisational, unorthodox candidate, prone to implausible claims about wages, budgets, and growth. But his economic strategy did not just come from nowhere. Reporters and voters paid little attention to it, and the candidate himself never talked about it in detail, but there was an actual intellectual foundation beneath Trump's bravado on the economy. His eclectic core of advisers drew up an econometric analysis, purporting to show how Trump's preferred blend of tax cuts, immigration crackdowns, restrictions on foreign trade, and expansions of oil drilling would work together to crank up growth and restore the good jobs that had gone away for so many Americans.

I had been invited to Manhattan to hear how those pieces all fit together and to get an earful about how I and everyone else in Washington was getting the Trump recipe all wrong. I also received a template for evaluating Trump and his economics-of-division strategies once he took office. It would become a handy guide to all the ways that Trump's efforts to reward elites and play different groups of workers against each other would fail to produce a new and bright future for the middle class. Far from it.

The office and the artwork were owned by Wilbur L. Ross Jr., a maverick investor who had built his career as a bankruptcy specialist before launching his own firm. Ross liked to buy struggling companies, restructure them, and then sell them at a profit. He had been a player in the steel industry, in coal, and, at one point, in a successful effort to help Trump keep control of three Atlantic City casinos when they were threatened with foreclosure. He was nearly eighty years old, and he was now one of the architects of the effort to construct a coherent economic plan out of Trump's gut instincts on policy.

At the time, Ross claimed to be a billionaire. He had made the Forbes 400 list of America's wealthiest people for years, with a personal fortune estimated at nearly $3 billion. His art collection alone was valued at around $150 million. It included several of Mori's works and two dozen paintings by the Belgian surrealist René Magritte, who is famous for, among other works, a painting of a pipe that is captioned "Ceci n'est pas une pipe"—*This is not a pipe.* He had sold WL Ross & Co. years earlier to a larger firm for a reported $100 million with escalation clauses, and he still maintained a corner office at the company. It looked north over the leaves of Central Park, which were changing orange and brown in the fading warmth of midfall. By the window stood a table covered in framed photos of Ross with politicians he had supported over the years, first as a Democrat and now as a Republican. There he was with senators, presidential candidates, a speaker of the house. President Bill Clinton. The table was stuffed like a hunter's trophy walls.

Ross was waiting in the office when an assistant showed me in. I had never met or talked to him before; unlike most campaigns I had covered, which would put their top advisers on the phone for hours to patiently walk through the specifics of policy proposals, the Trump operation had shown relatively little interest in fleshing out its plans with reporters. Trump's initial tax proposal had run just four pages, lacked key details, and promised to relieve seventy-five million Americans of the obligation to pay federal income taxes. Instead of filing tax returns every year, the Trump plan crowed, those households would get a one-page form to send to the IRS saying, "I win." Campaign officials were in no hurry to fill in the blanks, on that plan or most any other plan their candidate had offered. They were happy to let Trump's brash—bordering on impossible—promises stand on their own.

He was going to eliminate America's trade deficit with the world by dramatically increasing exports to foreign trading partners and reducing the amount of manufactured products the United States imported from abroad. He was going to eliminate the federal deficit and balance the budget—no, even better, he was going to pay off the entire federal debt, more than $19 trillion worth, in eight years.

Independent experts rarely bought those claims. Trump never produced a plan to reduce the debt, but several think tanks across the ideological spectrum issued analyses that found that his tax cuts would add trillions to the debt over the course of a decade. Some economists warned that his trade policies, which included large threatened tariffs against trading partners like Mexico and China, could tip the global economy into recession. Usually, a Republican presidential nominee draws intellectual support for a campaign policy agenda from all corners of the conservative movement, including free-market analysts in Washington and elsewhere. Trump was finding relatively little of that, because his agenda did not fit neatly into a traditional Republican box. His business-pleasing tax cuts clashed with a trade policy that corporate leaders and conservative thinkers largely rejected. He was making promises that even the most ardent tax-cut fans struggled to defend, like claiming his proposals would juice annual economic growth to as much as 6 percent, which would have been its highest rate in more than thirty years. But publicly and privately, his close advisers were convinced that Trump's plans would shatter expectations—and frustrated that almost no outside experts agreed.

That's how I ended up shaking hands with Ross, in his tailored suit with a coat hung neatly behind an office door, and the lanky man who joined us in his office, an economist named Peter Navarro.

A few weeks earlier, Navarro and Ross had published a thirty-two-page analysis purporting to quantify how Trump's plans to cut taxes, rebalance trade, increase drilling for fossil fuels, and peel back federal regulation of business would work together to grow the economy and create millions of jobs—including bringing back manufacturing jobs that had been outsourced to China and other countries over the last several decades. It was the closest the campaign would come to the book-length policy manifestos that past candidates, Republicans and Democrats alike, had put forth. They had written it together, two men who had never met in person until the Republican National Convention in July, Ross the "international private equity investor," as the report said in its footnotes, and Navarro a business professor at the University of California at Irvine, the only member of Trump's inner policy circle at the time with a doctorate in economics.

The report was a map of how they and Trump saw the economy and a promise that his plans would invigorate growth without adding to the budget deficit. In an interview that September, Navarro had described it as "the whole chessboard." When its release failed to soften the criticism the campaign was taking from all sides over its plans, Navarro invited me to Ross's Sixth Avenue offices to make the case that the Trump view of the chessboard was correct, and that corrupt think tanks were conspiring to deny the truth about the prosperity that Trump's policies would bring.

"It's a very important element of the campaign," Navarro had told me on the phone. "Voters aren't getting the truth." He offered to host me in New York so that he and Ross could explain the truth that their models showed.

It was a clear morning in Midtown, the temperature in the mid-sixties and the sun brushing the leaves in the park. Ross welcomed me into his office. He sat next to Navarro. I sat across from them. Ross spoke first in a soft, almost grandfatherly, voice. Navarro waited patiently for him to make points, and when Ross would finish a thought, he would jump in with punchy little lectures, like a professor when class time is running short. Often he laughed in the end, in exasperation at his adversaries.

We started off talking about think tanks—"They're kind of in a time warp, where they're used to doing the same thing over and over and over again," Ross said, "and there's an institutional mentality against change"—but soon we were talking about the chessboard, and how the Trump team saw all the pieces moving toward the sort of middle-class boom that was now long in the rearview mirror of American history. Almost no academic economists in America saw the economy working the way Navarro, Ross, and Trump did. Trump viewed trade deficits—the difference between how much is imported from trading partners and exported to them—as damaging to growth; few economists agreed. No school of economics embraced both sharp corporate tax cuts and the

threat of steep import tariffs as a recipe for enhanced domestic investment. Navarro understood that he was an outlier in his profession. And
he was certain that he and Trump were right, whereas everyone else was
wrong.

"What's cool about Donald Trump is he's coming in from a business
point of view—not a business school, not a government—he's coming in,
he breaks down all siloes, he understands, as Mr. Ross has said, that all
revenues spring from the private sector, and if you go to generate those
revenues, you have to do it holistically and integratedly with policy," Navarro said. (By "policy," he was including energy, trade, and regulations,
and not just changes in tax rates.) "It's weird," he continued. "That paper
we did is the only attempt anyone has made to get the whole picture.
That's embarrassing for the country."

Revisiting that "whole picture" is instructive. It shows clearly how
Trump and his team imagined they would transform the American economy upon winning the White House: rolling back decades of globalization, reshaping the incentives for where multinational corporations
would build plants and hire workers, and restoring a blue-collar economy
in which Americans built more and drilled more and bought more things
from other Americans. Not from foreigners in countries that had long
been ripping America off.

The document also provides a scorecard for assessing how far short of
those promises Trump fell in his first years in office, even before the pandemic hit. And he did fall short, by a lot.

"Donald Trump's economic plan proposes tax cuts, reduced regulation,
lower energy costs, and eliminating America's chronic trade deficit," the
Navarro-Ross document, dated September 29, 2016, began. "Trump's goal
is to significantly increase America's real GDP growth rate and thereby
create millions of additional new jobs and trillions of dollars of additional
income and tax revenues." It was a nerdier version of what the candidate himself had said not far from Ross's office, in his campaign kickoff
speech at Trump Tower: "I will be the greatest jobs president that God
ever created. I tell you that," Trump had said. "I'll bring back our jobs

from China, from Mexico, from Japan, from so many places. I'll bring back our jobs, and I'll bring back our money."

Bringing back jobs has proven more difficult than candidate Trump imagined. Global supply chains that evolved over several decades have not simply unwound or evaporated overnight. Manufacturing jobs have not flocked back home from abroad. Trading partners have not meekly bowed to tougher demands from the White House. Workers' incomes rose in the first three years of Trump's presidency, but not by nearly as much as he promised, and largely not for the reasons he said they would.

All of those shortcomings were evident even before the events of Trump's fourth spring in office. In March of 2020, Trump presided over the fastest and steepest contraction of economic activity that the United States has seen in the modern statistical era. The outbreak of the COVID-19 pandemic blew a crater in the American economy as business activity and much of daily life shut down to slow the spread of the virus. The nation entered the month of March with one sort of economy and ended it with an almost unrecognizable one.

It is important, particularly as policymakers debate how to rebuild the economy post-pandemic, to dismantle a myth that Trump proclaimed even as the crisis deepened. The president loved to say that he had engineered the greatest economy in the history of the world—implying that workers would have been historically happy and secure, if only the virus had never crossed the American border. That's wrong.

The economy on the eve of the crisis was the product of three years of Trump policies, and it was nowhere near as strong—or as transformative for workers—as Trump claimed. It is hard to imagine any president, or any policies, sparing the nation from recession amid the outbreak. But the early indifference that Trump and his team showed toward the virus almost certainly worsened its damage to Americans' health and their personal financial situations.

Let's evaluate them both in turn: the pre-COVID and post-COVID realities for American workers under Trump. The former was nowhere close to what Trump claimed. The latter was disastrous.

Before the virus struck the United States, Trump liked to brag that growth on his watch was "booming" and that America was enjoying its "best economy ever." Neither was true. Annual economic growth did not top 3 percent—not 6 percent, just 3 percent—for even one of Trump's first three years. Unemployment continued to decline as it had in years prior, eventually reaching its lowest point in a half century before the virus hit. But the typical worker never saw anything close to the hot pace of job and wage growth that the country experienced in the late 1990s. On measure after measure of growth—for the economy as a whole, for job gains, for real average hourly earnings, and for the typical worker's wages—the economy in Trump's first three years did not look special at all. It looked almost identical to the economy in the first three years of Barack Obama's second term. That's true even though Trump was enjoying a historically strong tailwind from Congress and the Federal Reserve.

The gains that the middle class enjoyed in Trump's first three years flowed from extraordinary amounts of fiscal and monetary stimulus. They were the product of tax cuts and spending increases financed with borrowed money, combined with interest rates that stayed historically low for an economy with such low levels of unemployment.

Few of the predictions that Navarro and Ross (and by extension Trump) made in 2016 came to pass during those first three years. Instead, Trump's economic program ballooned the federal budget deficit by several hundred billion dollars a year above what forecasters had expected before the election, validating warnings from some of the think tanks that Trump's advisers called corrupt. The trade deficit was larger at the end of 2019 than it had been at the end of 2016, even though Trump imposed an escalating series of tariffs—taxes on imported goods—that contributed to a global slowdown in trade. Tax cuts did not come close to paying for themselves. Economic growth never approached the fantastical levels that Trump had promised. It never even cracked the lower bound of his advisers' expectations.

While Trump succeeded in enacting much of his agenda, the policies he pushed as president failed to transform the economy the way he and his team said they would.

It's all right there on the chessboard.

On pages 3 and 4, the Trump plan lamented what some economists had called a "new normal" of economic growth in the United States—the downshift that has characterized the American economy in the twenty-first century. Trump's team declared there was no reason for that downshift to be permanent. They were certain they could engineer much faster growth, and not just in a short burst. For years and years and years.

At every turn, their optimism was overstated. The document declared that Trump's energy plans, which included opening vast stretches of federal land to drilling, would add nearly $100 billion each year to the economy. For each of his first two years in office, the entire mining industry grew by only $6 billion per year. The estimate was not just wildly off. It was also directionally wrong: growth of the energy sector under Trump slowed markedly from its pace in Barack Obama's second term, when advancements in hydraulic fracturing (fracking) technology spurred big investments in American oil and gas drilling. In Trump's fourth year, as oil prices plunged amid the COVID-19 pandemic and a global supply glut, the sector veered into a deep contraction, idling rigs and shedding jobs in the United States.

Team Trump also overestimated how companies would react to the large reduction in corporate income tax rates that was the center of Trump's tax plan. Ross and Navarro had not drawn up the campaign's tax policy blueprint. For that, Trump had tapped Arthur Laffer, an economist who had advised President Ronald Reagan and scores of other politicians on tax-cutting plans, and a team of his disciples. Laffer was convinced that high personal and corporate tax rates were holding back the economy, much as they had been in the years before Reagan took office. Cut those rates, he told me over a long lunch in Washington during the campaign, and massive growth will follow. Trump's tax plan reflected that philosophy, as did the tax-cut package he signed into law at the end of his first year in office. Trump and his team never stopped promising that an avalanche of corporate investment would flow from the cuts. Lower tax rates, they said, would entice companies to build new factories in the United States and shut down the ones they had built overseas.

"Reducing the U.S. tax," Navarro and Ross had written in the chessboard document, "will help close the current offshoring gap."

None of that played out as Trump and his advisers predicted. The tax law Trump signed in late 2017, which was the signature legislative achievement of his first three years in office, was stacked with the sort of incentives that Trump said would drive domestic investment and growth. It reduced the top corporate rate from 35 percent to 21 percent. It gave a separate tax break to owners of businesses that are not organized as corporations, a large group that includes most American small businesses but also many big real estate companies (like hundreds of Trump's own companies) and Wall Street investment houses. It allowed multinational companies easier access to cash they had parked on the balance sheets of their overseas affiliates, in order to reduce their tax liability. It even allowed companies to fully and immediately deduct from their tax bills the cost of any new investments they made in the United States.

And what came of all that? Investment increased—for about half a year. Then its growth rate began to fall. Early in 2019, it turned negative. Researchers at the International Monetary Fund issued a report finding that the boost to investment from the Trump tax cuts had been "smaller than would have been predicted based on the effects of previous U.S. tax-cut episodes." By the end of Trump's third year, investment had fallen for three consecutive quarters. Even accounting for the brief surge in 2018, real private nonresidential fixed investment grew less per quarter after Trump's tax cuts were enacted than it had under Obama—in either of his terms. There was less total investment in the economy than you would have predicted if you had simply assumed Trump would maintain the average pace of investment growth that America had seen in the years after the 2008 financial crisis. That all came before the pandemic kicked in.

Companies headquartered in other countries did not step up their investments in the United States as Trump had promised they would. Foreign investment in America grew at a slower pace in his first two years than it had in Obama's second term. Trump frequently claimed otherwise, telling reporters and supporters that countries like Japan were dumping cash into America at rates no one had ever thought possible. But he was contradicted by official statistics from the Commerce Department and sometimes even by his own photo opportunities. In the summer of 2019, when Trump was on a presidential visit to Japan, the Japanese prime minister gave Trump a map showing investments by various Japanese companies across the United States. Trump brandished it gleefully, on the trip and again when he was back in the White House. But the investments portrayed on the map, when you counted them up, came to less than twenty thousand jobs. A drop in the bucket for the American manufacturing workforce.

Not even statistics produced by groups that supported Trump's push to reverse outsourcing could show a major effect from his policies on the flow of American jobs. A nonprofit called the Reshoring Initiative, which attempts to track the flow of manufacturing jobs into and out of America by combing news coverage and corporate announcements, reported in 2019 that companies had announced plans to "reshore"—meaning, move back from abroad—just under 145,000 factory jobs in Trump's first two years in office. That was the best showing for any two-year period in the group's data, which stretched back past the early days of the China shock under President George W. Bush. But it was still less than the annual job growth the United States had enjoyed in a typical *month* in the Obama era. And the bulk of those reshoring announcements had come in 2017, before Trump had signed the tax law.

Trump claimed early and fleeting success at accelerating manufacturing job growth. After climbing slowly in the recovery from recession, factory job creation had stalled in Obama's last two years, partly the result of a fall in oil prices that had chilled the energy industry's expansion. In Trump's first two years, factories started hiring again. The nation added 450,000 manufacturing jobs. It was still well short of the millions of jobs Trump had promised to bring back, but it appeared to be a start. But then it fizzled: in Trump's third year, manufacturing employment flatlined.

The overall effect was far more modest than Trump had promised. He did not, after all, reverse the decades-long shift of the United States from a production economy to a service economy. In 2019, the share of private-sector employees who work in manufacturing fell below 10 percent for the first time since the government started tracking the statistic in 1939.

Further analysis showed that the factory jobs that were created on Trump's watch were not, for the most part, going to the working-class white voters in the industrial Midwest who had powered his campaign victory. A Washington think tank called the Economic Innovation Group broke down the first two years of manufacturing gains by county and found that they were highly concentrated in the Mountain West and the oil patch, not the distressed parts of states like Ohio. The big drivers were tech companies, like Tesla, which opened a large new electric-car production facility in Nevada. Trump's own economic team acknowledged this, even as the president kept telling rallies in the Midwest that he had brought manufacturing back for them. Kevin Hassett, the first chairman of Trump's Council of Economic Advisers, told me in an interview in 2019 that there was a difference between what he called "creative-destruction" parts of the country, where jobs had been wiped out by recession but other jobs had popped up quickly to replace them, and "destruction-destruction" parts, where jobs were destroyed and new ones were slow to appear. Manufacturing growth under Trump, Hassett said, was "not necessarily disproportionately in the destruction-destruction places."

He was correct, though you wouldn't know that from how Trump boasted about manufacturing in rallies in Michigan and Ohio.

The manufacturing slowdown was related to the Trump team's largest policy miscalculation: the supposed ease of renegotiating the terms of global trade to better advantage American workers.

Trump has long been fixated on the trade deficit, in a way that befuddles economic experts. Most economists do not view a persistent trade deficit as a problem for presidents to target, because it depends on a variety of factors, like the relative strengths of nations' economies and currencies. (The smallest the trade deficit has been in recent years was during the Great Recession, when Americans could not afford to buy as many imports, a fact many economists cite as evidence that low trade deficits are not signs of economic strength. Sure enough, the trade deficit began to fall in 2020 as a new recession took hold.) Trump and his team thought otherwise. They saw the trade deficit as perhaps the largest structural problem facing the economy. It was money being spent on goods that could have been produced in the United States—should have been produced, in their view—and thus represented a loss to the country. There was no question, Ross and Navarro told me in our interview, that reducing the trade deficit would supercharge the economy.

"In plain terms, reducing the trade deficit means increasing the money workers will have in their paychecks and consumers will have in their pockets," Ross and Navarro had written. Prices on American-made goods would fall with lower taxes, lower regulatory burdens, and lower energy costs, they added, and distressed workers would be the winners: "In these ways, all of Trump's policy reforms will work together to increase wealth and the concentration of wealth among the poor, working, and middle classes of this country."

Getting the boost, they said, would be simple. It just required some hard-nosed negotiation.

It was not simple, even when negotiations succeeded. In the chessboard report and our interview in Ross's office, Navarro had railed against a trade deal the United States had signed with South Korea, which took effect in 2012. When Trump won the election, Navarro went to the White House as a special trade adviser, and he helped push for a fast renegotiation of that agreement with the Koreans. In September of 2018, Trump signed a revised agreement. Independent analysts called it a modest improvement on the previous deal. Trump and his team called it a big win for workers.

In the year that followed, the American trade deficit with South Korea *grew* compared with the year before.

The overall American trade deficit also grew in 2018. It contracted in 2019, as both imports and exports declined amid Trump's increasingly stringent tariffs—and retaliation against them from China and other countries. But in dollar terms, adjusting for inflation, the trade deficit remained higher than it had been at the end of Obama's tenure.

Economists widely blamed Trump's trade war for dampening business investment and sowing uncertainty in the economy.

After his election, Trump had appointed Ross to run the Commerce Department. Ross had stayed in that job, even when it exposed a deception he had pulled off for a decade. Ross was not a billionaire. His financial disclosure form showed dramatically less wealth than he had been reporting to *Forbes* all those years. He was tossed off the Forbes 400 list. But he stayed in Trump's orbit, and he helped Trump impose tariffs on imported steel and aluminum. Then he watched the tariffs hurt the industries he was trying to help.

In 2018, Ross had recommended that Trump place tariffs on imported steel and aluminum in order to protect industries that his department had deemed vital to America's national security. Those tariffs raised prices for American consumers and manufacturers, who were stuck paying more for the same metals than their counterparts in Europe and across the world. A few steel mills said they would increase production and hire more workers. Trump staged a rally at one of them, in Granite City, Illinois, and often told supporters that he had saved the industry. Reality was more grim. Steel and aluminum manufacturers continued to struggle. As tariffs persisted, large metals companies' stock prices dipped. Several factories idled production and announced layoffs. At the end of 2019, more than a year and a half after Trump announced the tariffs, there were fewer workers in American steel and aluminum plants than there had been when the tariffs were imposed.

The metals tariffs were the first major strike from Trump's administration in what economists quickly came to see as a multifront trade war. The adversaries in that war were spread across the globe. Trump forced a renegotiated agreement with Mexico and Canada, which Democrats in Congress agreed to pass after demanding that the administration include stricter labor standards for workers in multinational companies' factories. He traded shots with European leaders. They placed tariffs on Kentucky bourbon and Harley-Davidson motorcycles, he taxed French wine. But the major foe was China, and it put up a much bigger fight than Trump and his team had expected.

Trump and his team wanted China to overhaul its approach to trade: buying more American exports, allowing more American companies unfettered access to its markets, ending state subsidies for industries that competed with the United States, eliminating the theft of American intellectual property by Chinese companies, and more. To force the issue, Trump imposed tariffs on a growing list of imported goods from China. "Trade wars are good," he wrote on Twitter in March of 2018, "and easy to win." He expected Beijing to quickly back down. Instead, after more than a year of turmoil in markets and on the global stage, he settled in late 2019 for a so-called Phase One deal with the Chinese that few economists hailed as a game changer for growth in America.

Here, it is worth quoting at length from the chessboard. It illustrates the faith that Trump's advisers had in the idea that the world's second-largest economy would simply bow to the demands of a bellicose new president, the way Trump's bankers had in so many of his real estate negotiations.

"China is likely to pose the biggest challenge," Ross and Navarro wrote. "That said, the US is still China's biggest market, and the Chinese Communist Party runs a huge risk if it chooses to destabilize its own economy, and undermine Party control. For example, China cannot cancel imports of American soybeans because there is not enough global excess supply of soybeans to replace the American output." (They did cancel them, in retaliation for Trump's tariffs.)

"If China paid a premium to divert supplies from other countries, the US would simply fill the market void created so there would be no net impact on US exports." (The administration was forced to send billions of dollars in aid to American farmers whose income from exports suffered as the trade war went on.)

"Our view is that China's leaders will quickly understand they are facing strength on the trade issue in Trump rather than the kind of weakness on trade that has characterized the Obama-Clinton years. Just as these Chinese leaders have been exploiting American weakness by cheating in the trade arena, they will acknowledge the strength and resoluteness of Trump and rein in their mercantilist impulses." (They did not.)

"Ultimately," Navarro and Ross wrote, "our view is that doing nothing about unfair trade practices is the most hazardous course of action—and the results of this hazard are lived out every day by millions of displaced American workers and deteriorating communities." But the administration's trade approach created new hazards of its own. It sowed uncertainty for companies in the United States and around the world, which several economists suggested had a chilling effect on domestic investment. It contributed to a global slowdown that fed back to the American economy; customers abroad suddenly could not afford to buy as many American exports. Tariffs forced many American multinationals to raise prices on the goods they manufactured in China and sold to customers in the United States, or to pay to relocate their supply chains to other low-cost countries like Vietnam. There was little sign that those shifts drove factory work back to the United States.

I tracked all those effects as they unfolded, from my new job as an economics reporter in the Washington bureau of the *New York Times*. In the fall of 2018, I flew home to Oregon to talk with executives at a Portland company that found itself caught in the crosshairs of the trade war. It was Columbia Sportswear, a major seller of rain jackets, snow boots, and other outdoor gear, nearly all of which were manufactured abroad—a product of the outsourcing wave that had displaced American factory workers over several decades.

Columbia's chief executive, Tim Boyle, was livid about Trump's tariffs. Trump had told companies that if they didn't like the tariffs, they should move their factories out of China and back to America. I asked Boyle if he would ever consider it.

"There is no way," he said. "Zero. None."

"This migration to Asia has been happening since the sixties," he continued. "And so everybody who made investments in machines to make fabric or extreme, you know, plastics to make nylon or any kind of textile products—all those investments have been in Asia. All the technology." To make a shirt that fit someone, that American consumers would want to buy, Boyle said, "That's a technical expertise in tailoring that doesn't exist here anymore."

Trump was right that structural shifts had hurt American workers, particularly those without college degrees, over the course of several decades. He was wrong to think he could reverse those shifts overnight, easily, just by talking tougher than previous presidents. The trade war was not easy to win. His promises were not easy to keep.

A candidate who said he could get the economy growing at 4 or 5 or 6 percent a year saw, in his first three years as president, a growth rate that never came close. At the end of his third year in office, annual growth was veering toward 2 percent, and his economic advisers were forced to concede that it had fallen short of their forecasts, which predicted 3 percent annual growth for nearly a decade. As the year of his reelection campaign dawned, most economists were expecting the Trump economy to grow at a rate below the "new normal" level—2 percent a year—that his advisers had mocked during the campaign.

The advisers were undaunted. In February of 2020, they unveiled a new set of economic projections that once again featured 3 percent growth per year as far as the eye could see. They waved off concerns about the fall in business investment, which they called a temporary blip due to uncertainty over the Trump trade strategy. (They also called that strategy "perfect.") They played down any possibility that they might once again be proven overly optimistic, for any reason—including the outbreak of a virus that was already spreading from China to Europe and beyond. In a late-January television interview, Wilbur Ross suggested that the virus could "help to accelerate the return of jobs to North America," particularly the United States, as companies looked to move production out of China. He did not seem concerned that the virus could spread to American production lines. No one else in the administration seemed to be, either.

"I don't think corona is as big a threat as people make it out to be," the acting chairman of Trump's Council of Economic Advisers, Tomas Philipson, told me and a group of reporters in a late-February briefing. Public health threats did not typically hurt the economy, he said. He suggested the virus would not be nearly as bad as a normal flu season. Someone asked what *was* his biggest concern for the economy, if not the virus. "Currently," he said, "I don't think we have a lot of concerns."

That nonchalance continued to infect the administration's response to the virus even as it spread across the United States. In the early weeks of the outbreak, administration officials insisted publicly and privately that the threat was overblown. A senior administration official called me one afternoon in early March, when the American death toll from the virus was still limited mostly to one senior-living facility in Washington State, to stress how strong the economy was. Supply-chain disruptions from China were by themselves stoking talk of an American recession. Some economists and lawmakers were beginning to call for the federal government to pass a stimulus bill to juice growth and safeguard against the downturn. The official said no way; the economy didn't need stimulus, and besides, temporary measures to boost growth never worked anyway. Those delays cost the country time and resources in its efforts to contain the virus and its economic damage.

Near the end of March, Trump signed a $2 trillion economic rescue package that had flown through Congress. It dwarfed the cost and scope of the 2009 stimulus that had helped cushion the blow of that recession. Mayors and governors across the country had shut down entire sectors of the economy—schools and churches and bars and diners and all but the most essential workplaces—in hopes of slowing the spread of the virus. Those decisions, and the public health panic over a virus that was filling hospitals beyond capacity and growing deadlier by the day, threw millions of people out of work. They threatened the survival of thousands of businesses, large and small. The rescue package was meant to be a lifeline to sustain workers and families and firms until the lights came back on for the economy. And when the bill passed, a lot of economists worried aloud that it might not be large enough to work, at least not for very long. It took only a couple of weeks for the critics to be proven correct.

Trump did not flinch at blowing up the budget deficit with the bill, and he welcomed the accompanying moves by the Fed to cut interest rates to zero and pump trillions of dollars of liquidity into the financial system. His campaign bluster about paying off the debt had given way to a presidential addiction to stimulus: tax cuts and spending increases and the sort of accommodative monetary policy that he had denounced when Barack Obama was president.

The simplest way to describe the economic results of Trump's first three years in office is this: in order to keep wages rising and unemployment falling, he borrowed revenues from future taxpayers and pressured the central bank to lower interest rates in order to stimulate an economy that was well on its way to experiencing the longest expansion in American history. As a result, economic growth improved modestly and briefly.

When Trump took office in January 2017, the unemployment rate was as low as it had been in 1998, amid the late-nineties tech boom. But economic growth had slowed in 2016. Business confidence had slid, partly as a reaction to a string of new financial, environmental, and labor regulations that the Obama administration was issuing. Business owners tend to dislike regulation, and when Trump won they quite rationally expected that a new era of regulatory rollback was on its way. Their economic confidence and investment, reported in industry surveys, shot up. You can make a case that this psychological boost, born of expectation of deregulation, was the biggest impact Trump had on the economy before the tax law passed. It helped reinvigorate growth temporarily.

After the tax cuts came a period of unprecedented fiscal and monetary stimulus. The cuts bathed corporations, shareholders, and workers in hundreds of billions of dollars of cash that they otherwise would not have had. That's because the cuts in tax rates were not sufficiently offset by the closure of loopholes used to avoid taxes—or by any other kind of tax increase—to be what budget experts call "revenue neutral." The budget deficit swelled. It grew more when Trump and Congress agreed on a series of increases in defense spending and nondefense domestic programs, shattering spending caps that Obama and congressional Republicans had agreed to put in place years before.

All the while, Trump was browbeating the central bankers at the Federal Reserve, who set America's interest rate policy. The Fed had started to raise rates after years of leaving them near zero. Low rates encourage economic activity, as opposed to savings, and officials had seen them as necessary to stoke growth after the recession. Now officials were trying to get back to a more "normal" level of rates. Trump was furious. He wanted lower rates, to generate as much growth as possible. On Twitter and in public appearances, he denigrated the Fed chairman he had appointed, Jerome Powell, and called for lower rates. Fed officials swore they were ignoring those calls, but they weren't ignoring the trade war and the global slowdown, which they worried were threatening American growth. The central bank stopped raising rates and started cutting them.

Typically in American history, Congress pumps up the budget deficit and the central bank cuts rates when unemployment is high or rising, in order to ward off or dig out of recession. It is extraordinarily rare to see a combination of rate cuts and deficit growth in a period of rock-bottom unemployment. But that is exactly the combination Trump dialed up, and it helped him deliver faster wage growth. In the summer of 2019, two of my *Times* colleagues and I built our own crude model of fiscal and monetary policy over time. We concluded that after adjusting for the economic conditions he inherited, Trump had enjoyed more fiscal and monetary stimulus than any president since Jimmy Carter, who was in office at the end of the 1970s. Trump's advisers had fundamentally rejected the idea, in 2016, that the economy needed that sort of stimulus. All Americans have gotten from past attempts, Navarro and Ross wrote in the chessboard report, "is a doubling of our national debt from $10 trillion to $20 trillion under Obama-Clinton and the weakest economic recovery since World War II."

Median incomes stalled in 2018. The growth that Americans did see in their paychecks under Trump was a reminder of the power of tight labor markets to lift all workers—a product of companies having to pay more to attract the people they need. But it was not sustainable. The Fed ended 2019 with little room left to cut interest rates. The federal deficit had topped $1 trillion for the fiscal year. Yet growth was sliding again— even before the virus triggered a recession. The pandemic gave America an unneeded reminder of the fragile existence that tens of millions of people and families endure every day. When COVID-19 began to spread, the typical worker had a three in ten chance of not being able to take even a single paid sick day from her or his job. The less those workers earned, the higher the odds their employers offered no paid leave. At the end of March, as the outbreak flooded New York City and much of the country closed for business, a research firm called Civis Analytics surveyed thousands of Americans about how the virus was affecting their lives and livelihoods. The more a respondent earned, the less likely she or he was to report losing a job or income as a result of the virus. Low- and middle-income earners were far more likely to have missed a rent or mortgage payment amid the outbreak. Black and Latino respondents were hardest hit. They were less likely to have the option to work from home and more likely to have lost their jobs. They had relatively little financial cushion to ride out the crisis, particularly when compared with white Americans who enjoyed significantly higher levels of savings and wealth on average.

They were also more likely to die—and to be put at risk of infection. New York health statistics showed black and Latino residents of the city were dying of the virus at vastly higher rates than white residents. A raft of research showed men of color and women of all races were disproportionately manning the front-line "essential" jobs that were sustaining the flow of food and other supplies for a nation that was sheltering in place to avoid infection. The least advantaged Americans had been effectively conscripted into the highest-risk work of keeping the nation running, at the same relatively low wages they'd earned before the crisis hit. But the conscripted workers weren't rebelling against their circumstances: polls showed black Americans, Latinos, and young women of all races were far more supportive of stay-at-home orders than older white people.

More than a decade had passed since the last financial crisis, three years of it under Trump. But the inequities and insecurities in the economy hadn't changed much at all.

If you reject the idea of an inevitable "new normal" of wage stagnation or decline for the middle class—and I reject it, just as Trump's team did in 2016—then it follows that something is still structurally broken in the economy. Something that will still be broken once the economy begins to heal in earnest from the coronavirus recession, and something that Trump and populist politicians like him will never solve with quick fixes. It follows that a different approach might be able to repair that structural break, but Trump showed no inclination to try one. He, like his team, was invested in selling the results of the approach he continues to push, no matter what those results might be. Which is exactly what they had accused their critics of doing on that fall day in Midtown.

"The research," Ross had said, late in the interview, referring to the research conducted by economic think tanks, "is being tailored to fit the dogma rather than the research being done and that leading to the dogma. It's the reverse of the way that things ought to be done. It ought to be done, let the research drive the conclusion. Let's not have the conclusion drive the research we put out."

Navarro interjected, looking at me. "Not to be too hard on you," he said, "but you've been guilty of this." He referenced an article I'd written that drew on models that showed the Trump tax plan blowing out the budget deficit. "Just introspectively," he said, "ask the question: Why don't journalists ask the question? Is it that journalists don't have the training to see through that? I mean I'm kind of curious about that. When you look at this stuff, does it take me and Wilbur to kind of walk [you] through all of this to see it? Or is it not at least somewhat obvious that there's a stench here?"

I told them that I had been covering campaigns for a long time, and that I was skeptical of all candidates' claims about what they could do for the economy. I said I was trying to understand their claims better, to better evaluate them. I told them that their trade plans, in particular, were novel for a presidential nominee. Journalists, I said, did not have a lot of experience evaluating those sorts of plans and how they might affect growth. Ross agreed.

"I'll tell you why there isn't the experience," he said. "It's pretty simple. Nobody ever looks back on the trade deals that were made and says, okay, here was your theory what was going to happen. Here is what actually did happen. Let's try to figure out the difference between the two."

"It's not that hard," he said.

Trump and his team have never applied that sort of introspection to their own policies. They rarely admit errors. They call data points that undermine their message "fake news." They have shown little patience for solving large, complex problems, be they trade relations with China or the national sacrifices needed to defeat the health and economic menace of a pandemic. Again and again, Trump has settled for gimmicks that lean heavily on marketing. He has convinced a group of white workers that they are better off thanks to him, but he has not made them better off.

All of that lay years ahead of us, the advisers and me, on that clear-sky fall day in Midtown. Our interview ran long. The host excused himself for another meeting. I watched Navarro help him into his coat.

Ross left through the lobby, leaving Mariko Mori's orb, and its bright future, behind.

11

Restoring the Riches of This Land

HOW TO GET THE MIDDLE CLASS BACK ON TRACK

America is once again engaged in the process of rebuilding its economy from a devastating recession. It cannot afford another feeble and prolonged rebound, in which the gilded chambers of the economy recover faster than all the others, and it need not have one. The pandemic recession pushed more than twenty million Americans out of their jobs in a single month. Policymakers can and must make it their mission to put those people back to work—and to open new pathways for those workers to add the highest possible value they can to the country. To do that, our leaders must avoid the errors of the last recovery and heed the

lessons of the nation's great postwar boom, the last time America delivered lasting prosperity and security for the middle class.

This is where to start: invest in people. You don't just bail out airlines
and flood the financial system with money to keep it functioning. You don't
keep businesses whole but leave individuals to slowly scrape up the pieces of
their shattered careers and dreams. You don't harness the politics of fear to
lash out at the immigrant doctors who manned ventilators during the pandemic or the farm workers who kept the produce flowing to Amazon's delivery trucks. You don't keep turning a blind eye to the centuries of systemic
oppression that have kept the black women who don nursing scrubs and
ring up groceries from earning and saving enough to buy their own homes.

The recession reminded the nation where its essential strength lies.
It reminded the powerful that there is a group of workers who have long
served as the country's human safety net. They worked the factories
through a great war and the emergency rooms through the outbreak.
They have pulled us through, time and again. If you want to bring the
nation not just out of the pit of recession, but into the light of a new
Golden Era for all, you invest in those workers. They will take us there.

You invest in people like Ed Green and his daughter, Jazmine, who
stayed on the job as "essential" workers throughout the crisis—Ed on
the highway crew, Jazmine managing a pharmacy store. You invest in
the people who carry on their strong backs, in their nimble hands, inside their sharp and curious minds the potential to generate growth.
The people who would solve problems, improve their surroundings, add
more value to their employers and communities and families and selves,
if only they were empowered to. The people who are barred or blocked or
steered away from doing what they are best at.

Those workers drive middle-class success in the United States. If you
look for periods in the postwar era when typical Americans saw their incomes rising faster than the cost of living, you'll see that two conditions
were almost always present: low unemployment and strong growth. Investing in people is the best and most sustainable way to get both those
back. It would have been the right strategy for middle-class revival even
before the recession hit, and it is even more critical now.

Some of what you invest is money. Government will need to invest in getting everyone in the country back to work once it is safe for them to do so. Consumer spending and business investment will need support as they slowly emerge from the cavern of the crisis. Children and young adults will need better education and training to backfill what they lost when schools closed for months. Adults will need help mastering new trades to replace the jobs and career tracks that died in the recession. Workers and small businesses will need a stronger set of social insurance programs, to ensure the next downturn does not require the make-it-up-as-you-go legislation that this one did. We'll get to all of that in a bit.

You can also invest a lot without spending a dollar. You invest effort in helping workers find their way to the jobs that fulfill and motivate them, and in helping innovators develop new ways of tapping the grand potential of human labor in an age when companies too often treat their employees as though they're disposable.

You invest time, and your own hopes and dreams, in people who don't share your skin color or life experience. Like a University of Tennessee economist I know named Marianne Wanamaker, who, along with her husband and two children, has invested in a refugee family from Burundi that settled in Knoxville. She and her husband have helped the family solve paperwork problems related to their immigration status. They have helped the family's three young children in school. "They're so bright," Wanamaker told me in the fall of 2019. "Their future is limitless."

But a half-year later, after schools had shut for the pandemic, Wanamaker told me she was worried; every day without classroom instruction, those young children fell behind their wealthier, white peers, whose families could afford more books and software and other resources to enrich their learning. Millions of children across the country, whose bright futures are clouded by the difficulty of growing up poor, will need additional investment from their communities in the years to come.

Most of all, we need to invest the time to help each other understand what centuries of racial and ethnic and gender division in this country attempted to obscure, and what one prolonged Golden Age of capitalism revealed: that workers need one another.

These are the truths of our shared economy: that walls have held entire groups of workers back, that they still hold workers back, and that when those walls fall, the *entire* working class surges forward.

Distressed white workers in America would benefit from better schools, better opportunities, and better jobs for distressed black workers. Both groups would benefit from embracing immigrants and from encouraging them to climb the ladder of human potential to the heights that America makes available—and which so many other parts of the world do not. Nonwhite workers would benefit from a renewed surge up that ladder for the working-class whites in Ohio, in Southern California, in all the places where American Dreams were interrupted by outsourcing or automation.

Those white workers should also understand that the evolving demographics of the United States—the aging of the workforce and the growing share of people who are not white in the overall population—make it impossible for white people to rebuild the middle class on their own.

There is no sustainable future for a working class that allows itself to be divided on identity lines. That is particularly true for white workers. There simply are not enough of them—not enough workers in the labor force now, not enough babies growing up to join and then replace them decades from now—to generate a sustained level of even 3 percent growth per year, which is the lowest bound of what Donald Trump and his economic team promised America their policies could achieve in perpetuity. The American workforce is becoming less white and less male, and to keep up a strong pace of growth it needs two things: more workers than it already has in the pipeline, and for all its workers to generate more value, in economic terms.

I am making an argument here about one of the most mysterious forces that experts observe in the economy: productivity. It's a measure of how efficiently the economy works, from factories to restaurants to lines of computer code. In the Golden Era of the middle class, productivity grew rapidly. The economy got better and better every year at producing and marketing and selling things—at meeting the needs of its people through the marketplace. That rapid improvement fueled rapid economic growth, which delivered raises for workers that grew faster than the cost of living did. People were the key to that productivity growth: women and black men and immigrants and everyone who had been blocked from doing their best work for the economy, then were gradually allowed to. In our current century, productivity has slowed. Investing again in people, and in breaking down the social and legal forces that are once more blocking them from doing their best work, is the way to revive it.

If you could choose the raw materials to build another middle-class expansion that is as rich and as durable as the first few postwar decades were, you would want to start with a pool of workers who were ready to deploy their full talents but for some reason were blocked from doing it. You would want people who were clamoring to come to this country to work, to invent, to start businesses. You would want workers who were capable of doing so much more than the jobs they were stuck in, whose talents were going to waste. You would want people with dreams, but whose path to achieving them was littered with obstacles.

America has all of those.

The silver lining of several decades of middle-class malaise in the United States—and even, perhaps, of the pandemic recession—is that we have vast untapped potential right here in front of us. We have millions of workers who are held back by discrimination, by social norms that should be scrapped, by the overt denial of opportunity from people in power who can't stand the idea of anyone being allowed to compete with them on a level plane. Workers who are held back by government regulations in some cases and the absence of government intervention in others. Held back by the political divisions that have blinded workers to their most natural allies in the pursuit of a better life.

To reignite an economy that once again values all workers for their talents, America must restore the upward flow of talent that powered growth and prosperity after World War II. It must restore it for women, for black men, for immigrants, for all nonwhite workers. And it must restore it for working-class white men, too.

White male workers need to acknowledge that racism and sexism still hinder women and workers of color in America today. And those workers need to see how white workers without college degrees have been, in a different but still important way, also disadvantaged by shifts in the modern economy.

America needs to invest in all those workers, and those workers need to invest in each other.

And America needs to do that even though Donald Trump, by inflaming racial discord to gain and keep political power, has made the task more difficult.

12

Winston-Salem, 2019

"HOW DID WE STEAL SOMETHING YOU THREW AWAY?"

I saw him for the first time in five years in the cool of a liquor store, the air-conditioning blasting against high-eighties heat, bars on the windows, the streets falling dark as cars slipped into the half-full lot. "That's one bad thing about the South," he would tell me later, after his shift ended and we'd driven a few miles up the wide, sidewalk-free road to an Applebee's for beers. "They don't really believe in lighting streets." The next night I found myself on the white side of town. It was lit up like a fireworks show.

When I arrived in Winston-Salem it was a Friday evening. The liquor store was busy; my legs were stiff from hours on the road. I waited to get his attention and watched him joke with the customers. They came from all walks. They were baby-faced or middle-aged or pensioners who had just cashed an end-of-week check. The young ones bought armloads of party supplies, and the older ones bought bourbon and brandy in single bottles. Everyone knew exactly where to find what they needed. They headed straight for it when they walked in the door, wading into the bottles that fanned out in rows around a crescent-shaped room, spaced as neatly as if it were a factory floor. On Saturday mornings, I was told, third-shift workers from the town's remaining factories line up outside the door before the store opens at ten a.m., to stock up before they go home to sleep.

Ed Green was standing behind the counter in a blue polo shirt with "ABC" stenciled on the breast, his beard graying more than I remember, his belly a bit trimmer, half-frame glasses on his eyes, and a smile cracked across his face, like always. He was on his feet for at least the twelfth straight hour, halfway through his second job of the day. Like always.

The crowd thinned momentarily, and he motioned me over. He shook my hand. How's the new gig? I asked. "Pays better than baseball," he said, and the smile spread even wider.

It was nine days after a predominantly white crowd at a rally in Greenville, North Carolina, located nearly two hundred miles west of here, had heard President Trump demean a quartet of black and brown Democratic congresswomen, all of whom were American citizens and only one of whom was an immigrant. The audience responded with a chant of "Send them back!"—as in, back to the countries they had supposedly come from. It was one day before the president would wake up to a Fox News segment about another House Democrat, who had criticized the conditions under which immigrants were being held in America's border detention facilities. The congressman was a black man whose Maryland district included impoverished parts of Baltimore with large black populations. "Why is so much money sent to the Elijah Cummings district when it is considered the worst run and most dangerous anywhere in the United States," the President of the United States would fume in a Saturday morning tweet. "No human being would want to live there."

No human being.

It was late July 2019, and Ed Green was still cobbling together a middle-class income by juggling multiple jobs, as he had been doing for the better part of two decades. He still had the day job with the state, fixing roads. But he no longer swept up the ballpark.

A couple of years before, he said, the baseball club had contracted out their janitorial services. The new company subcontracted the jobs. Employees like Ed saw their hours cut and their wages fall. "It's good for a college kid, somebody who's retired, doesn't need a bunch of hours," Ed said. "They pay minimum wage. So somebody trying to pay the bills, you need something more consistent." He saw it coming. He heard about the position at the liquor store from a friend at his day job while laying tar on the highway. "I guess," he said, "I'm old enough to be able to see when a company's going bad."

Is this job easier, I asked. Harder? He shook his head.

"Next year I'll be sixty," he said. "I shouldn't still be working like a twenty-year-old."

But you are, I said.

"Yeah," he said. "But I work smarter."

He made $10.75 an hour at the liquor store, he told me, and worked about thirty-five hours every two weeks. That comes to just under $10,000 a year. The total hours he worked were down to the equivalent of about one and a half full-time jobs.

The highway crew gave him a raise just before Christmas, nearly $10,000 a year. It was due to economic necessity, a sign of how free markets can still deliver for workers when the labor market is tight. With all the growth in Winston-Salem and the resulting construction, private companies were springing up all over the place and hiring away the government workers. The state had to increase wages just to keep a crew out on the roads.

Ed never got to enjoy the money. His wife's kidneys were failing. Less than a month after Ed's raise was announced, doctors told her she needed to quit working and spend nine hours a night hooked to a dialysis machine while she waits on a list for a transplant. "The bills just keep coming in," he said. She stopped drawing a salary. He had to pay to add her to his health insurance. The raise was swallowed by medical bills. He kept working the second job. "She'll try to stay up for me" after late shifts, he said, "but most of the time she's knocked out."

His wife had just started drawing disability pay from the government. A nonprofit helped with some of the medical costs. Caring for her was close to another part-time job. Every three months, she needed a thorough eye exam at the hospital, to make sure her kidney disease did not claim her sight as a complication. She had her eyelids popped open and a solution injected that made it impossible for her to drive. Ed drove her to those appointments. He also had driven her to her appointments when the dialysis began, because it was mucking with her memory and they needed to know what the doctors said. He missed some work, which he almost never had for his own ailments. If and when a kidney donor was found, he planned to miss some more. They would have four hours from the time they received the call to make it to the hospital for the transplant.

Ed told me this while we sat at the bar at Applebee's, a few miles from the liquor store up that poorly lit road. We had driven north after he'd closed the store for the night, clinging alongside US Highway 52, Winston-Salem's black-white dividing line. I nursed an IPA, he sipped a Blue Moon. The Red Sox were leading the Yankees on a television over the bar. He caught me up on the developments of the last few years of his life. His wife's illness. His daughter graduating from college. The gentrification of Winston-Salem's downtown, which he and his road crew were paving the way for.

The beer was almost gone when I asked him about something we'd only ever discussed glancingly, but would, over the next couple of days, address head on. I asked how, in his life, racial discrimination had held him back. He did not tell me the full story—not yet. He did tell me he had been seeing progress in recent years, for him and his children. A city and state and nation beginning to make strides toward equal opportunity for black Americans.

He could feel the progress, he said. "Up until now."

"Now," Ed Green said, "you've got a guy in office who's saying, 'No, they're bad.'"

Nearly 150 years after emancipation, nearly 50 years after the Civil Rights Act, black Americans still do not have the same economic opportunities as white Americans do. They are paid less for the same work when compared with similarly educated whites. Their wages have grown more slowly over the last several decades. They are still woefully underrepresented in some of the highest-paying occupations in the economy. They are less likely to own homes, to hold stock shares, to be admitted to elite universities, to sit in corporate boardrooms, to practice law or medicine, and to amass the full Game of Life security blanket that we associate with middle-class stability. The United States still discriminates against its black citizens systematically, and black Americans report that the discrimination has been inflamed by a president who delights in bullying people who are not white.

Donald Trump has retweeted white nationalists from the White House. He has used his social media platforms to taunt and criticize black athletes. He has singled out a group of female, nonwhite Democrats in Congress for repeated attacks, including the ones that provoked the "send them back" chants in North Carolina in 2019. In the summer of 2017, white nationalists marched in the streets of Charlottesville, Virginia. Protesters met them; violence ensued; in the melee, a neo-Nazi white man rammed his car into a crowd, killing a young woman, Heather Heyer. Trump condemned the violence but told reporters there were "very fine people on both sides" of the skirmish. He reportedly called African nations "shithole" countries and, in an echo of Ronald Reagan's "monkey" comments so many decades earlier, complained that after seeing the United States, immigrants from Nigeria would never "go back to their huts." In the fall of 2019, as Democrats intensified an investigation into his conduct in office that was a prelude to impeachment, Trump called the inquiry a "lynching."

In the winter of 2019 the Pew Research Center asked 6,637 Americans a detailed series of questions about race relations in the United States. More than seven in ten black respondents said those relations were "generally bad." A similar number said Trump had made them worse. More than eight in ten black respondents said the legacy of slavery continues to affect black Americans a great deal or a fair amount. Just under eight in ten said the nation has not gone far enough in giving blacks equal rights with whites. Half of black respondents expressed deep pessimism about the prospect of black Americans *ever* achieving equality.

Economic statistics showed just how far away equality was. Trump loved to tout the decline of the black unemployment rate on his watch—but by the end of 2019, it was still two full percentage points higher than the unemployment rate for whites. The typical black worker still earned $217 less per week than a typical white worker, a difference of more than twenty percent. The typical white family still had ten times the wealth—the combined value of all its investments, real estate, and other assets—than the typical black family. Even when economic forces were dragging down working-class whites, they still enjoyed some advantages over similarly educated black workers. Whites without college degrees had lost wealth over the course of the twenty-first century. But statistics from the Federal Reserve showed that at the median, they still had more than eight times the wealth of similarly educated black Americans.

It is worth lingering on these gaps. They underscore the persistence of discrimination and the stifled potential of America's workers who are not white. And they undercut a growing belief among a slice of white Americans, most notably among Donald Trump's working-class, white base of support, that black Americans have overtaken white workers and discrimination now flows the other way.

In the Pew poll from 2019, Republicans overwhelmingly downplayed the possibility of discrimination against black Americans. A third of them said the country has gone "too far" in giving black Americans equal rights to whites. Another poll released a few months later, by the nonprofit Public Religion Research Institute, found that nearly six in ten whites without college degrees said discrimination against whites is as large a problem as discrimination against black Americans.

"There is a perception on the part of many whites in America that blacks have caught up or even moved ahead of them, and that it has occurred in ways that are not meritorious," the economist William Darity told me. "That perception is not consistent with the data." And, he said,

"It has the political effect of providing greater support for politicians who openly profess racism."

Darity is one of America's foremost researchers on the effects of discrimination on workers in the American economy. He was the coauthor of the late-1990s study that included examples of newspaper help-wanted advertisements from 1960 that openly called for white or "negro" applicants. He is now a Duke University professor and an expert in the racial wealth gap. In our interview, he told me about the gulf between black and white Americans and why so many whites struggled to see it.

He started by reframing the wealth gap in terms of income security. If you lost your job tomorrow, and sold everything you owned to replace your income, how long would that money hold out? The typical white American could make it three years: median white wealth is triple the median income for a white household. The typical black American would last no more than six months. This was the summer of 2019. It was a prescient analogy.

Darity traced that divide back to Reconstruction, to the federal government's unwillingness to deliver on its promise of land and livestock to the formerly enslaved workers who had been emancipated. He carried it forward, through the murderous theft of black capital in the Jim Crow era and the suppression of black homeownership after World War II by the government's redlining practices. He saw the immediate aftermath of the Civil Rights Act as a fit of progress, snuffed soon after it sparked. "The upcycles," he told me, "have not been particularly pronounced." He said the election of Barack Obama and the visible success of black athletes had given whites a mistaken picture of how much ground black Americans had actually gained. The country had never eradicated discrimination. It seemed to be growing back stronger than ever.

Darity is a liberal economist and an outspoken advocate for increased federal spending to redress racial disparities. The data he cites is not partisan or ideological; it is the cold truth of an economy that continues to hold black workers back.

His findings are supported by work from more conservative economists, like Marianne Wanamaker, the University of Tennessee professor.

She spent a year in the Trump administration as a staff member of the White House Council of Economic Advisers.

Wanamaker grew up in western Tennessee, in a small town where churches were segregated by race and schools were decidedly not. She was white, and from an early age she could see discrimination around her in town and hear it from the mouths of extended family members who lived deeper in the South. "My grandmother was from Mississippi, and we would often go to small-town Mississippi for a few days in the summer," she told me. "The world seemed different there. Things seemed less integrated, even though the town was about the same size as where I grew up. I remember my own family members talking in a derogatory way about black people in their town. I remember my parents reminding us on the way home that that was not the way we were going to talk in our house. But of course it stuck in my mind that there were people I loved who felt very at ease sharing these incredibly racist comments with me, even as a child."

Wanamaker excelled in math as a student. In college, by the fortune of a faculty-advising assignment, she was introduced to economics. She was hooked and pursued a career in economic history. Questions of race were still stuck in her mind, still upsetting her. "As an academic, you take your life experiences and try to throttle them into a paper," she told me. "We're all looking at our life experience and saying, Is there a story here?"

In the spring of 2017, shortly before she joined the economic team in the Trump White House, Wanamaker and a Vanderbilt University economist named William Collins published a working paper through the National Bureau of Economic Research that told a stunning story about the persistence of racism across American history. They had fused century-old census records and more recent survey data to assemble a picture of intergenerational mobility from Reconstruction to today. Their data allowed them to see how likely it was for a black or a white man to grow up to occupy a higher position on the nation's income ladder than his father had, and how that likelihood had changed across several generations. They did that by observing which occupations sons held as adults compared with their fathers.

Wanamaker and Collins found that in the aftermath of emancipation, the sons of poor white men were far more likely to climb the economic ladder than the sons of poor black men. (At the turn of the twentieth century, in the South, the sons of poor white men could expect to end up earning more as adults than the sons of even the richest black men.) That gap never closed. In terms of economic mobility, the penalty for being born black is the *same today as it was in the 1870s.*

A year later, Republican staff researchers at the congressional Joint Economic Committee would reach a similar conclusion. They would publish a map of "social capital" across the United States, a geography of what they considered the ingredients to sustained economic success. One of the researchers overlaid it with a map of cotton production in the antebellum South—a map of slavery, basically. The two matched up neatly. Areas with high concentrations of enslaved workers before the Civil War, which are now home to many black descendants of those workers, have some of the lowest social-capital scores in modern America.

Wanamaker's data showed that if there had been even one generation of durable progress in relative mobility—one group of black sons who were afforded merely the same opportunities to get ahead as boys who were like them but white—America's long-running gap in black and white earnings would have all but vanished. "You would have essentially leveled the playing field," she told me.

It did not happen, no matter what white workers might have been told today. Even the gains of civil rights, which lifted black men to occupations they could not reach previously, were insufficient to bridge the opportunity divide.

As Darity, who is black, had told me, the era of black progress in the late 1960s did not last. "It was fundamentally over by the time of the Reagan presidency," he said. "I would argue that the Reagan presidency begins an active reversal of the policies that might have contributed to change." That reversal was now being accelerated, he said, "by the climate of explicit racism that has been promulgated by the current president."

Some of the barriers black Americans face today aren't the same as the ones they faced in 1960. They are not explicitly barred from attending certain colleges. There aren't job postings that say only whites need apply. But the public schools black students attend often remain segregated and underfunded. Occupational discrimination is real, but less advertised. Black Americans who do rise up the ladder sometimes face backlash from whites who suppose, against everything research tells us about how discrimination continues to hold black Americans back, that they must have made it only because of a quota. Black people remain underrepresented in America's universities—particularly in the science and technology fields that America's leaders have stressed are the path to the best-paying jobs in a globalized and high-technology economy—and overrepresented in the country's prisons. Decades of policy choices have led to each of those outcomes.

We can see the economy-wide barriers to advancement for nonwhite workers—and the potential for huge strides for American workers if those barriers fall—in a highly educated profession that keeps detailed statistics on its own patterns of discrimination: economics. The economics profession has a particularly acute race problem, but one that illustrates challenges that are widespread across the economy.

Nearly a third of the American population was black, Latino, or Native American in 2018. But that group made up less than one-twelfth of economics professors, according to data from the American Economic Association, which is the governing body of sorts for academic economists. Those groups were similarly underrepresented among the ranks of Americans who earned an economics degree, be it a bachelor's, master's, or doctorate, over the preceding two decades. Universities awarded nearly 470 doctoral degrees, a requirement for nearly all elite economics professorships, in the 2016–2017 academic year. Only 15 of them went to black students.

I have written about those disparities for the *Times*, and when I do, I always hear from white, male economists who contend that they are not signs of discrimination. Some economists like to say that they are, as a profession, as rational as free markets. They award degrees and teaching positions to the best candidates. If there were a group of better candidates who were being discriminated against, for race or other reasons, then *some* competitor university would snap them up and reap the benefits.

That is how rational actors supposedly behave in a free market: inefficient behavior like racial discrimination is punished by competitors and thus driven out of the marketplace. Therefore, the argument goes, low representation of black, Hispanic, Native American, and other nonwhite students in the profession must be evidence not of discrimination but of differing preferences or abilities among racial groups. (There's an old joke about an economist walking past a five dollar bill on the street and refusing to pick it up; his brain tells him it can't be a real five dollar bill, because if it were, someone else would have picked it up before him.)

There are so many things wrong with that argument—historically, culturally, even economically—that it's hard to know where to start. The simplest way to say it is, if discrimination were irrational and easily competed away, America would have eliminated it long ago. But we don't have to fall back on theoretical arguments. We have data on discrimination in the field. In 2019, the American Economic Association, increasingly rocked by allegations of racism and sexism in the economics discipline, conducted a survey of its membership. It was a voluntary survey and, I should note, not a random sample like a national opinion poll. But its respondents roughly matched the profession on several demographic lines, and its implications were unmistakable for the leaders of the profession.

Nearly half of black economists reported they had been discriminated against or been treated unfairly in the field because of their race. Only 4 percent of white economists said the same. Respondents were allowed to elaborate on their answers in anonymous comments. "Economics is dominated by people who have little concern about the consequence[s] of racism, and people who have the concern are excluded," one respondent wrote. "I would not recommend my own (black) children to go into this field," another wrote. "It was a mistake for me to choose this field. Had I known that it would be so toxic, I would not have."

Much of that toxicity is systemic; the ladder you have to climb to advance in the economics field—like so many fields in the United States—was built by white men for white men, and in large and small ways it continues to advantage white men. (Highly educated white men are the staunchest defenders of those long-maintained systemic advantages.) Here is one example: to earn tenure and professional acclaim, economists must get their research published in academic journals. Some of those journals are more prestigious than others. Arguably its most prestigious journal, the *American Economic Review*, has never had a top editor who is black.

Here is one more example, from a respondent to the association's survey: introductory economics courses are taught in many colleges and universities in a way that fails to serve black students who come from less advantaged backgrounds than white peers. It is one reason why economics doesn't attract as many black students, from the beginning of college, as other science and technology disciplines. "We need to focus on colleges with large populations of underrepresented groups and start teaching the intro economics courses in a way that students with weaker high school backgrounds can grasp AND get excited by," the respondent wrote. "Teaching the intro courses in lectures of hundreds of students with ONLY multiple choice homework and exams is doing a serious disservice to the students and to our profession. We will not get a more diverse profession if we cannot target college students more effectively."

There is a reason that so many colleges still teach economics in the same way they did when the students were primarily white men, and why economics departments still maintain a certain process of tenure that runs through elite academic journals that are policed largely by white male economists. Economists call it "path dependence." It's the idea that past is prologue, that systems develop and harden over time and are difficult to change. It is easy to see why that is the case: the people who set the rules of a particular institution, be it the practice of law or the governance of the nation or the academic discipline of economics, tend to be people who successfully navigated those rules and thus see little reason to change them. Or, even worse, who recognize that changing the rules would threaten their hold on power. That is true even when changing the rules would create better outcomes for society, or the country, as a whole.

Sometimes you can see path dependence, physically, in the world around you. I saw it in Winston-Salem, when I went back to visit Ed Green.

Seventy-five years after black women led the strike that crippled production at the R.J. Reynolds tobacco plant and delivered lasting benefits for black and white workers alike, Winston-Salem remains starkly divided by race. It is divided geographically, with whites clustered downtown and on the west side of town and black and Hispanic residents spread across the north and east sides. Policy decisions have cemented that divide. Decades ago, workers cut a four-lane highway called US 52 through what had been a poor black neighborhood, partitioning the largely black residents on the east side from the largely white ones to the west. Another working-class black neighborhood was razed to build BB&T Ballpark, home of the Dash, the minor-league baseball team that once honored Ed as its employee of the year.

I drove down US 52 to meet Ed for lunch on my second day in town in July 2019. It was a Saturday. He had lined up an extra shift at another liquor store—not his usual store but one that needed additional help on a hot weekend. We met at a juice bar for smoothies; he was still watching his health. He told me that in his weekday job on the highway crew, he was helping to pave a thoroughfare that will connect a medical research park to a batch of loft apartments downtown. Some of them were newly built; some were carved from the bones of the R.J. Reynolds tobacco plants that had once employed his grandparents and the ladies of Local 22. Young people were moving into those condos and apartments and taking jobs in that research park. They were mostly white. "The highway's just for them," he said. Businesses were sprouting up to serve the new arrivals: coffee shops, microbreweries, distilleries, cozy concert halls.

In Ed's neighborhood, east of US 52, there was no similar surge of activity. Home values had not budged much since the recession. Ed and his wife rented a brick rambler that online real estate sites valued at about $60,000.

Three of their children lived in the area: a daughter who managed a CVS store, a son who was a supervisor for the Veterans Administration, and another daughter who worked in the Hanes apparel factory. A grandson had just graduated high school, and he was preparing to start at Winston-Salem State University in the fall of 2019 with a plan to study sports medicine. A granddaughter was visiting from Florida, along with one of Ed's sons, who was in town to help Ed's wife with her health issues. The son worked as a technician for Nielsen Media Research, the company that calculates ratings for TV shows. He has skipped around the country earning raises from the company, relocating from Florida to Washington, D.C., to Sacramento and then back to the lower taxes and lower housing costs of the Sunshine State. He was thirty-three years old and thinking of moving to Winston-Salem, where houses cost even less. All six of Ed and his wife's children are college graduates, and they all wanted to own homes someday.

None of them did. Yet.

The neighborhood the Greens live in is majority black. It is undervalued in comparison with similar areas that have predominantly white residents, according to researchers at the Brookings Institution in Washington, D.C. Homes in heavily black neighborhoods are worth thousands of dollars less than comparable ones in white neighborhoods, a pattern that repeats in large and diverse metro areas across the United States. It is not just the real estate that is diminished by segregation. Nearly half of Winston-Salem's black residents live in a majority-black neighborhood. The schools in those neighborhoods churn out students who have an educational proficiency rate that is half that of the schools in all-white neighborhoods. If you are black and live in the city, you are more than seven times as likely than a white resident to live in an area of concentrated poverty.

The previous night Ed had started to tell me about the discrimination he has experienced during the course of his career. Over our blended-fruit liquid lunch, I asked him about it again. "The job I'm on now," he said, "in my department there's thirty-five people. Out of thirty-five people, there's two Hispanics and five blacks. Out of the whole department, there's only two minority supervisors."

Why do you think that is?

"You know, life is changing," he said, "but you still have the good old boys club here." The supervisors who hire a guy just because they know him, Ed explained, and not because he's the best worker for the job.

He had long recognized the discrimination around him, and he had taken steps to shield his children from it. He had deliberately named his son Jordan. "I specifically picked that name so that his name doesn't stop him from getting a foot in the door," Ed said. No one would think twice about calling back a job applicant whose resume said "Jordan Green." Ed was worried that wouldn't be the case for a Tyrone or an Abdullah. He had been hopeful, he said, that if Jordan had a son, he would not need to worry about what to name him. But he was unsure now. The president of the United States was berating a black congressman on Twitter. And some white people around town seemed much more comfortable than they had been in the past calling their black neighbors names.

We got to talking about Trump and his white working-class supporters, and Ed told me there was something about their economic grievances that he did not understand. He did not see how they could suddenly start complaining that black or immigrant workers were taking jobs from them. Think about landscaping, he said. (I thought back to the Trump fans I'd interviewed in Virginia, complaining that Latinos had taken over their industry.) It used to be a hard, low-paying job that fewer white people wanted to do. Now the pay has improved, he said, and the workers are mostly nonwhite, and whites seem angry. "How can we steal something," Ed said, "you just threw away?"

When he left lunch to go back to work, I found myself thinking about things of value being thrown away. About black workers, still held back by the segregation and prejudices that many white Americans will tell you the country left behind long ago. About the decisions America's leaders make every day, at every level of government, to perpetuate discrimination simply by maintaining systems of schooling and hiring and opportunity that were built to work for white men, and which now exclude others— not just nonwhite men, but women of all races, too.

About $5 and $20 and $100 bills, strewn across city streets, just waiting for someone to see that they're real enough to pick up.

13

SoHo, 2019

UNCOMMON CAPABILITY

In a crowded corner of a thin building in lower Manhattan, Deborah Jackson and her team run what you might think of as a boutique financial firm that specializes in one particular, undervalued asset: American women. They have no trouble finding promising leads for more of that asset to invest in. America is awash in women who are undervalued by the people who run and fund businesses.

Here is a simple way to measure just how much the United States economy is missing out on by failing to fully harness the talents of American women. The Bureau of Labor Statistics reports that in 2018 there were just under twenty-seven million women in the United States between the ages of twenty-five and sixty-four who had gone to college and earned at least a bachelor's degree. They easily outnumbered similarly educated men in the population because women had, for nearly two decades, been flocking to college at much higher rates than men. But the women's advantage disappeared if you zoomed in on the American population and looked only at the people who were working or trying to find a job. There were essentially an equal number of men and women with college degrees in that group of workers, which economists call the labor force. The gender advantage evaporated because a much larger share of women were not actively trying to work—sometimes by choice, and sometimes not. That fall-off, from the number of women with college degrees in the population to the number of them in the labor force, represented a huge loss for America's families and workers, and ultimately its middle class.

Consider: if the labor force had engaged prime-aged, college-educated women to the same degree that it engaged men, the United States in 2018 would have had more than 3.6 million additional, high-skilled workers who were eager to help the nation grow.

If each of those women had been paid the typical salary for a female American worker with a bachelor's degree, that pay would have added up to more than $200 billion a year.

If each of those women had earned the typical salary for a *male* American worker with a bachelor's degree, the pay would have totaled nearly $300 billion a year.

If *all* of America's prime-aged, college-educated women were as engaged in the labor force as men, and if each woman from that group earned the typical salary for a male college graduate, the additional pay each year would top $700 billion. The gains would be even larger, on every count, if you expanded the numbers to include all eighty-six million prime-aged women in the labor force, and not just the ones who graduated from college.

A steady increase in female labor-force participation was a big driver of the growth and income gains of America's Golden Age for the middle class after World War II. It was part of a virtuous cycle of opportunity and talent for American women. They were honing skills and building knowledge by increasing their rates of attending and graduating from college, then going on to work more outside the home after graduation while also gaining access to occupations and career paths that had been closed to them for much of the nation's history. By the early 2000s women had surpassed men in college attendance and graduation. They had narrowed, though not eliminated, the disparity between how much a woman and a man earned for doing the same job.

What if you had told a friend in 1995 that over the next twenty-five years, a combination of expanding trade, emerging technology, and deliberate policy choices would give a big economic advantage to the most educated workers in the American economy? And also that, with each passing year, more and more of the most educated Americans would come from one particular group of people? Your friend might well have concluded that the most educated group would dominate the job market over the next quarter century. Those Americans would work more and earn more, because the economy was increasingly set up to reward their skills. Right?

Wrong.

Instead of accelerating over the last twenty-five years, economic progress for American women has slowed. The share of women between ages twenty-five and fifty-four who were working or looking for work peaked in 1999. It fell throughout the first decade and a half of the 2000s, even as trends in the economy and in education increasingly suggested that employers should have been looking to female workers to fill their jobs of the future. It fell for women with bachelor's degrees and, somehow, for women with graduate degrees. Only toward the back half of the 2010s, in the waning months of Barack Obama's presidency and continuing through the Trump presidency, did the rate begin to climb again. It remains well below the participation rate for men and the participation rate for women in other rich countries, like France and Canada. And it is nowhere close to the level you would expect, given the advantages that the twenty-first-century economy should be granting to American women over comparatively less-educated men.

The participation rate is a window into the impediments for women, particularly women at the top of the education ladder, that have spread like ivy through the American economy in recent decades.

On paper, female workers should be getting ahead of men, given America's trends in technology and education. Instead, women continue to earn less and work less than men. They remain woefully underrepresented in some of the most lucrative fields in the economy, including computer science and finance. They are promoted less often at all levels of corporate America, particularly in the ranks of top executives. They are barely an afterthought to venture capitalists.

Women remain, as a group, America's most underappreciated economic asset. They are blocked, by new and complicated forces, from maximizing their talents and deploying them in ways that would accelerate productivity and growth and deliver a new era of sustained income gains to the middle class.

For a while, these developments, particularly in labor-force participation, puzzled many economists. They saw a larger share of women joining the workforce in other rich countries, and they wondered why the United States, which had been a leader in opening its economy to female workers after World War II, was suddenly going backwards. The first few times I wrote about the issue, the stories framed it as a mystery that economists were trying to figure out. What in the world was behind the reversal? What uniquely American problems were pushing women away from work and keeping working women out of better jobs with higher pay?

In recent years, economists have made a lot of progress on that puzzle. They still concede that they don't understand certain things about the forces holding women back, but they've developed—and broadly agree on—several explanations for what's going on. Many of them are exactly what you'd expect from an economic system that has been guided for centuries by lawmakers and business leaders who are predominantly men.

Some of the forces holding back women are similar to the ones holding back black workers, including path dependence, underinvestment, and overt discrimination. Some, like sexual harassment and assault in the workplace, are sinister remnants of a boys'-club economy that allowed and even encouraged powerful men to abuse female subordinates. Some are the product of social norms and government policies failing to adapt to the changing economic reality as fast as women have—in particular,

America's struggle to support women as they have children and raise families, and who find themselves slipping behind male colleagues as a result.

Some people, mostly men, doubt that every one of those impediments is actually real. They say that women's choices—on issues as varied as what college majors to pursue, whether to pause their careers to have children, and how much work/life flexibility to demand from their employers—account for nearly all the gap in pay between the sexes. The digital archives of the *Wall Street Journal* editorial page are stuffed with articles dismissing or downplaying the role of discrimination, bad policy, or other barriers in holding back women's advancement in the economy. In one such op-ed, from 2014, a pair of white male researchers at the conservative American Enterprise Institute wrote that gender pay-gap claims were "economically illogical." If women were paid dramatically less than men, they wrote, "a profit-oriented firm could dramatically cut labor costs by replacing male employees with females. Progressives assume that businesses nickel-and-dime suppliers, customers, consultants, anyone with whom they come into contact—yet ignore a great opportunity to reduce wages costs" by hiring women.

"They don't ignore the opportunity," the researchers concluded, "because it doesn't exist."

Sound familiar?

Even if those men were correct, and women's choices were steering them toward lower-value work than men in the labor market, those choices would nevertheless be hurting the American economy. If women were capable of working and earning more, but simply *chose* not to, policymakers could stoke higher growth—which could help the economy deliver higher wages not just for those working women but for all workers across the country—merely by finding ways to encourage women to make different choices.

But let's be clear: the argument is absolutely incorrect. The choices women make in the American economy today and the economic outcomes they experience are often forced on them by a system that is still optimized for powerful men. Prejudice and discrimination may be economically irrational, but they have persisted for centuries. There is no reason to think that the free market finally defeated them in the 1960s. There is also no reason to think that a market that has grown and evolved over time under the direction of white male leaders should inherently offer equal opportunity to women or workers of color.

A vast array of studies demonstrate this, including research from the International Monetary Fund, the Organization for Economic Cooperation and Development, the Brookings Institution, and economists in every major wealthy nation in the world. One of the first economists to sit down and talk for hours with me about the challenges facing the middle class was Heather Boushey, the head of a progressive think tank called the Washington Center for Equitable Growth. She has written exhaustively on the subject in books and technical research papers; her work helped form the backbone of a women's-economic-empowerment plank of Hillary Clinton's 2016 presidential campaign platform. She has shown how paid parental leave for women after childbirth boosts labor-force participation, family incomes, and economic growth.

Some of the best work on the "market failures" that result from women lacking access to paid time off after childbirth and being forced to quit their jobs to care for an infant comes from Aparna Mathur, an economist at . . . the conservative American Enterprise Institute. She has shown that a lack of leave can cause families to make inefficient choices—for themselves and the broader economy—about how much to work and when, which hurts parents and children alike. As COVID-19 ripped through the American economy in the spring of 2020, Boushey and Mathur led the call among economists for Congress to ensure that all workers had access to some form of paid leave to care for themselves or their children amid the outbreak—a critical move for safeguarding public health and for helping families avoid drowning in the flash flood of the recession. In late March, Mathur signed on to the White House Council of Economic Advisers, where she told me she hoped to win more support for a paid-leave push.

Cold, hard evidence of barriers to advancement for women, overt and discreet, has even been compiled by employers who have examined their own hiring practices. A recent example comes from one of America's top clusters of bright minds and highly educated talent, Northwestern University, an elite private university just north of Chicago.

In 2016, Northwestern's administrators launched a task force to examine why, despite more than two decades of efforts to diversify hiring, the university still employed men in 70 percent of its tenure-track faculty positions. An internal report found that the university's share of women faculty placed it in the middle of its competitors: below more diverse universities like Yale and Johns Hopkins but above the University of Chicago and Stanford. A follow-up report from 2018, which a faculty member sent to me after I published a story in the *New York Times* on accusations of sexual harassment against a prominent Harvard economist, warned that Northwestern's share of women faculty would stagnate if officials failed to fix problems in their hiring and retention efforts. "These numbers suggest," the report said, "that Northwestern has a gender equity problem."

That 2018 report was produced by a subcommittee. It marshaled the tools of social science research, including data collection and a wide range of interviews, to learn where, exactly, the university's efforts had gone wrong. What it discovered was "both explicit and implicit bias in hiring practices."

Women on the Northwestern faculty, the study said, frequently reported that when they had been interviewed during the search process, interviewers asked about spouses and children—but did not ask the same questions of men. When they were out for dinner with members of the search committee as part of the interview process, the conversation sometimes turned aggressively sexual. Some men on the hiring team, women reported, made comments about looking up women's skirts. One female candidate was asked if she was "a breeder." Another said that at her recruitment dinner, some of the men asked what she did in her spare time. Dance, she said. One of the men immediately responded, "'Oh, are you a pole dancer?'" she said. "And it started the conversation if I was a stripper."

We could linger here, for pages and chapters and easily an entire book, on all the different ways that the modern American economy impedes progress for women. We could talk about the persistence and prevalence of harassment in the workplace, as my Pulitzer Prize–winning *Times* colleagues Megan Twohey and Jodi Kantor have detailed in their powerhouse reporting on abuse of women by the Hollywood mogul Harvey Weinstein and others. We could talk about all the ways that women's careers suffer when they try to balance them with children and family, as my colleague Claire Cain Miller has shown over and over in the pages of the *Times*. Economists have increasingly concluded that outdated and inadequate policy support for mothers in the workplace drag down female labor-force participation in the United States when compared with similar countries that guarantee access to parental leave and provide more affordable child care. We could talk about the biases that male managers continue to harbor against promoting women, as shown by studies. We could go further back in women's careers, to college, and review the ample evidence showing that many science and engineering departments have failed in their efforts to attract sufficient numbers of young women to what we are often told are the most important and lucrative majors in the United States today—this despite the fact that young women have for years outperformed young men, as a group, on some key high school science and math tests. At every turn, we would find the ingrained effects of path dependence and resistance to cultural change. In economics, for example, several of the most widely read introductory textbooks are four times more likely to mention a man in their pages—as a reference, as an example, as anything—than to mention a woman.

We could do that, but let's not. Let's look, instead, at the vast untapped potential that women hold, for themselves, their families, and the American economy.

Let's look at the economy the way Deborah Jackson sees it, from her cozy corner office in the New York City neighborhood of SoHo.

To call it an office is slightly generous. The headquarters of Jackson's company, Plum Alley Investments, is a sixth-floor sliver of a coworking space, smaller than some Manhattanites' walk-in closets. It has two long rows of tables, light wood, and a bay of windows with the shades drawn.

At the end of the room is a whiteboard with a long list of names scrawled across it. They are all start-up companies that are run by women.

Jackson enjoyed plusher confines in the first half of her career. She graduated Columbia Business School and joined Goldman Sachs, the powerhouse investment bank, in 1980. The first time I talked with her, she told me what she remembered from her earliest interviews at the firm: the lettering stamped on the glass doors of its headquarters just off Wall Street. "Uncommon capability," it said, and for a long time, she bought into it. She worked in Goldman's municipal finance division, which arranges loans for local governments, hospitals, and other not-for-profit organizations. She flew first class on trips to meet potential clients and sealed deals with red wine and red meat at the 21 Club, a plush New York restaurant. She loved the work; she felt as though she was solving problems and making a difference. But after a while she didn't feel that way anymore. She left Goldman for a smaller firm, she launched her own investment-banking practice, and then, just before the Wall Street crash of 2008, she left the financial industry entirely. She called it a retirement. It sounded more like burnout. "It just lost its interest for me," she told me. "It just became work."

Volunteering in her spare time after the crisis, Jackson began to meet young entrepreneurial women. The more she saw of their energy, the more it impressed her. She helped organize gatherings of women who were skilled at computer coding. And then she launched Plum Alley, which was first a sort of business accelerator for women launching start-up companies but has since morphed into a modern, feminist outpost of the industry where her whole career began: finance.

The reason that every successful capitalist economy needs a financial system is, more or less, plumbing. Financial institutions help deliver money from people or organizations that have an excess of it to businesses, entrepreneurs, home buyers, and other borrowers who don't have enough of it at any particular moment. Like pipes, carrying water from reservoirs to thirsty plants. It's great in theory. It's not so easy in practice. A lot has gone wrong in America's financial plumbing since Deborah Jackson first hit Wall Street in 1980. It grew too big and complicated, and the men who ran it overloaded some pipes with risk. Along the way, the plumbers—who are predominantly men—somehow managed to collectively ignore an entire garden full of entrepreneurs who have struggled to attract the capital they need to nurture and grow their businesses. That group is women. Deborah and her team can recite all the ways investors have passed them by.

They have a whole PowerPoint deck on it. The first statistic is stark. In 2018, it shows, venture capitalists in the United States distributed $131 billion to start-up businesses, hoping to seed the next Google or Tesla. That money went to nearly nine thousand different companies. Just over 2 percent of them were founded entirely by women. Another 12 percent were founded by a mixed-gender team of entrepreneurs that included at least one woman. The rest, 86 percent, were companies founded entirely by men. The male-only teams reaped $116 billion from the venture capitalists. The women-only teams got $3 billion. The amount flowing to women-only teams on which at least one founder was not white was almost nothing.

You can't blame that disparity on what industry leaders sometimes call their pipeline problem: the fact that university science and engineering departments award far more degrees to men than women. The share of women receiving computer science and engineering degrees is dramatically larger than the share of female-founded companies that received venture funding in 2018. You could easily blame it on a boys' network. As Plum Alley notes later in the slide deck, a recent magazine spread of America's top venture capitalists—the folks who hand out the money to start-up founders—featured thirty-three men and two women. In pitch meetings, company founders tell Jackson and her staff, men are often asked promotional questions: *How big could you get?* Women are often asked precautionary ones: *Have you considered that this could all go wrong?*

That's if women make it to those meetings at all. A 2018 Morgan Stanley report surveyed investment firms and found that investors were far more likely to consider pitches from men than from women. They were much more likely to consider white business owners than entrepreneurs of color. They perceived female-owned and nonwhite-owned businesses to be riskier investments, even though that's false on both counts; female-owned businesses, the report noted, tend to outperform the market, and businesses owned by nonwhite entrepreneurs fare just as well as those owned by whites.

Jackson considers those facts a failure of the financial industry—and an opportunity for her investors. She has turned Plum Alley into a sort of investment club for people who believe in the underappreciated potential of women who start companies. She has eight full-time employees, split between New York and San Francisco, who aggressively scout women-led start-ups that are looking for capital. She has brought together a network of affluent women, and some men, who invest in the companies that her team identifies as prime opportunities for growth, job creation, and social impact.

In the fall of 2019, when I visited the SoHo office space, there were eighteen companies on the Plum Alley whiteboard, in industries that included artificial intelligence, gene editing, water and air quality, and clean energy. It is a small-scale start to freeing a large amount of trapped talent in the economy. And it is not in any way a charitable cause. It's a business bet.

"We try to find underrepresented, underappreciated founders," Jackson told me, in a small shared lounge of her coworking space. She is white, with long, light-colored hair; she was wearing black flat shoes with green trim and pink flowers, a combination I'd never seen in my scattered visits to venture capitalists on Sand Hill Road in Silicon Valley. She continued:

> But we don't compromise on quality. Or competence. A number of our
> founders have degrees from prestigious institutions. When you know the
> companies and the founders, they are kind of the crème de la crème of
> talent. And in many cases, a number of these companies have progressed
> now so they're attracting some of the—what we call the "big boys." How-
> ever, they could not get their attention in the first rounds. And now that
> they've proven something and they're kind of a hot company, moving
> ahead now, they're getting the attention of the bigger firms. I think it's
> only a matter of time until this portfolio performs quite well and probably
> outperforms other portfolios.

Two other bets are underpinning that prediction. One is that women are not just overlooked by venture firms; they're more focused than men on leveraging innovative technologies to solve large social problems like chronic disease or climate change. The boys who have been venture-capital darlings in recent years have often built companies that burned cash to no apparent end (like WeWork) or delivered new twists on old vices (like the vaping company Juul).

Referring to the start-ups on her funding list, Jackson said, "Every single one of these companies has a component of, 'We are going to make the world better.' Women care more about the social impact than men—I think the data all shows that." That's not a do-gooder strategy, she explained. It's a faith that more value can be created and more durable companies can be built by solving the largest and most pressing problems society faces.

The second bet is a trickier one, because there is no way that Plum Alley, or one hundred smallish investment firms like it, could tip the odds by pouring money into the market. The bet is that the structural forces that have kept women from founding more companies and drawing more funding can be broken or at least bent. That all the women Jackson and her team invest in will not find themselves dashed against the rocks of an economy where men can more easily access money and mentoring and where male founders are surrounded by examples of other men who blazed entrepreneurial trails.

If enough people invest in women founders, Jackson said, just maybe, "you will have a massive number of women in the STEM fields that become role models. You know, there's all this money going to [efforts to] teach girls in middle school how to code. I'm so supportive of that. I think that's great. But it kills me because right now we have women in STEM and technologists that are not getting funded. So if they don't get funded, they will fail and they won't be role models. And then why would anybody go into that business, if [they] think [they] have no shot at it?"

That's true not just of start-ups. It's true of engineering more broadly, and science, and math, and, yes, economics. America has made great strides in tearing down some of the social and psychological barriers for women to advance in certain fields; very recently, for the first time, women made up the majority of new students in medical school. In the laggard sectors of the economy lies a great hope for productivity gains and growth. A chance to help a multitude of talented women finally do what they are best at, to the benefit of everyone around them.

America's opportunity is not just that women could be working more than they are. It's that they should be creating more, hiring more, solving more problems, figuring out the best ways to put men (and women) back to work.

Here is another way of quantifying that opportunity. This one comes from Morgan Stanley, in a 2018 report. If revenues for companies owned by women and Americans of color were on par with those groups' participation in the labor force, the investment bank's researchers calculated, the United States would have an additional $4.4 trillion of economic activity every year.

In the fall of 2018, shortly before Morgan Stanley released its report on what it called "The Trillion-Dollar Blind Spot" in the American economy, researchers at the International Monetary Fund completed a study on the macroeconomic effects of reducing gender discrimination around the world. It was a wonky and understated manifesto on the potential benefits of empowering women in the economy—the benefits that would accrue not just for women but for everyone. Increasing inclusion for women in the economy, the IMF researchers wrote, boosts growth. It raises productivity. And it helps men too. "Greater gender diversity is likely to boost male incomes," the researchers wrote. "This makes discrimination against women in labor markets not only economically inefficient but also directly costly to men."

Unlocking trillions of dollars of potential is far too much for one boutique investment firm to manage on its own. It's too much for the network of investors that Deborah Jackson is assembling, men and women both, and for the founders and employees and customers of the companies Plum Alley Investments is helping to fund. It is a start, though, one of thousands of efforts across the nation to bridge the gaps and roll back the boulders that impede multitudes of American workers from helping themselves—and all of us.

Jackson has mapped that beginning, with dots for each of the companies she is helping to support. They are clustered on the coasts, particularly in California, but there are a couple in the middle of the country. One from Chicago, she tells me, pointing. One from Minneapolis. And a vastness of open space around them.

Jackson's small but growing effort is, unsurprisingly, rooted in the urban, educated, multiracial hubs of innovation that increasingly dominate the American economy. Her money has gone where the high-end entrepreneurs are. Vast expanses of America never pitch her investors. They are not on the radar in SoHo.

Those left-out places are the last piece of the country's broken puzzle of opportunity. And there's a good way to get them all on the map. It involves a different sort of investment in people.

14

Turners Falls, 2019

SILENT FACTORIES, EMPTY ORCHARDS

Kevin Hassett still has a favorite fishing rock where the Connecticut River thunders off a small cliff and plunges toward Long Island Sound. It sits across the basin from the dam and the fish ladder and the start of the canal that slices through a village named Turners Falls. On the banks of the canal lie bombed-out old factories. They're a remnant of the great industrial town that was already fading when Hassett was a boy who loved to fish here—of the work and production and *identity* that so many small towns across rural America have lost in recent decades.

Hassett grew up one town over, in Greenfield, in the 1960s and 1970s. The village of Turners Falls was founded as a planned industrial community, with mills as a centerpiece, one hundred years before that. Water, not fish, powered its economy. Men cut the canal to gin the hydropower that electrified the mills that built the glory days of western

Massachusetts manufacturing. In an early warning for factory towns across the nation, those glory days were already fading by the time Donald Trump's future chief economist was born.

The factories that now stand silent in Turners Falls—or do not stand at all—once churned out lumber, cotton products, Bowie knives, and, above all, paper. The workers who manned them lived in a flat grid of colonial houses a short walk away. At the village's zenith, in the early 1900s, there was an electric streetcar downtown, an opera house that seated one thousand, and direct rail service from New York City. By the time of Hassett's youth, those were all memories. Tales of a town that had seen the economy pass it by.

The glory days are not coming back, not in any way that resembles how they once were. But there is a renewal budding along the banks of the canal nonetheless, one that could flourish with a heavy dose of the best hope left for the large stretches of rural America that have been left out of the twenty-first-century expansion: immigrants.

In the spring of 2019, Hassett invited me to accompany him to his hometown, to see the ruins of what had been and to talk about how to spark a revival. More than most wayward sons, he brought with him a power to change the town's fortune, potentially for the good. He was at the time fifty-seven years old and the chairman of the White House Council of Economic Advisers. The top economist for the president of the United States.

Stories of past factory glory enchanted Hassett in his youth, as the son of schoolteachers who watched his slice of industrial America slip more and more into decay. He saw members of a cultlike hippie commune, led by a musician who called himself Rapunzel, turn a downtown theater into their headquarters. They bought and ran a pizza parlor, record store, and several other shopfronts. Hassett and his friends drank beer from kegs in a large sand pit on the edge of town. He captained his prep school's track team, once racing the future king of Jordan to what Kevin swears was the only tie of his career. Like many future economists, he played more than a few rounds of Dungeons and Dragons.

Mostly, he says, he spent his free time outdoors. He fished the rivers and the falls. He hiked the hills and forests and stream banks. He explored, relentlessly and curiously, what appeared to him to be the ruins of a once-great economy.

Why, he wondered, did it all go away? And what might bring it back?

On the day we visited the ruins, nearly all the factories that had once lined the canal were shuttered or leveled. The poverty rate in Turners Falls was stubbornly high. Manufacturing employment in Massachusetts had fallen by more than half over the course of the last forty years.

Hassett had helped to set a plan in motion that he hoped would reverse those trends. It was based on a theory of tax cuts, leveraging the power of capital investment, and, ultimately, rich people pouring money into places and neighborhoods that aren't currently home to a lot of rich people. I wanted to see how that hypothesis was actually playing out on the ground, in one of the many once-great factory towns that Trump had promised to bellow back to life. And I had a theory of my own, centered on another sort of capital that could renew the small towns and sprawling counties that have been bypassed by the twenty-first-century economy.

America's economic inequality—and its untapped potential—is increasingly place-based. In the past two decades, punctuated by the Great Recession and its aftermath, a shrinking number of counties in the United States have contributed a ballooning amount of the country's job and business growth. Rural areas had to wait years longer than cities and suburbs to begin to recover from the recession, and by some measures, nearly a decade after the recession ended, they still had not regained what they lost. They have not seen their residents get back to work nearly as fast as those in small or large metropolitan areas, the Federal Reserve noted with consternation in 2019. Too many rural economies now depend heavily on the residents of large metro areas, who visit their towns or buy their products. In the spring of 2020, many rural areas—even in states like South Dakota without stringent restrictions on economic activity—saw unemployment spike and their economies contract, as the pandemic froze their best customers in place in the city.

It is a particularly dire situation for the start-up businesses that America is counting on to create high-paying and middle-class jobs to replace all the ones it lost in its decades-long bleed of manufacturing work. After the Great Recession wiped out businesses across the country, the recovery brought start-ups to only a few select urban areas, largely concentrated among America's "superstar" cities, like San Francisco, New York, and Chicago. In 1999, according to census data analyzed by the Economic Innovation Group, a Washington think tank devoted to issues of regional inequality, 125 counties supplied half of the nation's new business formation. In the recovery from the Great Recession, that shrank dramatically. Only twenty counties generated half the new business growth, on net, for the country. Even the state of Texas, with a proud history of vibrant rural economies, saw a concentration of activity after the 2008 recession. More than four out of five new Texas jobs in that recovery sprung up in one of four Lone Star metro areas: Dallas, Austin, Houston, or San Antonio.

Many rural counties were ravaged by the opioid epidemic, which ripped like wildfire through small-town pharmacies and medicine cabinets, setting off a chain of addiction and death. That epidemic is largely responsible for the spike in what the economists Anne Case and Angus Deaton call "deaths of despair," which also include suicides and alcohol poisoning. Case and Deaton, both emeritus professors from Princeton, have traced the surge in those deaths and shown that they have led to an astounding reversal in the United States. For years, as medical technology advanced, Americans had been living longer and longer. Now, though, white middle-aged Americans without college degrees are living shorter lives than they once did. Opioids are the agent of many of those early deaths. But Case and Deaton do not see drugs as the cause. They see decades of deterioration of the quality of rural life for Americans who did not go to college.

That quality includes declining wages since the 1970s, Case and Deaton wrote in a 2018 rejoinder to a critic of their work. Also, they wrote, it includes "the decline in labor force participation, the decline in marriage rates, the rise of cohabitation, the rise in out of wedlock births, and of parents living apart from children that they barely know. We discuss the decline in the quality of jobs, the increasing lack of opportunity for people without a [bachelor's degree], as well as changing religious practices. We discuss the decline of unions, and the consequent loss of the local, national, and workplace voice that workers once had. We discuss that many less-educated people have lives that are economically and socially inferior to those of their parents."

Kevin Hassett moved away from Western Massachusetts for college and graduate school and an economics career, which took him to a think tank and eventually the White House, where he stood out in part for pro-immigrant views that many of Donald Trump's other aides did not share. But he never stopped thinking about his hometown.

In the middle of the morning on our tour, Hassett and I parked on a slab of asphalt near a small canal, a trickle compared to what we would see later in Turners Falls, and waded through mud and weeds to the center of what had been the Greenfield Tap and Die. One hundred years ago, the factory standardized the production of nuts and bolts, which workers had previously cast by hand. The tap cut the grooves for nuts, the die did the same for bolts and screws, and together they revolutionized mechanized production around the world. The Greenfield plant drew its electricity from a set of turbines that tumbled in the waters of the canal, which was sluiced off from the Green River. The power was so plentiful, and the plant so innovative, that it grew into the largest tap-and-die factory ever to exist in the United States. It nurtured a growing middle class in industrial Massachusetts.

Employees, a historian named Rebecca Ducharme noted in a review of the plant's economic contributions, often worked thirty years or more there. The plant sponsored parades, carnivals, and a baseball team. It offered employees disability benefits, help finding housing, an apprenticeship program, and, through years of union pressure that sometimes culminated in strikes, relatively good wages. It was also a cornerstone in the construction of America's twentieth-century war machine. During World War II, the factory's efforts to ramp up production of parts for tanks, planes, guns, and shells were so vast that the company chronicled them in a monthly newsletter for employees.

When we arrived, there was almost no trace left of any of that. One of the former factory buildings had turned to puddles and weeds and long flat slabs, littered with spent Michelob Light cans. Homeless men lounged under the trees across the canal. We walked around the parking lot, talking about the war and the factory and the workers whose ranks dipped from the thousands in the 1940s to a few hundred in the 1990s to basically no one at the turn of the century. The plant went out of business, was recognized as an environmental hazard, was bought by local officials, and was eventually demolished. "This place here—it's a potentially great industrial site," Hassett told me as we trudged, boot-clad, through the wreckage. He had a friend on city council; there were hopes, he said, of bringing life and jobs back.

We returned to the car and drove to Turners Falls, a few minutes away. We parked near an old railroad bridge that had been built by the Keystone Bridge Company, of Pittsburgh, Pennsylvania, in 1880, and then rebuilt—probably after a flood washed a section of it away—in 1936 by the Phoenix Bridge Company of Phoenixville, Pennsylvania. We stepped out into the sun.

Hassett is freckled with subtle reminders of his family's Irish heritage. He has a small belly hanging over what remains a runner's lanky frame. He wears glasses and smiles constantly. He is perhaps the most affable nerd I have ever met in Washington, in a decade of gravitating toward affable nerds in a city that is rarely affable or, shockingly, nerdy. He is relentlessly, unflappably cheerful, in budget briefings, television interviews, even the thick of arguments about whether the burden of corporate taxes falls on companies or workers. A running theme of his research, long before he joined the Trump administration and helped architect a multitrillion-dollar tax overhaul, was his finding that when the government taxes big corporations, workers actually bear the cost. The first time I interviewed him, he explained how cutting corporate tax rates would relieve workers of that government burden, delivering a superboost of income growth to middle-class families whose incomes had tumbled during and after the Great Recession. This trip was partly about that—about showing me how, in Hassett's view, portions of the new tax law could deliver jobs and wage gains for the Massachusetts middle class. But it also showed me a side you don't normally see of presidential economists, an exploration of identity that Hassett said all Irish Americans share: a quest for understanding, for home.

That quest, in the early-afternoon sunlight, took us along a path toward the railroad bridge. Hassett regarded it and all the other relics we encountered on the walk as he did the vine-covered statues that characters stumble on in J. R. R. Tolkien's *Lord of the Rings*: as a lost city of men, once great, now fallen into ruin. He called those relics the "bones" of the town, and he loves to walk among them, like a mad archeologist, plotting their reanimation. "Look at the size of those stones," he said, pointing to a large cluster off in the trees that had probably been the walls of a great building or the feet of a different bridge. "Think what they had to do to move them here."

The water was high and green and frigid. We paused on the bridge. "They had a massive lumber presence in Turners," Hassett said, gazing out onto the water. "They had a sawmill up above the falls. That was gone before I was sentient." We stepped off the bridge and onto a path. The day was warming. In a large puddle near the trail, frogs called to each other. They sounded as though they had just woken up from a long hibernation, with new life on their minds.

We walked back to the car, pausing to stare across the high, cold water, and finally made our way to the village of Turners Falls, which is a subsection of a larger town now called Montague. It was the reason for our trip. We were on our way to see the ruins of what the village had once been, and what Kevin believed it could be again.

We drove through the former millworkers' neighborhood. The once middle-class craftsman houses were peeling and rotting in places. Windows were boarded up. We saw a drug deal go down on a corner. It almost certainly involved opioids, he surmised. We found our way to the falls and a dam that was still iced over from the winter, where several factories loomed on the waterfront, along the great canal, a century and a half old. Those mills used to churn out paper and cotton and cutlery. They have all fallen silent. The last of them closed in 2017. The town didn't know what to do with the reams of paper it left behind; one day, city officials say, they let local artists in, to carry off as much of the stuff as they could. "The mills are the problem everyone has been trying to crack for twenty years," Walter Ramsey, the planner for the town of Montague, which contains Turners Falls, told me as he prepared to give us a tour of the canal-front properties. "Industrial use here—we don't see it as viable."

Several years before he went to the White House, Hassett helped devise a plan to revive mills like these in towns like Turners Falls, the cradles of blue-collar, middle-class America that have rusted and crumbled from their postwar heyday. He fleshed out his plan in the West Village of New York City, in the townhome of a technology billionaire who had a novel idea about harnessing the vast amounts of wealth just sitting, untaxed and underproductive, in the bank accounts of rich capital owners from Wall Street to Silicon Valley: real estate developers, megafarm barons, hedge fund managers, start-up founders, heirs to monopolists long dead. Hassett carried that plan into the Trump administration, and the tech billionaire built a lobbying and research machine to promote it, including the Economic Innovation Group. Working together, they all helped slip the idea, for a program known ever-so-optimistically as "Opportunity Zones," into what would become the president's signature legislative and economic accomplishment, the 2017 tax cuts.

The idea behind the zones was to strategically reduce certain taxes on the windfalls that wealthy Americans receive when they sell stocks or homes or other assets (called capital gains)—if those wealthy Americans chose to invest money in areas like Turners Falls. In short, the zones would theoretically entice capitalists to turn their gaze, and money, to places that struggled to attract investment in the decade following a financial crisis that only briefly scathed Wall Street but scarred large tracts of America for life.

A lifetime of research—of complicated theories and formulas, all pointing to the power of capital investment, and tax cuts, to deliver big gains for workers—had convinced Hassett the plan would work. He was sure that the problems of industrial Massachusetts were solvable with simple, mechanical tweaks to the taxes investors had to pay the government from their investments in these distressed places. Tax advantages would rebalance the incentives of the economy, he told me probably hundreds of times, to once again favor towns like Turners Falls and the sons of blue-collar workers that he—and I—had grown up with.

There was little sign on our visit of it working yet. Ramsey, the town planner, was excited about the zones; he had invited Hassett to town after reading about them, and about Hassett, in a story I'd written for the *Times*. Turners Falls had been designated an opportunity zone by the state. But the Trump administration had been slow to issue regulations governing investments in the zones. Hard data on this question was difficult to come by because the tax law had required no measurements of how or where money invested through the program was being spent. But it appeared that not much money had flowed into zones nationwide by the end of 2019. There were still high hopes, which Hassett harbored and expounded even after he left the administration midway through 2019, that big investors would start showering money on left-behind areas, including rural ones. But in Turners Falls, in the spring of 2019, not a single opportunity-zone investment had yet been made. No new mills were on their way to the canal. The following spring, Hassett was headed back to the White House, to try to help craft policies that might keep thousands of manufacturers across the country from closing for good in the pandemic.

What do you do with a mill town without a factory future? You might give up on it and encourage people to find work somewhere more dynamic. That's what many policymakers and thinkers have proposed in recent years: to entice Americans to move, en masse, to areas that afford better jobs and more opportunity. There's no immutable law of capitalism that says towns cannot or should not die of economic irrelevance. Instead, there's a concept called "creative destruction," through which the economy is improved; it's all about the most successful companies growing and thriving, and the least successful ones withering and dying, to be replaced by new ones with better ideas, which in turn could drive some other company out of business. Create, destroy, rinse, repeat. Why shouldn't cities be the same way? If Ohio elected a governor cold-blooded enough to say, "Well, Toledo, you've had a good run, but your population is shrinking and your major companies are fleeing and the economy seems to be moving on from your whole manufacturing fixation, so let's just give all your tax dollars to Columbus and see if it can build itself some more fancy new restaurants and housing developments with those funds"—well, why not? What's wrong with letting a place die?

A lot, actually. Starting with the people you might be sentencing to die with that place.

Many Americans today are trapped in parts of the country that are underperforming—and they have no intention of leaving. That underperformance can be as damaging to a young woman following her dreams, maximizing her talent, and *doing what she is best at* as any bad social norm. It can drag a middle-aged man off the economic ladder he spent his lifetime climbing. It can also hurt his children. Growing up in an underperforming area, research by the Harvard economist Raj Chetty and a team of colleagues has shown, makes it harder for children to advance economically as adults.

If we want to reinvigorate the middle class, we need to bring new life to the patches of the country that have wilted in the shift to a more globalized, urbanized economy. We need to bring opportunity back to rural America, before it vanishes for good and leaves millions of workers stranded.

A focus on rural renewal would certainly help Trump's base voters, the alienated white working class spread across the industrial Midwest, the forests of Southern Oregon, and elsewhere. But rural areas are not just white. As the economist Olugbenga Ajilore—my former neighbor in Toledo, who now works at a liberal think tank called the Center for American Progress in Washington, D.C.—likes to note, one-fifth of Americans live in rural areas, but those areas differ wildly in terms of diversity. Some are home to large populations of black, Hispanic, or Native American residents. Those areas offer a sort of double bonus: if we could get their economies moving again, we would unlock the potential not only of trapped white men without college degrees, but of women and workers of color as well.

We need to get those regions' economies moving because it's unrealistic—and wrongheaded—to expect people to move away from them in bad times. "When regions are faced with adverse changes in labor demand, some residents may respond by migrating to more prosperous areas," Federal Reserve officials noted in 2019, in typically dry economist terms, adding that what you should expect to see in that case is a shrinking labor force with relatively stable participation rates. That's not what we've seen. In rural areas, labor-force participation is declining. Research suggests that people have been moving less often in recent decades. They are not chasing the economic opportunities that economists would have expected them to, a disconnect that led to some labor shortages during the oil and gas fracking boom in states like North Dakota. And they're not leaving distressed towns and counties behind. Taken together, such trends "could amplify the labor market effects of local shocks and lead to persistent disparities" between rural economies and everyone else, the Fed has warned.

The economist David Autor, godfather of "hollowing out" research, says there is a good economic explanation for this as well—a reason why Americans without college degrees are not flocking to cities the way they once did. Urban areas, he has shown, no longer offer the premium wages and better jobs that used to lure those workers from their rural hometowns, largely due to the decline of manufacturing.

There are noneconomic reasons too. People don't always like to move. They own houses. They belong to churches. They ran track in high school with the ladies who now get together every Thursday for coffee downtown. Sometimes their families and friends still live where they grew up. They enjoy the glow of holiday dinners and the ease of convenient, and often free, child care. Some economists have been surprised that people don't move toward opportunity more often. I'm surprised that so many folks move in the first place, given how many people I know who have lived in the same town or neighborhood or on the same block for nearly all their lives. "People are just not as mobile as the stories make them out to be," Autor told me in his office in Boston. "There's a lot of squandered talent in the world. That's one of the great threats to our system."

For as long as I've been writing about struggling economies, dating back to my time in Ohio, economists have told me that the best way to help restore those economies' glory days is through a policy designed around helping people move. Not helping them move out of economically depressed areas and toward more opportunity. But helping people move in—and bringing opportunity with them.

They have a particular sort of new arrival in mind.

City leaders have been slowly executing a renewal strategy for Turners Falls over the course of a decade. They've tried to lure young and valuable workers to create and fill high-paying jobs. They hoped those jobs would seed new activity that would grow through the rest of the community. They had a ready supply of educated workers nearby, in a ring of five liberal arts colleges that draw students and crank out graduates in this part of the state. They were pitching those graduates on a relatively low cost of living, a relaxed quality of life, and the sort of outdoor amenities—hiking and fishing—that were once the highlights of a young would-be economist's childhood. It was slowly bearing fruit, the town leaders told me.

Other towns are not so fortunate. So many rural areas across the country have tried strategies to attract local college graduates, often to no avail. (It will not surprise you that many of the most vibrant rural economies that remain in America include—and increasingly revolve around—college towns.) College graduates tend to go where there are large concentrations of companies that hire highly paid workers for what economists call high-skilled jobs, and where there are other college graduates and workers whom they can befriend or date.

For these reasons, in most cases regional inequality appears self-reinforcing. Rural areas with few college graduates in their existing workforces cannot attract either other college graduates or the companies that want to hire only college graduates. Their workers who did graduate college are more likely to move elsewhere to chase opportunity than their workers who did not graduate college. So those areas gradually lose businesses, dynamism, and population. Their home values fall. Vacancy rates rise.

Another economist I've known for a long time, Adam Ozimek, recently published a proposal to break that cycle. He did it through the Economic Innovation Group, the think tank focused on regional inequality. Unlike the group's opportunity-zones plan, which aims to drive financial investment to distressed areas, Ozimek focused on human capital: attracting the sort of people who have the power to spruce up an economy through the full force of their talents. "There are few policy options to address seismic demographic changes and the socioeconomic problems they cause," he wrote. "One is available and can have a direct impact: immigration."

At present, immigration exacerbates regional inequality because the highest-educated and most entrepreneurial immigrants, just like their native-born counterparts, cluster in superstar metro areas. Ozimek's idea is to allow—not force, but allow—struggling communities to change that equation by offering what he calls "Heartland Visas" to skilled immigrants. Recipients could travel anywhere in the country that they like, but they would need to live for a specified amount of the time in the community that issued them the visa. Their presence would change the dynamics of the area, on purpose.

"A new human capital pipeline for the heartland would do much to counteract the profound demographic challenges that shrinking communities face in their housing markets, municipal finances, entrepreneurial ecosystems, and labor markets," Ozimek wrote in his report, coauthored with two of the staff members from the innovation group. He noted that about a quarter of America's entrepreneurs are immigrants. But he said the benefit would far outstrip new business formation. "More skilled people in sheer numerical terms are needed to spark durable turnarounds and counteract the economic drag of population decline itself. Skilled immigrants, who are typically young, well-educated, and innovative, can meaningfully enhance local efforts to kickstart the process of economic revitalization."

The best economic evidence we have concurs. Immigrants, it shows, are an economic solution, not the cause of a problem.

Donald Trump has sold working-class Americans a lie about immigrants. Economic research shows that they do not, over any long-term horizon, take jobs from Americans or depress wages for the middle class. Immigrant families are no more likely to be a "drag" on taxpayer-funded social services than native-born Americans are, a review by the National Academies of Science, Engineering, and Medicine concluded in 2016. The research often cited by politicians who preach immigration restrictions finds only that some surges of relatively less-educated immigrants serve to reduce wages for other, previous waves of immigrants and for native-born Americans who dropped out of high school. Much other research contradicts these findings and shows that immigrants boost jobs and wages for native-born workers. A study published in 2019 by Princeton economist Leah Boustan and several coauthors examined immigration restrictions imposed by the United States in the 1920s and found that those restrictions did not boost wages for American workers. They actually reduced them, and they hastened the adoption of new technology that put some American workers out of a job.

Meanwhile, economists have published volumes of papers on the benefits that immigrants bring to economies. They work hard, they pay taxes, they innovate, they create jobs, they buy things, and they generate economic activity. And right now in America—particularly in shrinking swaths of rural America—we need them. Not just ones with advanced degrees, who are the cornerstones of Ozimek's plan, and not just in rural areas. But we especially need those immigrants in those places. The prescription that immigrants can help revive left-behind America was true when my colleague Josh and I wrote about Ohio in 2005, and it remains true now. America needs to attract and keep more of the world's top brainpower. We need their work, and we need their talent. We need their ability, by kick-starting the economic-revitalization process in struggling rural towns, to unlock the potential of workers trapped in jobs that don't use their full skills and don't pay them a good wage.

The National Academies summed it up well in that 2016 report. "Immigration is integral to the nation's economic growth," it said.

"Immigration supplies workers who have helped the United States avoid the problems facing stagnant economies created by unfavorable demographics—in particular, an aging (and, in the case of Japan, a shrinking) workforce. Moreover, the infusion by high-skilled immigration of human capital has boosted the nation's capacity for innovation, entrepreneurship, and technological change. The literature on immigrants and innovation suggests that immigrants raise patenting per capita, which ultimately contributes to productivity growth. The prospects for long-run economic growth in the United States would be considerably dimmed without the contributions of high-skilled immigrants."

This is an area of vast consensus among economists, even though polls show that many Americans do not believe it. Even some of Trump's earliest advisers knew it to be true.

At the end of my interview in Wilbur Ross's Manhattan offices in the fall of 2016, after Ross had excused himself to another meeting, I sat and talked for a while with Peter Navarro, the lone academic economist on the Trump campaign team and the future White House trade adviser. He had just spent an hour telling me how Trump's trade, tax, and energy policies were going to produce booming growth. I had some lingering questions: Won't your immigration policy work against that? Where are you going to get workers if President Trump cracks down on arrivals and accelerates deportations?

Navarro started by blaming immigrants (incorrectly) for high unemployment among black and Latino Americans. In inner cities, black and native-born Latino workers "are like at the tip of the spear of illegal immigration, because disproportionately they're the ones who lose the jobs," he said. "Because those jobs the illegals take tend to be lower income, lower educated."

He told me that the administration's policies would draw a large number of native-born Americans who had given up looking for work in the weak recovery from the recession back into the labor force. And he said he had recently completed a cost-benefit analysis on Trump's proposed wall along the border with Mexico. In the analysis, he said, "You start with the violent crime stuff. We want those people out. Because those people create social costs, in terms of rape, robbery, mayhem, whatever. But also if you incarcerate them, you're spending money there. So those people are a net plus, plus, plus if you get them out of here." The next group of immigrants, he said, was a drag on the economy because they did not generate enough in taxes to pay for the government benefits they draw. He said that group included immigrants here illegally and through legal channels.

"Mr. Trump," he said, "has been pretty clear how he just wants to deal with the violent ones first, and then work his way down the pyramid."

Then Navarro turned to higher-skilled immigrants. Attracting them, he said, was the goal of nearly every other country like the United States, and should be the goal here. "So, there will be and can be immigration," he said. Reporters, he added, were always getting Trump wrong. "It's not like he wants to shut the border down."

He said that if tech companies legitimately needed skilled people to fill jobs, they could get visas for them. "It's a process," he said.

That did not turn out to be true. Under Trump, immigration plunged to its lowest levels in a decade. His administration reduced the number of refugees it would accept from war-torn countries and other areas from which people were forced to flee. Trump proposed the framework of a plan that would have admitted fewer legal immigrants to the country every year. On several occasions in his first three years on the job, he threatened to shut down the border with Mexico entirely. Each time, aides talked him out of it, worrying about economic disruption.

Economists warned that the moves would hurt the American economy, right away and in the future. Rural areas continued to fall further behind superstar metros. Millions of people waited on the outside of the American economy, blocked from helping it prosper and grow.

Kevin Hassett is a traditional conservative economist whose pro-immigration stances earned him a backlash from some of Trump's supporters even before he started his job in the White House. He tried not to contradict the president once he arrived. But sometimes he could not help himself.

We drove to Turners Falls together on a clear early-spring morning. The temperature had fallen to near freezing the night before, but the sun was out and the fields were warming. It was the perfect weather, Hassett explained, for sugaring the maple trees. We drove through town and beyond it, spying men in overalls with plastic hoses and buckets who were tapping the trees to extract what he swore, defensibly, was the best syrup in New England. We snacked on rich maple candy from a storefront at one of the sugar farms, then we drove back toward town through the countryside, past the farm that his maternal grandfather was forced to sell during the Great Depression, past a sagging bar where he said he used to see Natalie Cole sing when she was a local prep school student.

He pointed out other farms, naming their crops, both current and long gone. He named the economic plague that had visited them in recent years. Instead of an invasion, it was an absence—of immigrant laborers who no longer found their way to the trees.

That's "a lot of maple syrup," Hassett said, motioning out the driver's-side window to one of the fields, describing what we were seeing. "A lot of orchards that aren't harvested anymore because they couldn't get the migrant workers."

Sunbeams glinted off the window. I stared out at frosted fields that were thawing, ready to start another season of growth.

"Everywhere you go," Donald Trump's top economist said, "there's an orchard that's empty now."

At some point on the tour, Hassett told me the story of how Turners Falls got its name. I read up more on it after I returned home. It is bloody and sad. It is one kind of immigrant story, for a town that could now use another.

They named Turners Falls for a British captain who slaughtered sleeping women and children at a fishing basin above where the Connecticut River crashes down in a cold spray from forty feet above. The captain was William Turner, and he was engaged in what was known as King Philip's War, a late seventeenth-century clash between Native Americans and the Massachusetts Bay Colony settlers, who had arrived uninvited decades before. The tribes and the colonists had worked out an initial, uneasy coexistence at first. But in an escalating competition for land and food, distrust grew among the English, some of their tribal allies, and rival tribes led by the Wampanoag.

As so often happens when different groups see resources as stretched and come to believe there is only a finite amount of prosperity to be had, war broke out.

The Wampanoags' leader was named Metacom, but the English called him King Philip. He had been battling the settlers for nearly a year when Turner and his soldiers made plans to ambush what they knew was an encampment of unarmed civilians, in retaliation for natives capturing English soldiers in a raid and making off with their cattle. The settlers and the natives were hungry and exhausted; both sides employed a starve-them-out strategy, raiding food supplies and disrupting the planting cycle. The tribes had a fallback at the falls, where shad and salmon ran thick from the ocean toward Vermont to spawn. Their people pulled fish from the water by day and slept in divided camps at night, with women, children, and old men resting apart from the armed men whose job it was to fight. It was the spring of 1676.

Captain Turner's soldiers arrived at the falls undetected in the middle of May, marching overnight under cover of a thunderstorm. A report from a colonial journalist named Roger L'Estrange tells what happened next. The English fired into the village huts at dawn. Historians report that when the defenseless occupants rushed out, the colonists strangled them, or ran them through with swords, or drove them into the river. Some were children, five years old or younger. "Many of them were shot dead in the waters," L'Estrange wrote. Others tried to flee in canoes, but they were shot as well. "The stream of the River being very violent and swift in the place near the great Falls," L'Estrange wrote, "most that fell over board were borne by the strong current of that River, and carried upon the Falls of water from those exceeding high and steep Rocks, and from thence tumbling down were broken in pieces." The English found more than two hundred natives dead in the river below the falls or on its banks. At that point, only one white soldier had fallen.

And then, quite quickly, the battle swung against Turner. Sounds of the fighting had roused tribal warriors camped nearby. They counterattacked, killing dozens of Turner's men and pushing them back from the falls. Turner died in retreat, shot crossing a smaller river that eventually feeds into the Connecticut. His body lay in the water for days, until his men found the courage to retrieve it and bury him.

The war wound down after that. When it ended in a peace treaty, both sides were devastated. War halted the whites' fur trade and jolted their heavily agricultural economy. It would take decades for them to recover. The southern New England tribes suffered far worse. A quarter of their population was dead. Many of the survivors fled the region, the beginning of a multicentury westward march of dispossession and suffering for tribes who occupied the land that the English settlers would eventually declare a new nation.

Almost everyone who fought with or against Captain Turner at the falls that day lost in the end: the fallen warriors and soldiers, the slain children, the people forced to flee the fishing lands they had loved.

More than three hundred years later, Turners Falls needs a new immigrant story—and this time, everyone can win.

15

Washington, D.C., 2007–2019

NO QUICK FIXES, EVER

The night before I started my first job in the nation's capital, as a correspondent for the *Chicago Tribune* newspaper, an old friend took me on a driving tour of the city. We had been colleagues in Denver, and he was still the Washington reporter for the *Rocky Mountain News*, which, like so many other wonderful things in the heart of America at that time, was nearing the end of a slow death. When my friend picked me up, he tossed me an oversized blue sport coat, which had until recently belonged to the disgraced lobbyist Jack Abramoff, who had bribed members of Congress and defrauded Native American tribes. (My friend acquired the jacket through some strange sequence of unpaid cleaning bills.) I climbed into his passenger seat, and we drove toward Capitol Hill.

He parked on an overlook and motioned me out of the car. It was a clear night, and the dome of the Capitol shone silently in the glow of floodlights. "Take it in," he told me. "Really take it in." And I did. I let myself soak in the kid-from-Oregon awe of that dome and those lights, of the Washington Monument and the Lincoln Memorial at the other end of the mall. Wasn't this the top? Wasn't this what I had been working for since I had started writing obits and wedding announcements as a teenager?

It's a thing the city can do to you, with or without a lobbyist cloak. It feeds your highest ideals and your most naked ambition, and it fuses them all together so you're unsure which is which.

My friend broke the spell. "Okay," he said. "Let's go. Tomorrow, that's just a place where you work."

I have now worked in Washington for more than thirteen years. I have been a professional reporter here for as long as I was a reporter everywhere else—in Oregon, California, Colorado, Ohio—combined. I have raised a child in its suburbs, bought a home, and attended a few of those D.C. press dinners and cocktail parties that everyone in the country loves to hate. They're not my favorite.

We can't talk about fixing the middle class without talking about Washington, a city that allows middle-class Americans an illusion of proximity to the people who decide every day whether to work in their best interests. It is an inspiring city and an absurd one. You can ride the metro train all summer and find yourself packed in with school groups from Kansas or Louisiana or France. You watch them climb the escalator at MacPherson Square to make a tourist pilgrimage past the home of the most powerful leader in the world, where they gaze through the fence rails at the president's front lawn. You can go to a ball game and see defense contractors peddling war machines on the scoreboard between innings, realizing that the advertisers care about reaching only a few people and that you're not one of them, and that the intended targets must be listening, because those ads are everywhere. You can pay a lot of money for a beer in a hotel bar with the president's name on it and watch a familiar cast of television characters flit around you, but good luck flagging one of them down for a chat about the policy issues actually affecting your job and family.

Disillusionment with Washington—the feeling that it doesn't work for regular people, that it changes good people who were sent there—helped elect Donald Trump. Like so many politicians before him, Trump has made the city his foil.

But it's important to parse what he, and everyone else, means by "Washington." They're not talking about a city, really. They're talking about power, and about a political system that perpetuates the interests of those who have long held it.

It's a crucial distinction. You can hate Washington, fairly, and then throw your hands up when your preferred outsider—Trump or Obama or George W. Bush or Bill Clinton or whoever—fails to change it. It's a valid frustration. But what you're really frustrated with is a political system that is unresponsive to the hopes, dreams, and needs of people like you. You're frustrated that the federal government takes a quarter of your paycheck before you ever see it but doesn't listen when you tell it you have a problem. What makes Washington so insidious, as a location and as a proxy for the political system, is its ability to sort the concerns of the powerful from the concerns of the least empowered and to almost always deal with those of the powerful first. That hasn't changed under any of the three presidents who have occupied the White House since I got here.

Nine months after I arrived in the city, the *Tribune* sent me to Florida for a story I'd pitched on the state's imploding housing market, which a couple of economists had told me could pull the state and the nation into recession. I saw how a wave of foreclosures and a sharp drop in home prices were already crippling the Tampa economy. I wrote that over the preceding year, "Construction laborers worked less and spent less. Homeowners tapped less equity to buy cars or boats. Several planned downtown condo projects, including one by Donald Trump, ground to a halt." I quoted a local real estate developer: "It's bloody," he said.

Blue-collar construction workers were some of the hardest hit by the recession that followed. Two million of them lost their jobs nationwide. Those who kept working saw their wages drop by more than any other sector of worker, according to research on private payrolls by Erik Hurst, the University of Chicago economist, and his colleagues. Those workers lost their homes, their savings, their credit ratings. Congress never gave meaningful relief to homeowners who were left underwater on their mortgages, and neither did Obama, who took office in the depths of the crisis—despite a mountain of economic evidence that suggested the best way to end the recession and speed the recovery was to help borrowers climb out of their holes.

It is by now a well-worn story of that recession: Washington bailed out the banks but not homeowners. It helped the powerful first. Then the powerful, as they often do, used the disparity to stoke anger in America—anger at the banks, yes, but also anger at the underwater borrowers. The latter launched a political movement, the Tea Party. The former just became a talking point that almost every candidate reeled off on the trail.

Trump's condos in Tampa were never built. Some prospective buyers, who had plunked down deposits, lost hundreds of thousands of dollars. Jack Abramoff is back working in Washington today. The city has only grown richer and fatter since I moved here, in spite of recessions, some brief federal budget tightening, and the arrival and exit of various brands of political types who all claim to represent the forgotten American but never seem to forget to bank a lot of money before they leave town.

The financial crisis did not upend America's economic or political hierarchies. It reinforced them. Its aftermath reminded politicians that the easiest way to keep the current system working on behalf of the powerful is to divide the poor and the middle class into factions and let them go to war. It's easier to turn Americans against each other than it is to focus them to change a system that perpetuates legacy power dynamics. It could easily happen again in the years to come.

No presidential candidate, alone, can fix that. No new congressional majority has the incentive to. The same is true in state legislatures across the country, which suffer from the same fealty to entrenched interests as Washington. The people most empowered to change the system are voters—individuals who can reject, on a personal level, the politics of division and embrace the ideal of helping each other to help ourselves.

That's not a policy prescription or a partisan endorsement. It is in a sense a very Oregon way of looking at the economy—a forester's view of the forest, which is there to be experienced and worked and replanted and nurtured and loved. It is a call for the vast majority of Americans— the less empowered, the people who have been knocked back on the beach every time a sneaker wave smacks the economy—to start taking care of one another. Not just people who look like them, or who vote for the same political party they do, or who watch the same cable news network. Not just the baggers in their own grocery stores or the drivers delivering their packages or the nurses in their local hospital wards.

It's a call for less vilification and more collective heroism.

Narrative journalism is the art of telling reported and true stories using the dramatic structure of a novel. There is always a hook, a climax, a conclusion. There is always a hero. There is almost always a villain. Among the masters of the craft, there is an enduring fixation on the storytelling style of Hollywood westerns, circa John Wayne. "Who is your 'white hat'?" a superb former editor of mine used to ask, meaning, Who is your protagonist, your Gary Cooper riding into town to set things right? "Who is your 'black hat'?" It is a clean and easy and effective way to tell stories. But it is not, in my experience, an accurate reflection of how the world usually works.

Our greatest heroes are almost always flawed. The people we call villains are sometimes not the bad guys at all.

A lot of books and cable-news segments and campaign speeches about the middle class focus on whomever the writers or anchors or politicians claim has broken it. They make villains out of immigrants, out of black people, out of feminists, out of corporations, out of foreigners or socialists or the very rich. I am guilty of this. I have on several occasions made villains out of my parents' generation, the baby boomers, whom I blamed for running up government debt and heating the planet with carbon emissions and hoarding the spoils of America's middle-class Golden Age for themselves.

Let me tell you: It works. It is a time-honored, market-tested approach. It gets people to pay attention. It gets crowds riled up.

But it doesn't give us a deeper understanding of our problems or help us solve them. It just works at selling something.

There are villains of sorts in my story of the economy, a group of mustache-twirling rogues in black hats who derailed decades of middle-class progress after World War II. I am not going to tell you it's all boomers; I confess that in my previous complaints I underrated their role in the civil rights push that opened new and important opportunities for women and Americans of color. So there are boomers in my villain group, but also millennials, and also Generation X-ers, like me, and even the last remnants of the dying group of Americans who came of age in the Second World War, and whom Tom Brokaw famously called the Greatest Generation. (When my son read Brokaw's book as a seventh grader, he said he could not reconcile the "Greatest" label with the internment of Japanese Americans during the war.)

I will tell you about my villainous group, starting with the fact that I am, statistically, a member of it. The people who have steered America away from shared prosperity and into a new era of rising inequality and increased economic insecurity are, in the broadest sense, powerful white men with college degrees. To co-opt a favorite pejorative of today's political class, let's call them elites. They—we—are the batch of Americans who have hoarded the treasures of economic progress over the last several decades.

I will tell you how that group, which you can rightly deride for its greed, has hurt itself and this nation by erecting new barricades to opportunity and by failing to reinvest in the people and places that were marauded by the economic forces elite white men set loose on our economy.

And I will tell you why the cycle of vilification is destructive for the country and its hopes of building another golden age of shared prosperity.

First, the bad guys. It's fair to think of elite white men with college degrees as the antagonists of the middle class for the past forty years, even if many, or even if all, of them did not intend to be and do not see themselves that way. College-educated white male elites are the legacy inheritors of the advantages that the United States economy has imparted to white men from the time of English colonization forward. No matter how much any of them complain about "reverse discrimination," data shows us clearly and convincingly that elite white men earn more, own more, and have more access to the most lucrative occupations in the economy than any other group—more than men of color, more than women of all races and ethnicities, more than white men without college degrees. A subset of white elites has used those advantages in recent years to enrich themselves without adding value to the economy.

When I worked at the *Stanford Daily* newspaper in college, we ran what I recall was a fair number of advertisements from Goldman Sachs. It was the late 1990s, the internet was young, and a printed student publication was still one of the best ways for a big investment bank to recruit scores of talented soon-to-be graduates to join its ranks. A bunch of the grads did, and they made a lot of money, even through a stock crash and a financial crisis and two decades of slow growth punctuated by recessions that swept millions of people out of the middle class.

Wall Street was, in the 1980s, 1990s, and early 2000s—and still is today—a money machine for white male college graduates. The industry hires women and nonwhite men too, but big financial firms continue to be dominated by white guys like the ones I went to college with—guys like me. The same is true of America's executive suites and some of its highest-paying professions. College-educated white men constitute the vast majority of the so-called top 1 percent, who over the last several decades have captured a rising share of the income and wealth generated by a growing American economy. Their windfalls have often come at the expense of typical workers. Sometimes those windfalls reflect entrepreneurial skill, or hard work in school, or inherent talent. Sometimes they reflect the inherited advantages of whiteness in America. Too often they flow from an activity that economists call "rent seeking," which is a nice way of saying "making yourself rich without creating any real value for the economy or society."

Elite white men have too often expanded their economic advantages not by adding extra value to the economy but by finding increasingly sophisticated ways to siphon away the value created by others. In corporate boardrooms, which remain dominated by white men, executives pay each other higher and higher compensation packages, in ways that economists have shown are untethered to the health of their businesses. Elite white men have found new and innovative ways to lobby the government for favors, direct and indirect, that have helped make the economy less competitive and less efficient, hindering growth. They drove the policy shifts, under Democratic and Republican administrations alike, that allowed the finance industry to more than double in size while not measurably improving its services to investors like middle-class pensioners. Wall Street elites crashed the economy into recession in 2008 and continue to divert huge chunks of money from more valuable uses. A 2012 analysis from economists at the International Monetary Fund concluded that the American financial sector had grown so large that it was slowing economic growth. Perhaps the most prominent researcher on the size and economic value of Wall Street, a French economist at New York University named Thomas Philippon, has concluded that the American financial industry is oversized relative to its value for the economy, to the tune of hundreds of billions of dollars each year. He has also shown that declining competition across the American economy is hurting investment and growth.

If you want to blame someone for the ills of the middle class, blame the most powerful members of this group. College-educated whites now hold about 70 percent of America's total family wealth, according to the Federal Reserve, while whites without college degrees hold just over 20 percent. That's a dramatic and fairly recent shift. In 1989, the groups' share of total wealth was essentially even. Since 2000, elite whites have widened what was already an expansive advantage in income and net worth compared to similarly educated black and Latino Americans— even before the latest recession hit. Some of those elite men bankrolled the protests in the spring of 2020 that called for "reopening" the economy even before testing and medical advancements made it safe to do so, effectively demanding that more marginalized Americans be forced to choose between risking their health and keeping their jobs.

If the American economy is not rebalanced to better serve all workers, rather than mostly elite whites, the consequences will be severe.

For all the time we spend in America talking about the middle class, we don't talk much about why we need one. So many of its virtues are obvious. We don't need to dive into the fundamental rationale for why it's good for people to feel secure in the knowledge that they will have a place to sleep and food to eat and medical care if they get sick or injured. And yet some prominent individuals in America will downplay the importance of getting as many people as possible all the way through the Game of Life with their middle-class comforts intact, and instead will tell you that the best thing for a country is a combination of high inequality and high economic mobility. Ideally, the argument goes, the best economy you could design would steer massive riches to the people at the very top, in order to encourage risk taking and innovation, and would give everyone a fair shot at joining that rarefied group.

In the United States today, we do not live in anything close to that kind of system. When you talk to working-class people—men and women, black and white, native born and immigrant—you hear a wide range of thoughts on how the economy should work and whether the government should get more or less involved in correcting it. You hear resentments about government benefits and frustrations with jobs that don't provide satisfaction, the fulfillment of a hard day spent doing meaningful work. Everyone wants themselves and everyone else to have a fair shot, but no one seems to be able to agree on what a fair shot means anymore.

On some things, we should be able to agree. If you're no more likely to do better than your parents did, compared to your ancestors 150 years ago, that's not a fair shot. If you are penalized in the workplace for your decision to bear children because the laws of biology assign that task to you and not to your colleagues who are men, that's not a fair shot. If you spend half your life perfecting your skills in a good and valuable job and then one day that job no longer exists, and you're nearing retirement and staring down an economy that suddenly seems to lack any use for your talents, that's not a fair shot.

The United States of America is a nation that was founded on a land theft of historic proportions and was built to prosperity in part on the backs of women and men who were enslaved and forced to work. These inconvenient facts loom over every history book, every argument for American exceptionalism. They contribute to the wide gaps in income, property ownership, and other economic outcomes along racial lines, even today. It can both be true that America is a land of opportunity, the greatest opportunity the world has ever seen, and also be true that opportunity in America has always been more open to a particular class of white men than it is to anyone else.

And yet there is real money in denying those facts. A lot of people get paid for apologizing for the "winners" in the new economy, for patting everyone else on the head and saying, "Sorry, that's just how the system works. If you want to be paid like a superstar, be a superstar. If we didn't pay stars so much, no one would work hard enough to be one." A lot of economic superstars like to believe that anyone who works hard enough and follows their dreams can grow up to be a millionaire. Data and history and the plain evidence of the people you talk to all over the country show that's not true. Certain people are born with much higher odds of reaching superstardom through no effort of their own. Others are born at the bottom of the ladder with the odds stacked against them. And what used to be the safe haven in between, the warm embrace of the middle class, is smaller and colder than it used to be.

That's an unsustainable system, even for the stars. Wide-ranging economic research shows us that the health of the American economy rises and falls with the vibrancy of its middle class. Among the findings: Middle-class workers spend a greater share of their incomes, a powerful engine of economic growth, than rich and wealthy workers do. Their children are vastly more likely to grow up to be entrepreneurs than children of poverty or extreme wealth, according to the nonprofit Kauffman Foundation, because the middle class offers a sort of Goldilocks upbringing for future risk takers. It offers the time and resources for children to invest in their own skills, like their schoolwork, but not enough comforts to drain kids' motivation to creatively seek to climb the economic ladder through invention and ingenuity. A healthy middle class has historically been associated with rising levels of growth and income across countries, the economist William Easterly has found. The International Monetary Fund reported in 2011 that more equal distributions of income in nations are "robustly associated" with longer spells of economic expansion.

Perhaps most importantly, in these fractured times of American and global politics, strong middle classes breed political and social stability. It is not always a straight correlation; near the end of the Golden Age in the late 1960s, the United States was riven by protests against war and for gender and racial equality. But on a variety of fronts, the middle class is a stabilizing force. "Societies with a strong middle class experience higher levels of social trust but also better educational outcomes, lower crime incidence, better health outcomes and higher life satisfaction," the Organization for Cooperation and Economic Development wrote in a 2019 report, citing several studies. "The middle class champions political stability and good governance. It prevents political polarization and promotes greater compromise within government." The report warns that middle-class people increasingly say the economy is unfair because they see so much income and wealth flowing to the rich, while their own lifestyles—that middle-class security blanket—have become more expensive.

The bottom line there is hard to miss. The growing concentration of income and wealth among a group of (largely male, almost entirely white) elites is a recipe for social discord that could easily rebound to hurt the rich—especially if the recovery from the latest recession further thins the ranks of the middle class and widens the gaps between the rich and everyone else. A slowing economy will produce less wealth for everyone—again, including the rich. The economic practices of elite whites since the end of the Golden Age have been self-enriching in the short run. In the long run they could be ruinous.

Here is an appeal to that group. To elite white men who went to college, who earn large incomes, who have seen their fortunes rise as many of their fellow Americans' stagnate or fall back: you have a vested interest in the future health of the middle class, in stoking a revival of broadly shared economic prosperity. If not for moral or civic reasons, then for selfish ones.

Now here is an appeal to everyone outside the group: your revitalization will come faster and more powerfully if those elite white guys get on board.

Progress for disadvantaged American workers has always required standing up to power and, at times, defeating entrenched interests. The black women of the R.J. Reynolds plant had no realistic chance of talking their white male bosses into better pay and more humane working conditions. But there's a difference between taking action to kick open the doors of opportunity and falling back into a cycle of blame and complaint about perceived villains. For too long in recent history, demagoguing and scapegoating have done almost nothing to help rally Americans around the policies and practices and mindsets that we now know—that evidence shows us—provide the easiest and most fulfilling path to an economy that lifts all workers.

The black hat/white hat form of storytelling has died out in much of the American entertainment industry. We like our superheroes with a dark side now, our villains with a sympathetic twist. The last western to win Best Picture at the Oscars, *Unforgiven*, was so morally ambiguous that my father, brother, and I once spent days debating whether there was a single character you could call a "good guy" in the film. (We settled on one: the barber.) We cling to the spaghetti western trope only in newspaper narratives and political salesmanship; in the political arena at least, it's time to leave it behind. To the extent that we can escape the practice of dwelling on villains, it will be easier for us to do what it takes to actually solve the problem.

This is what it is going to take: we need to destroy all the barriers that block people from making the most of their talents.

Most writers at this point would try to sell you a package of policy reforms that would do exactly what they are recommending. They'd give you bullet points and revenue forecasts. Not a fully drafted legislative proposal, but the blueprint for one. Their own "full chessboard" view of the middle class and how to fix it.

What I want to give you instead is a guiding principle for renewal paired with the insights of an intellectually diverse group of some of the best policy thinkers I know.

In more than a decade spent on the reporting trail, investigating the questions that I Voltroned together to form this book, I have encountered many very smart economists with strong thoughts on how to blow up the barriers holding talented people back. Many of their ideas have widespread acceptance on one side of the political spectrum or the other. A lot of conservative economists agree with Kevin Hassett that corporate taxation holds middle-class incomes down. A lot of liberals say we should tax high earners significantly more and use the proceeds to invest in poor and middle-class Americans through direct transfers of income or expanded benefits like free college.

Melissa Kearney, a University of Maryland economist who partnered with David Autor on some of his early "hollowing out" papers, would reform federal tax rates to eliminate what is effectively a huge penalty on second earners, usually women, in two-income households—a penalty that deters some of the most talented women in the country from working. The Harvard economist Raj Chetty, whose research is leading the way on questions of economic mobility, has started experiments in moving people to opportunity—actually finding ways to physically relocate people from struggling neighborhoods to thriving ones.

Some of the solutions are themselves fodder for entire books, such as how to reduce the cost of American health care and how to bring down soaring housing prices in superstar areas like Silicon Valley.

Many are targeted at specific groups who are being held back. William Darity, the Duke economist who has exhaustively chronicled discrimination and its effects, proposes a suite of programs to empower black Americans to earn more and build wealth, including paying reparations to the descendants of enslaved people and providing a living-wage, government-guaranteed job for anyone who wants to work. In April of 2020, I tuned into an online conference call in which Darity said the pandemic recession had made those measures all the more important. The virus, he said, had exposed "the deep historical residue of health disadvantage that was already embedding itself in the black community." He predicted it would further worsen income and wealth inequality on racial lines. That inequality, he said, "has been horrendous in recent years, and I can only imagine those disparities would get worse absent any policy interventions."

Heather Boushey, president and CEO of the Washington Center for Equitable Growth, who was one of the first economists to talk at length with me about the middle class and how to revive it, favors expanding paid leave for parents and caregivers, reducing or eliminating the cost of child care for working families, and adopting a universal prekindergarten system, all to support working women and their children and to advance women in the workplace. As the pandemic unfolded in the spring of 2020, she pushed for new and permanent policies to safeguard workers on the front lines of the virus response—both to protect those workers and to give Americans confidence that the people taking care of them during the outbreak would be taken care of themselves. America's version of the pandemic economic crisis, she told me in an email that spring, "is deeper and more protracted because we lag behind all our economic competitors in ensuring that the people who make up our economy have access to what they need to be healthy." She said the countries faring best in the crisis had "paid sick leave, universal access to affordable health care, and a robust public health infrastructure"—along with income supports for workers and businesses that automatically ramp up when the economy contracts.

Some economists, like Matt Mitchell at George Mason University, a crusader against "crony capitalism" that favors the politically connected, support policies that reduce the ability of people and companies to engage in rent seeking from the government. Such policies include eliminating state occupational licensing requirements that prohibit people from working in certain fields, like hair braiding, without a particular government-approved training certificate, and killing tax loopholes and direct subsidies that benefit handfuls of companies that lobby hard to maintain their edge over would-be rivals. The government response at all levels to the 2020 pandemic only reinforced this view: to adapt to the new world of economic restrictions and the realities of the health crisis, officials suspended a lot of regulations that some economists say never should have existed in the first place. They allowed bars to sell take-out cocktails and, in some places, to deliver them to people's homes. They let doctors and other health professionals work in states even if they did not have a license there. Some areas extended that same ability to foreign doctors who were not licensed in the United States.

One of my favorite professional antagonists, a liberal economist named Dean Baker who delights in criticizing the reporting of the *Washington Post* and the *New York Times* on his personal blog, is an often lonely crusader for a similar change that would open elite white men to the same sort of labor competition that manufacturing workers face—by allowing doctors, lawyers, and other professionals who are trained abroad to more easily immigrate to the United States and ply their trades when they get here.

Late in 2019 I called Marianne Wanamaker, the University of Tennessee economic historian and former member of President Trump's Council of Economic Advisers, who has found no improvement in economic mobility for young black men dating back to Reconstruction. I asked her what policy change she would make to finally unblock the upward path for black men. She said that she, like some of her more liberal colleagues in the profession, supported universal prekindergarten. But, she said, "If you're going to address some of the core problems, you have to move back into people's lives"—on a personal level.

She was thinking of work toward racial reconciliation in a church congregation, or her own family's investment in their refugee neighbors in Knoxville. "The lesson of public policy is it can't really be effective when the problem is people," Wanamaker told me. "When the root cause of our problems is our own biases and how we treat people, the solution is not policy. The solution has to be us, and how we treat people and understand people and love people, and how we interact with them in society. That's a huge challenge. But it's not government's to solve."

I asked her the same question again the following spring. She told me the pandemic had made her more sympathetic to calls for universal health insurance funded by the government, and she expected support to grow for an increased social safety net overall. But she was still worried that government policy could not by itself conquer the problem. She was thinking about her refugee friends and their children, who were losing ground to peers with every day that schools were closed. "Crises like this really put the spotlight on the limitations of government (or maybe the fragility of programming) to address inequality in the current generation," she told me in an email, "when there are human capital and social inequalities amongst their parents."

I generally think government has a role to play in breaking down barriers to advancement; it's hard to see how women and black Americans would have made it even this far without federal civil rights legislation, for example. I also understand the hesitancy that many Americans feel about turning more of the task of balancing the economy over to politicians. American history is full of examples of political leaders using their power to block some groups from advancement. So I favor measures that meet a narrow test: Do they help people build their own human capital? Do they help them gain income and wealth and stability, so that they can survive the next recession, whether it is mild or severe? Do they defeat the power structures that hold people back? Do they help Americans do what they're best at?

Those sorts of policies would help disadvantaged Americans get through college, find jobs, and advance in the workforce. They would aggressively punish discrimination and tear down power structures that exist to protect white elites. They would foster and train a new generation of entrepreneurs, homegrown and imported, to disrupt the competition calcification of the American economy and create jobs that allow working-class whites—and everyone else—to return to the work that best utilizes their talents. They would discourage rent seeking, in part by diminishing government interventions into parts of the economy that are ripe for favoritism, and in part by diminishing the ability of opportunistic companies and people to game the economy for their own limited benefit, to the detriment of everyone else. They would protect against job losses in bad economic times and promote fair pay in good ones.

We should tax Wall Street trades more, to reduce the economic waste of a bloated financial system. (Economists call that "correcting an externality"; it's the same reason we should tax carbon emissions to curtail global warming.) We should equalize tax rates on the money you earn by working and the money you earn from investing, to stop rewarding the legacy beneficiaries of elite white privilege, some of whom can now coast on the wealth they've amassed at others' expense. We should experiment with a whole flurry of policies to support working women, be they mothers or not, in the workplace. We should increase immigration, particularly for highly skilled workers, and welcome more refugees. We should overturn restrictive residential zoning laws that boost high-end property values and reduce the supply of affordable housing for the middle class. We should force or incentivize some of the nation's great bestowers of human capital, elite colleges like Harvard and MIT and Stanford, to expand their enrollments and dramatically increase the number of low-income students they admit every year. (Their endowments are certainly big enough, and it's hard to imagine that an enrollment surge would dilute the value of their degrees. If it does, well, a lot of guys like me will be marginally worse off.)

If you add up all those initiatives you might make a dent in the problem. But you still won't be going far enough. This is where I agree—naively, perhaps, but earnestly—with Marianne Wanamaker. The big change we need is attitudinal. We need a national commitment to helping each other succeed and get ahead.

We need to stop ourselves and others from discriminating by race and gender. To stop vilifying the people who don't look like we do. Elite white Americans, in particular, need to work harder to help everyone else enjoy the same opportunities they do. Elite whites should acknowledge that they have benefited disproportionately from the economic changes of the last forty years, on top of the ingrained advantages that elite white men have enjoyed for centuries. If they are interested in helping lift others up to enjoy similar advantages in order to optimize the performance of the economy and keep delivering gains for people like them, they should be willing to pay higher taxes, to fund investments in human-capital accumulation for everyone else.

But more than anything, we all need to be more accepting of each other, more affirming. More uplifting.

It is a hopeful realization: that by helping each other reach our full potential, we'll help the whole country get its swagger back. But it is also a daunting one. We've never really achieved that goal as a nation, not in the booming 1950s or the civil rights era or ever. But I truly believe that we could.

Surveying the divide in economic mobility between black and white Americans, Raj Chetty and his team offered a similar prognosis. "Our results suggest that the most promising pathways to reducing the black-white gap are those whose impacts cut across neighborhood and class lines," they wrote. They cited mentoring programs for black boys as a promising example. And then they casually laid out some of the most intractable problems facing America today. What is needed, they said, are "efforts to reduce racial bias among whites, interventions to reduce discrimination in criminal justice, and efforts to facilitate greater interaction across racial groups."

It is up to you what that effort should look like, for you personally and for the country. For me it looks like this: building a nation where every child is invested in, where hard work is rewarded, where talent rises freely and easily, unhindered by discrimination. Where we are constantly refreshing our talent pool with new arrivals and better-developed home-grown kids. And where the upward flow of talent does not raise fears of a "winner take all" society.

The United States would be a very different country today if the shared prosperity of the postwar era, the upward talent flow that lifted everyone, had endured for another half century. The country would still experience anxieties, injustices, and flaws, but quite possibly a lot fewer of them. If we could eliminate all the "frictions" holding Americans back from rising to meet their full potential, the reward could be something like that alternate reality: an unbroken series of middle-class golden eras.

It would trigger much less anxiety about how high any one individual can climb on the economic ladder. History suggests we would experience less resentment of people who don't look or talk like we do. We would still have problems and strife and social conflict—it is hard to imagine otherwise—but they would play out against a backdrop of shared prosperity.

This alternate reality is difficult to envision in the scorched political climate that decades of middle-class decline has brought. Part of the problem is how lucrative it has become to sow division in America. Liberal readers send angry emails if you write a story suggesting that any of Donald Trump's policies have succeeded. Some conservative writers and anchors make a habit of inflaming racial tensions, erecting out-group straw men who are supposedly responsible for the struggles of their white, conservative audiences. This is not a new development. The workers who recalled the history of the sit-down work stoppage at the Reynolds factory in 1943 said that almost immediately after black women shut down plant 65, the white men who ran the plant installed separate entrances for black and white workers. In later years, when the factory union staged another stoppage, management recruited rural, white workers to replace them. They pitted white and black workers against one another in order to protect the profits of the white men who owned the factory. The tactics worked. Black and white workers never truly coalesced at Reynolds. The union was broken in the 1950s. The civil rights movement came late to Winston-Salem. Equality has not yet arrived.

It would benefit all of us to reject the forces of division. One way to think about them is that they're like pollution, or littering. We all prefer cleaner air and trash-free parks, but any one of us doesn't have much reason to burn less gasoline or toss our candy wrappers in the trash. It is a classic negative externality, in which the incentives for individuals run counter to what's best for all of us as a group. The only way to overcome it is by working together.

The Harvard economist Ben Friedman, in a lecture to the American Economic Association, made the case that shared economic growth is a positive externality, which benefits everyone even though individuals are not incentivized to pursue it. "These are externalities because there is no market where we trade tolerance," he said, "there is no place where one can buy an option on democracy; there is no explicit buy/sell price placed on expanded opportunity. As a result, families deciding how much to save and businesses deciding how much to invest have no reason to take into their internal calculus these aggregate-level consequences of their actions, consequences which we value not in market terms but in moral terms."

There are no easy solutions to this externality problem. It requires from each of us the hard work of trying to overcome biases, change policies, and modify our own behavior. To lift each other up for the good of us all.

"It takes powerful social movements, I think, to move these things," the University of Chicago economist Chang-Tai Hsieh, lead author of the breakthrough paper on how the upward mobility of women and black Americans supercharged the American economy in the postwar era, told me in an interview. "The sixties and the seventies in the US I think was a very special time," he said. But, he added, "I do think there is the potential for a similar burst if we had a similar type of revolution again, to tear down more barriers."

I cannot and will not offer you a simple solution for that task. I don't see a lot of complex problems around me being solved by simple plans. Like so much else in my career, I owe that perspective to Bill Woo.

Bill was my college mentor, my journalistic hero, and a great friend. We arrived on campus the same year, I as a scared freshman with way too much confidence in my writing abilities, he as an early casualty of what would become the corporate destruction of local journalism in the United States. He had been the editor of the *St. Louis Post-Dispatch* newspaper, the first Asian American to ascend to the highest job at one of the country's large daily papers, until he realized he wanted no more part in his bosses' slow march toward a smaller staff, shorter stories, and a diminished product that padded profits but shortchanged readers. He resigned, he and his family found their way to California, and he almost certainly saved me from a lifetime of studying and practicing law. (Sorry, Dad.)

During my freshman year, Bill was a visiting professor who taught a course in the Communications Department called Writing and

Reporting the News. It was a relatively small class, and you had to apply to get in. I was certain he wouldn't take me, but somehow he did.

The class met in the afternoons in an upper-floor room with no windows, a dozen or so disciples who hung on Bill's every soft-spoken word. He ran us through mock news events and forced us to write on deadline. To imbue us with journalistic ethics, he unspooled hours-long, perfectly crafted tales of his news-gathering youth in tones that barked with joy and fell to a whisper so low you could barely hear it over the hum of the air-conditioning.

In later years, Bill would drive me to a Palo Alto sports bar called the Old Pro or to a burger joint called the Alpine Inn, where we sat at a creek-side table. Once I was old enough to drink it legally, he would buy me a beer before noon then tell me stories about the way journalism once was and should always be.

Some days I marvel at the progression that he represented, the son of an American mother and a Chinese father. The history of great immigrant contributions to the United States includes the Chinese laborers who laid the railroad tracks that built the fortune of a man named Leland Stanford, who would use the money to create the university that would one day hire William F. Woo to teach journalism

He died of cancer in 2006, months before my son was born. I spoke at his funeral in St. Louis, told the mourners how he had inspired a whole generation of young journalists to pursue his ideal for the craft, what he called "the result of applied intelligence, a working set of values or principles and the interplay of points of view."

I told them how I had kept my assignments from his class, not because of the amateur writing I had produced but for the notes he had left me in the margins in a sharp, red ink. I think of one of them in particular almost every day.

"I really hope you keep this message with you always," Bill wrote. "There are no quick fixes, ever, for the things we hold dearest."

16

Green Family Home, 2019

EVENTUALLY, YOU GET MORE TIME

Ed Green has a goal for the day when he finally does not have to work so many jobs. He has a dream, one that his wife's kidney failure has deferred. It seems far now, as he sits across from me, worrying about the local hospital dropping his state-provided insurance plan, which would force him to drive an hour to Raleigh for her dialysis treatments. But he can see it, he can say it, he can imagine the day when he can get back to making it real.

He is going to go back to college. Earn his bachelor's degree. Maybe more.

After all these years juggling multiple jobs, Ed Green would like to be a labor lawyer. Someone who helps other people who work as hard as he does.

He has been thinking about it since before his children finished college themselves. He is sipping a beer and telling me how he'd worked it out.

"My original plan was, after they all were out, and the loans were all paid off, I'd go back," he says. "That's part of the bucket list. That's on hold now."

"I'll do it eventually," he says, "even if it's online courses. In four years, I'd like to semiretire, go back to school."

What does that mean, semiretire? I ask. Just one job?

"Yes," he says, "but that's better than I was doing six years ago. I had, like, four!"

He's learned a bit about labor law already through the union at his state highway job, where he's dealt with managers who want to lord their power over workers. "Sometimes they think they're above you," he says. "So you have to throw some knowledge at them, bring them back down."

He talks thoughtfully. Not fast, not particularly slow. He chooses a few words at a time. He rarely elaborates, until you ask him. As the beer falls closer to empty, I ask him how he does it. How he works so much. His son, Jordan, who also works two jobs, had asked him something similar.

"I was talking to my son today about it," he says. "As long as I get one day a week to sleep in, I'm okay."

He is hopeful for the future. He believes workers of color will be less restrained by discrimination. "We're in the process of the good old boys retiring, and the new regime coming in," he says. "The millennials—they're not color-struck. They're more, I know this guy over here, and he's Hispanic, I want him here because he can do the job. Not, I want some other guy because there's a friend of mine."

He is hopeful about his own health. He says his blood sugar levels are where they should be, and his weight is too. His doctor says it's because he won't slow down.

"I feel it, as I get older, wearing on me," Ed says.

His sixtieth birthday is just over the horizon.

"I try not to think about it."

On a Saturday afternoon, Ed's wife answers the door of their brick ram-bler on the distressed side of the highway that divides the black and white parts of Salem. Her husband is still at work. "I'm Mrs. Green," she tells me, and she invites me inside.

Jazmine Green, Ed's younger daughter, is sitting on the couch, watch-ing a flat-screen Panasonic perched atop a dark wood console with a faux fireplace inside it. She is combing out her daughter's hair. Her phone rings. She puts down the hairbrush.

"Sorry," she says to me, in a very Green family sort of apology. "I'm the manager on call this weekend."

Jazmine is a supervisor at a CVS drugstore in Winston-Salem. She has a degree in social work. "I've yet to put that degree to work," she says. "I'm still looking for that job, that career." What would that look like? I ask. "I don't know," she says. "I know I like to help people. I want to help the underserved community." A moment later, she adds, "As long as I'm helping, I'm happy."

None of the jobs she's found in the field pay enough to cover rent and parenting and student loans and any semblance of economic stability. "The thing that's holding her back is life," her father had told me the night before.

Her daughter has fallen asleep, mid-combing. She attends a perform-ing-arts elementary school, Jazmine says. She loves acting and dancing. She's been putting on shows ever since she could move. The two of them talk about her going to college someday, just like her mom did.

"I know where I came from," Jazmine says, "and I want better for her."

She tells me she understood growing up just how hard her father worked. He was gone a lot, she says. But when he wasn't at work, "He was present. Not just here. *Present*."

Jazmine tells me that Ed had a heart attack scare the month before and had to spend a night in the hospital. (He had failed to mention that over beers.) He left the hospital on a Wednesday. He was cleared to return to work the following Monday. But instead he went back the very next day, a Thursday. She has pushed him to slow down.

"I ask him all the time," she says, "is this something you have to do?"

Her brother is tending a grill on the sunporch, smoking burgers, chicken, and corn on the cob. Jordan Green is visiting from Tampa, where he lives with roommates despite having a good-paying technology job with the Nielsen company, the one that calculates television ratings. He has hopscotched across the country, earning a higher salary with each move, and has now found a city where the cost of living is relatively low and he can start to get ahead.

Jordan has two college degrees and an aborted career as a counselor at a community college. His last job in that field paid $32,000 a year, which is well below what a typical middle-class worker makes. Helping students, he says, is "where my passion was. But ultimately, what it came down to was, I have to make more money."

As they are for his sister, student loans are forcing Jordan's hand. He has to earn enough to pay them back. And to make regular trips to visit his daughter, who lives with her mother in Chicago. So he lives frugally. At the moment we are speaking, he is a thirty-one-year-old man with roommates, and he works a second job, at the Aldi grocery store in Tampa.

"I'm my father's child," he says.

He sees what it costs him and what it cost his dad. "It sucks, dude," he says. "In order to get ahead, you have to work so much."

We talk about Washington (where he used to live), and about work and our children. We talk about relationships; I tell him I've recently remarried. That my son, such a fan of Jordan's father all those years back, is doing well. He tells me about his daughter and the additional time he would like to have with her. We talk about his entrepreneurial dreams and his challenges in raising the money to fund them.

We talk about the pull between working hard enough to be comfortable and having the time to enjoy those comforts. "Eventually," he says, his voice turning briefly toward hope, "the money pays off, where you're able to get more time."

Dinner is nearly ready. I say good-bye to Jordan and Jazmine and Mrs. Green. I climb into my car and drive back toward Washington.

Ed still hasn't finished his shift.

Epilogue

I call my parents on the long drive home. My son is with them, near the end of an annual pilgrimage to the lakes and forests and grandparental charms of the Pacific Northwest. Smoke from the barbecue clings to my clothes. After we hang up I turn the car radio to the AM band, and as night falls it explodes with baseball games that warble in from New York, from Atlanta, from Cincinnati and Chicago and as far off as Quebec.

My dad coached Little League, but my mother taught me to love baseball. She gave me my first Dodger hat, a tattered blue cap that had been hers as a child. She obsessed over the playoffs, screaming at the radio when games got too tense. I, often unable to bear the pressure, sometimes retreated to the confines of cartoons with my brother in the other room.

My mother has long since made her peace with small-town Oregon, more than forty years after she moved there with no idea what she would do. What she ended up doing, I have come to realize, profoundly shaped how I see America and its possibilities.

I think of her while I'm on the interstate as I listen to the Mets close out a win and a minor-league game upstate comes down to the last batter in the ninth. I think of Ed Green and his wife and their children. I think about what parents pass on to their kids, the values of work and love and community.

My mother left the labor force to raise two boys, until both my brother and I were attending school full-time. In her spare time she volunteered at church, and she ran a shelter for women who were victims of domestic violence. Then she took a part-time job she was overqualified for, as a school classroom assistant. She wanted to be a school librarian, but even though she had a master's degree in library science, the state would not allow her to unless she also had a teaching credential. So she blew through a yearlong master's program in teaching, aced all her classes, and took a job running the library at a grade school a couple of towns over from McMinnville.

The students came largely from poverty, the daughters and sons of low-paid white workers and lower-paid Hispanic migrants who worked in the fields around Yamhill County.

She made a career, from her forties through her sixties, of helping those kids. Teaching them to read and love books. To master technology. To pursue knowledge. To find what they were best at, and to do it to the best of their ability.

She was building a middle class, one individual investment at a time.

Acknowledgments

I always marvel at the honesty and bravery of the people who answer a reporter's telephone call and agree to open up their lives. Each time it feels like a miracle, and I come away enriched. This book would have been impossible without the people who opened the fullness of their American stories to me, including Ambar Gonzalez, Deborah Jackson, Bob Thompson, and all of the people who have answered my questions about their lives and work over the past two decades, whether their names appear in these pages or not. I am chiefly and deeply indebted to Ed Green and his family. Ed has kindly and patiently agreed to every interview I've requested with him over the course of six and a half years, diligently tracked down details of his family history, and modeled a strength in the face of adversity that has filled me with hope. I cannot thank him enough.

I also owe a great debt to the scores of economists and other academics whose work poured the foundation for my understanding of the middle class and the American economy. There is no way for me to list all the researchers who have walked me through their fields of charts and data and carefully explained what was growing there and how it fit in with the vast literature of the profession. I've cited many of them whose work most directly informed the thesis of the book.

In the process of writing, I benefited in particular from conversations with Gbenga Ajilore, David Autor, Heather Boushey, Sandy Darity, Ryan Decker, Kevin Hassett, Chang-Tai Hshieh, Erik Hurst, Greg Kaplan, Melissa Kearney, Marianne Wanamaker, and Scott Winship. I appreciate all their efforts, even—in fact, especially—the times when they disagreed with my conclusions.

Several of my skilled friends and family members read early drafts of this book and improved it greatly with their suggestions, including my parents, my brother, Dan Tankersley, and sister-in-law, Becky Blanchard, and my friends Josh Boak, Bret Jacobson, Jay Hamilton, Lindsay Holst, Ryan McCarthy, Christi Parsons, and Meg Reilly.

Patrick Bernhardt has been a fountain of ideas and a sounding board for all things policy and journalism dating back to the fall when he was my editor at the *Stanford Daily*. Mike McDaniel helped me draw a vivid map of Yamhill County and of our shared childhood. I wouldn't have known where to start as an economics reporter, let alone as an author, without the advice of my favorite economist-turned-pastor, Nate Barczi. While I somehow had the foresight to save boxes of old notebooks filled with stories of the middle class, I could never have reconstructed many of the narratives you just read without the help of Whitney Shefte, my former *Washington Post* colleague, who drew out rich details from our interview subjects and thankfully held on to the videos that recorded them.

At regular intervals in my professional life, people have given me chances to work and learn and grow, for which I am eternally grateful. Jeb Bladine gave me my first professional newspaper job when I was fifteen years old. Yvette Saarinen somehow found the time in her editing duties to teach a high-school kid how to actually report. Bill Woo took me into his Stanford journalism course and mentored me over creekside beers. Sandy Rowe and Peter Bhatia hired me out of college and stuck by me even when I struggled to live up to their expectations. John Temple took a flier on me in Denver and sent me to the Colorado state capital to talk to the economists in the basement. Dave Murray said yes to a project pitch on the Ohio economy in the midst of a wild statewide campaign. Mike Tackett supercharged my career, bringing me to Washington and becoming a mentor for life. Ron Brownstein convinced me I was an econ reporter trapped in a politics reporter's body. Greg Schneider urged me to look beyond incremental stories and solve the mystery of why the middle class was not bouncing back from recession. Ezra Klein believed in my vision to build and edit a reporting team. Elisabeth Bumiller brought me back to writing, and Deborah Solomon has helped me succeed at juggling the competing demands of daily news and a book project.

Eight years ago, a young man cold-called me after reading one of my *National Journal* articles. His name was Nathaniel Jacks, and he said I should be writing books. He and his colleague at Inkwell Management, Michael Carlisle, waited years to develop the right book idea with me, and they have been incredible partners in bringing it to life. John Mahaney heroically edited my manuscript and many revisions, challenging me to sharpen my arguments and adapt them to the frenzy of a pandemic recession, cheerfully conveying his critiques and suggestions in early-morning phone calls. He and Clive Priddle, along with Peter Osnos and the rest of the team at PublicAffairs, invested in this story long before any of us knew how it would end.

Journalism is at its best a true team effort, and I have been blessed with wonderful teams of colleagues in my career. Thank you to all the reporters, editors, photographers, and other journalists who helped tell the stories that grew into this book. Thank you to Naomi Shavin, who carefully and cheerfully assisted in fact-checking this manuscript. Thank you to my economics teammates at the *Times* Washington bureau—Alan Rappeport, Jeanna Smialek, and Ana Swanson—for helping me survive our hurricane of a beat. And thank you especially to Ben Casselman and Neil Irwin, who have donated more hours and conversations and drinks to improving and encouraging this project than any friend could be reasonably asked to give.

I want to thank my parents for telling me I could do anything, for believing in me no matter what I did, and for modeling a life of curiosity and learning. I want to thank my brother, who wrote in a college graduation card that he couldn't wait to see the books I would write someday, and for supporting me in the couple of decades it took for me to deliver on that.

My extended family—aunts, uncles, cousins, late grandparents—have lifted me up with their love. So has the community at St. Barnabas, and, for that matter, all of McMinnville. I am glad to have grown up there, and thankful to my parents for finding it.

My son, Max, inspires and delights me, and I am so incredibly proud of him. He has accompanied me on reporting trips, advised me on my social media skills, and encouraged me to keep going on the book even when it seemed too daunting to complete. Part of my faith that things can get better in America comes from watching the compassion and thoughtfulness that he brings to the world every day.

My wife, Lily, is a gifted storyteller, a creative designer, a tenacious researcher, and a kind and patient partner. She has crafted this book with me at every phase of the process, from initial pitch through frantic final edits. There is no way I could have done this without her, and I love and admire her more than I can express here.

One last note: I wrote much of this book in the pre-dawn hours before my regular workday began. For much of that writing I had a single and devoted companion, a sweet shepherd mix named Schroeder, who crawled into my lap at a rescue shelter soon after I moved to Ohio and helped me through the nearly fifteen tumultuous years that followed. His calming presence on those dark mornings was a final gift before he left us, and I am thankful for that beyond words.

Bibliographic Essay

CHAPTER 1

The descriptions of Theodosia Simpson, her colleagues in plant 65, and the strike that crippled the R.J. Reynolds plant in 1943 are assembled from oral-history interviews conducted by the Duke University historian Robert Rodgers Korstad and several colleagues. The interviews were conducted between 1976 and 2000, and they have been archived online and made public for researchers by the University of North Carolina at Chapel Hill's Southern Oral History Program. My narrative of the strike and the events leading up to it weaves together the firsthand accounts of Theodosia Simpson, Robert "Chick" Black, and several other former workers who spoke with the interviewers.

The analysis of the peak usage of "middle class" and "hippie" is drawn from a Google Books Ngram Viewer search; both terms reached their height in the early 1970s.

Many of the historical examples of what the term "middle class" meant to Americans are drawn from Stuart M. Blumin's book *The Emergence of the Middle Class*, published in 1989, when he was a history professor at Cornell University.

CHAPTER 2

The history of Yamhill County and its logging industry is drawn from several sources, including the Oregon Secretary of State's historical fact page for the county; the Oregon Department of Forestry's *Oregon's Timber Harvests: 1859 to 2004*, compiled by Alicia Andrews and Kristin Kutara; versions of the US Forest Service's *Forest Statistics for Yamhill County, Oregon* and *Forest Statistics for Northwest Oregon*, published in October 1943 and July 1964, respectively; and the Oregon Office of Economic Analysis. I drew statistics on timber employment and wages, in Yamhill County and across the state, from a report that office issued in 2012 and updated in 2019, *Historical Look at Oregon's Wood Products Industry*, by Josh Lehner, an economist for the state of Oregon.

Observations of life in the county in the 1980s and 1990s are mine alone, though corroborated by conversations with several of my friends from childhood. My family history has been related to me by my parents and supplemented by Yamhill County property records.

Nicholas Kristoff's description of the county comes from his 2020 book with Sharon WuDunn, *Tightrope*.

The Prayer for the Oppressed is found on page 826 of the 1979 edition of the Book of Common Prayer, which guides services for the Episcopal Church.

CHAPTER 3

Median household income statistics, here and throughout the book, come from the Census Bureau's American Community Survey, Current Population Survey, and decennial census figures. I also use Census Bureau statistics throughout the book in reference to individual income and family income. Employment numbers for Ohio and other states, Toledo and other cities, and the nation as a whole are drawn from the Bureau of Labor Statistics database Current Employment Statistics, unless otherwise noted. Those statistics are also the source of wage and hours-worked data cited throughout the book, unless otherwise specified.

When comparing income and wage data over time, I typically adjust for inflation by using the Personal Consumption Expenditure Index, which is the deflator used by researchers at the Federal Reserve, and occasionally by using the Labor Department's inflation calculator that relies on the Consumer Price Index. In many cases, I have accessed inflation data using FRED, a vast collection of databases compiled and presented online by the Federal Reserve Bank of St. Louis, which is a godsend to economics reporters.

The Brookings Institution paper on ways to measure the middle class, *A Dozen Ways to be Middle Class*, was written by Richard V. Reeves, Katherine Guyot, and Eleanor Krause. My use of The Game of Life as a middle-class measurement tool follows a story I wrote for *National Journal* magazine, "This Isn't Your Life," in 2012. The Obama administration outlined its consumption-based measurement of the middle class in the February 2010 report of its Middle Class Task Force, published on the White House website. The "great whooshing" of fifteen million jobs is a calculation I made based on Bureau of Labor Statistics projections that the United States would create twenty-two million jobs in the decade that ended in 2010; in fact, it had created only seven million at the peak of the job market in that decade, before the 2008 financial crisis. I first published that calculation in *National Journal* in 2011, in a piece titled "What Really Happened to 15 Million Jobs?"

I spoke with Sherrod Brown about Hillary Clinton's and Donald Trump's prospects in Ohio in the fall of 2016, in a video interview for the *Washington Post*; he also predicted that the Cleveland Indians would win the World Series that year. (They lost to the Chicago Cubs in seven games.) The research paper that Josh Boak and I relied on for "Business as Usual," our series in *The Blade* of stories on the Ohio economy, was called *State Growth Empirics: The Long-Run Determinants of State Income Growth* and coauthored by the economists Paul Bauer and Mark E. Schweitzer.

CHAPTER 4

I first wrote about Bob Thompson and the struggles of Downey, California, for the *Washington Post* in 2014, as part of a series of stories called

"Liftoff and Letdown." In reporting much of that series, I was joined by a *Post* video journalist, Whitney Shefte, who helped to conduct several of the interviews, including a long interview with Bob Thompson. Bob's recollections of his childhood, life at the Rockwell plant, and Downey's role in the lunar program are his own but are supplemented by materials from the Downey Historical Society and by interviews with municipal leaders in Downey and space historians in Southern California.

The Brookings Institution report on the geography of the middle class, Alan Berube's *Where Does the American Middle Class Live?*, was published in 2018. Census data on the college wage premium was referenced in a Congressional Research Service report, *Real Wage Trends, 1979 to 2018*. The Pew Research Center data is from a 2012 report, *The Lost Decade of the Middle Class*. Time-series data on educational attainment is from the Census Bureau's Current Population Survey. Calculations on falling labor-force participation among non-college-educated American men come from a report by the Brookings Institution's Eleanor Krause and Isabelle Sawhill, *What We Know and What We Don't Know About Declining Labor Force Participation: A Review*, from 2017.

Historical California manufacturing statistics are from *The Evolution of California Manufacturing*, a 2001 paper by Paul W. Rhode of the Public Policy Institute of California. Joan Didion's masterful depiction of Southern California's rocket suburbs is from her article "Trouble in Lakewood," published in the *New Yorker* in 1993. Russ Murray's comparison of the North American plant to the Wright brothers' bicycle shop is from the historical tract *Cradle of the Cosmic Age*, published by the Aerospace Legacy Foundation.

The research by the Massachusetts Institute of Technology economist David Autor on the occupational polarization of the American labor market spans several research papers, many with coauthors, which have been published in refereed journals like the *Quarterly Journal of Economics*. A particularly readable summary for noneconomists appears in *The Polarization of Job Opportunities in the U.S. Labor Market*, published in 2010 by the Center for American Progress and the Hamilton Project.

CHAPTER 5

I first wrote about Ed Green in the second installment of the "Liftoff and Letdown" series, published in 2014 by the *Washington Post*. Again, Whitney Shefte assisted me with some of the interviews for that project. In this chapter and throughout the book, I rely heavily on Ed's personal recollections of his own life and his family history, supplemented in many cases by interviews with his family members—including his daughter Jazmine and his son Jordan—and by publicly available documents such as property records.

David Autor's 2019 remarks on labor-market polarization come from the annual Richard T. Ely Lecture, which he delivered to the American Economic Association at its conference in Atlanta. (He expounded on the lecture's themes later that weekend in an interview with my *Times* colleague Patti Cohen and me.)

For a good example of economists arguing that America's middle class has been doing just fine, see Donald Boudreaux and Mark Perry, "The Myth of a Stagnant Middle Class," or Michael R. Strain, "The American Dream Is Alive and Well," both published on the *Wall Street Journal* editorial page, in 2013 and 2020 respectively. The data from Thomas Piketty and Emmanuel Saez that showed no inflation-adjusted middle-class income gains in America from 1979 to 2014 came from the study "Income Inequality in the United States," originally published in 2003 and updated multiple times since. The study by Piketty, Saez, and Gabriel Zucman, "Distributional National Accounts: Methods and Estimates for the United States," was published in 2018. Both papers are referenced in a helpful Urban Institute paper by Stephen J. Rose, published in 2018, "How Different Studies Measure Income Inequality in the US."

The 2011 Brookings study *The Great Recession May Be Over, but American Families Are Working Harder than Ever*, which showed that additional hours worked account for all the income gains for American families since 1975, was written by Michael Greenstone and Adam Looney. I developed the Game of Life calculations on the millions of Americans who have fallen out of the middle class with the tremendous help of my *Times* colleague and frequent collaborator Ben Casselman. Census calculations are from the Current Population Survey / Housing Vacancy Survey.

CHAPTER 6

Lorraine Ahearn's portrait of Winston-Salem in the early 1940s comes from her 2009 *Greensboro News and Record* article "Strike: When Workers Broke Camel City." Ta-Nehisi Coates published "The Case for Reparations" in 2014. The *New York Times Magazine* published "The 1619 Project" in 2019.

As noted in the chapter, I draw my portrait of Winston-Salem's history, including its race relations, from a trio of books: *Forsyth: A County on the March*, published by Adelaide L. Fries and a long list of coauthors in 1949; *From Frontier to Factory: An Architectural History of Forsyth County*, published in 1981 by Gwynne Stephens Taylor; and *Forsyth County's Agricultural Heritage*, published in 2012 by Heather Fearnbach. I am certain that Fries would not have endorsed my retelling of the events, as her history downplayed the struggles of black residents, including the horrors of slavery. The accounts of "stemming" at the Reynolds plants and the role of black workers come from the interviews by Korstad et al. referenced in chapter 1.

The account of the violence that drove black North Carolinians from their homes in Wilmington are drawn from the *1898 Wilmington Race Riot Report*, published in 2006 by the North Carolina Department of Cultural Resources and principal researcher LeRae Umfleet.

Thomas N. Maloney and Warren C. Whatley's history of racism in Detroit during the Great Migration, "Making the Effort: The Contours of Racial Discrimination in Detroit's Labor Markets, 1920–1940," was published in 1995 by the *Journal of Economic History*. Maloney expounded on its conclusions in a 2019 interview with me. The Harvard University economist Claudia Goldin wrote about the proliferation of American high schools in the early twentieth century, and the resulting economic gains, in a 1998 *Journal of Economic History* paper titled "America's Graduation from High School: The Evolution and Spread of Secondary Schooling in the Twentieth Century." Educational attainment data, here and unless otherwise noted throughout the book, is from the National Center for Education Statistics, which is a division of the federal Department of Education.

Several polls conducted during President Donald Trump's time in office showed that Trump's Republican supporters were as likely—or more likely—to call racism against white Americans a greater problem than racism against black Americans. In a 2019 poll by Pew Research Center, more Republicans said white Americans face "a lot" of discrimination than said black Americans face "a lot" of discrimination. A 2019 Quinnipiac University poll showed that more Republicans called prejudice against whites a "very serious" or "somewhat serious" problem than said the same about prejudice against black Americans or minority groups in general.

The online exhibit published by the Schomburg Center for Research in Black Culture, a research division of the New York Public Library, about the history of black people in the city, is titled *Black New Yorkers*. *Newsday*'s 2019 investigation, "Long Island Divided," into continued real estate discrimination on Long Island, was by Ann Choi, Bill Dedman, Keith Herbert, and Olivia Winslow.

Claudia Goldin's pathbreaking research on the economic experiences of women spans a long list of academic research papers, speeches, and, most critically for this chapter, her 1990 book, *Understanding the Gender Gap: An Economic History of American Women*. Her "How well do you type?" insight is drawn from her Richard T. Ely lecture to the American Economic Association in 2006. The Sandra Day O'Connor anecdote was reported in Joan Biskupic's 2006 book, *Sandra Day O'Connor: How the First Woman on the Supreme Court Became Its Most Influential Justice*.

William A. Darity and Patrick Leon Mason's work that recounts discrimination in job advertisements is found in "Evidence on Discrimination in Employment: Codes of Color, Codes of Gender," published in 1998 by the *Journal of Economic Perspectives*.

Chapter 7

Labor-force participation statistics are from the Bureau of Labor Statistics and calculations by Krause and Sawhill (referenced in Chapter 4 notes). Estimates of how many Americans entered the middle class in the postwar era, by race, are from "Race and Ethnicity in the Labor Market:

Trends over the Short and Long Term," by James P. Smith, which is Chapter 4 of the National Academy of Science's *America Becoming: Racial Trends and Their Consequences*, volume II, edited by Neil J. Smelser, William Julius Wilson, and Faith Mitchell.

The seminal research study showing that the falling occupational barriers for women and black men lifted growth in the United States, "The Allocation of Talent and U.S. Economic Growth," is by the economists Chang-Tai Hsieh, Erik Hurst, Charles I. Jones, and Peter J. Klenow. It was published in 2019 by the journal *Econometrica*.

Lemonade Stand was developed by the Minnesota Educational Computing Consortium, the same group that produced arguably the greatest computer game of the 1980s, *Oregon Trail*.

The previously secret exchange between Richard Nixon and Ronald Reagan, in which Reagan disparaged black Africans, was released by the National Archives to the historian Timothy Naftali, who wrote about it for *The Atlantic* in 2019. For more on Reagan and the "welfare queen" myth, see Josh Levin's book, *The Queen*, published in 2019. Katharine L. Bradbury's work on the relationship between education, gender, and race, "Education and Wages in the 1980s and 1990s: Are All Groups Moving Up Together?," was published by the *New England Economic Review* in 2002.

David Autor recounted his journey to graduate school, to the field of economics, and to the study of how economic changes hurt workers in middle-skill occupations in interviews in 2019. This chapter relies on those interviews and on more than a dozen of Autor's published and working papers, chief among them "The China Shock: Learning from Labor Market Adjustment to Large Changes in Trade," published in 2016 by the *Annual Review of Economics* and coauthored by David Dorn and Gordon Hanson.

CHAPTER 8

I first wrote about Ambar Gonzalez in a 2011 feature story for *National Journal*, which was coauthored by Nancy Cook and Ron Fournier. Ambar's story was based on interviews with her and her family, and it has been supplemented by public documents, including property records. The survey that I took with me to Chicago was *National Journal's* "Heartland Monitor" poll; I am grateful to my former colleague Ron Brownstein for sharing that data, and so many of his other insights, with me.

I interviewed Patrick, the white man from New Jersey who would not allow me to share his last name, for a *Washington Post* story in 2014.

The Pew Economic Mobility Project's 2011 polling on racial differences in how Americans perceived whether they had already achieved the American Dream was contained in the report *Downward Mobility from the Middle Class: Waking Up from the American Dream*, by Gregory Acs.

The Harvard economist Benjamin M. Friedman warned that workers' souring assessments of their relative economic status could lead the country astray in a speech titled "Moral Consequences of Economic Growth: The John R. Commons Lecture," delivered at the 2006 annual meeting of the American Economic Association. It drew on his 2005 book of the same name. The study that found that the typical American who entered the labor force in 1983 earned less over a lifetime than a worker who started in 1967 was "Lifetime Incomes in the United States over Six Decades," authored by Fatih Guvenen, Greg Kaplan, Jae Song, and Justin Weidner.

Greg Kaplan's paper on the loss of meaning from work for some American men, "The Changing (Dis-)utility of Work," was written with Sam Schulhofer-Wohl and published in 2018 by the *Journal of Economic Perspectives*. His inspiration for that paper was a 2015 *Planet Money* podcast episode, "Why We Work So Much."

CHAPTER 9

This chapter draws heavily on reporting, data analysis, and source interviews I conducted in 2015 and 2016 as the economics correspondent for the *Washington Post*, some of which were reflected in stories I wrote for the *Post* in print and online during that time. In several instances, I co-authored those stories with members of the *Post's* polling unit, including Scott Clement, Emily Guskin, and Peyton Craighill; I am grateful for their unmatched ability to sift data for trends in public opinion and their relentless curiosity about the role of policy issues in motivating voters and driving election outcomes. I am also grateful to my then teammates at *Wonkblog*, Jeff Guo and Max Ehrenfreund, who directly and indirectly contributed their own analysis and reporting to several of the stories. My account of election night in the *Post* newsroom is from my memory and from conversations with my wife, Lillian Cunningham. She spent the entire night in the newsroom, at a desk that sat back to back with mine, finishing the final episode of the podcast she created and produced that year, *Presidential.*

The Chicago Council on Global Affairs published its findings about how immigration and economic concerns created a feedback loop that translated into support for Donald Trump in a September 2016 report, *America in the Age of Uncertainty.*

I conducted my interview on economic issues with Hillary Clinton in June 2016 over the phone; it was published by the *Post* the following month. I also spoke on the phone that year with Robert Bennett, whose pen name is Skookum Maguire and whose novel *The Aught-Sixers* depicts a group of disgruntled white men who take their guns to the border in an attempt to stop immigrants from crossing, a deed that turns fatal.

Peter Baker and Michael D. Shear are the authors of "El Paso Shooting Suspect's Manifesto Echoes Trump's Language," the August 2019 news analysis in the *New York Times* that declared that President Trump "has brought into the mainstream polarizing ideas and people once consigned to the fringes of American society."

I conducted my analysis of cable news's depiction of working-class voters by race using the GDELT Project's Television Explorer, which has provided me fodder for dozens of story ideas in the several years I have been using it. I conducted my analysis of 2016 *New York Times* stories about working-class voters by race using the newspaper's electronic archive. The only story the *Times* published in 2016 that included the phrase "working class black" and interviews with black voters was "Black Voters, Aghast at Trump, Find a Place of Food and Comfort," by Sheryl Gay Stolberg, which ran on October 30. For an illuminating and reflective discussion of media coverage of the 2016 race, listen to the January 31, 2020, episode of *The Daily* podcast, which features an interview with *Times* executive editor Dean Baquet and *Daily* host Michael Barbaro.

Jon Green and Sean McElwee's study showing how the choice in 2016 between voting and staying home was itself a product of economics is "The Differential Effects of Economic Conditions and Racial Attitudes in the Election of Donald Trump," published in *Perspectives on Politics*.

CHAPTER 10

My descriptions of Mariko Mori, her life, and her painting *The Last Departure* draw on several sources, chiefly *Mariko Mori and the Globalization of Japanese "Cute" Culture: Art and Pop Culture in the 1990s*, a paper by the art historian SooJin Lee, and a review by Holland Cotter of an exhibit of Mori's work in New York, published in 1999 in the *New York Times*. I still have the photo I took with my phone of the work hanging on Wilbur Ross's waiting-room wall.

The details of Ross's sale of his investment fund to a larger firm were reported by Katie Benner for TheStreet.com in 2006.

My account of the meeting with Ross and Peter Navarro is drawn from my notes and digital audio recording. I first wrote about it, and all the Trump campaign plans and documents referenced in this chapter, for the *Washington Post*. At the time of this writing, those documents, including the "whole chessboard" economic policy paper, are still posted online. Some portions of the meeting and an ensuing discussion with Navarro were agreed by both parties to be off the record and thus are excluded from all my writings about the meeting.

The think tanks that Ross and Navarro accused of undercounting the benefits of Trump's tax, trade, and other economic policy plans were the Tax Policy Center and the Peterson Institute for International Economics, both in Washington. For a snapshot of the widespread consensus in the economics profession that countries should not make it a point of economic policy to reduce trade deficits, see the December 9, 2014, survey on the issue conducted by the IGM Economic Experts Panel, which overwhelmingly disagreed with the statement "A typical country can increase its citizens' welfare by enacting policies that would increase its trade surplus (or decrease its trade deficit)."

My discussion of the effects of Trump's policies on the American economy over the first three years of his presidency are largely drawn from calculations and analyses I conducted as the policy editor at *Vox* and, since September 2017, as the tax and economics reporter at the *New York Times* in Washington. Some of that analysis was first published by *Vox* or the *Times*. In those stories, I have cited calculations on the pace and diffusion of manufacturing job creation that were completed by the Brookings Metropolitan Policy Program and the Economic Innovation Group, both think tanks in Washington. I have been blessed with extraordinary colleagues who have coauthored some of those stories, including Ben Casselman, Peter Eavis, Alan Rappeport, Jeanna Smialek, and Ana Swanson.

The International Monetary Fund's conclusions about the Trump tax cuts are contained in *U.S. Investment Since the Tax Cuts and Jobs Act of 2017*, by Emanuel Kopp, Daniel Leigh, Susanna Mursula, and Suchanan Tambunlertchai, published in 2019.

Arthur Laffer and I spent a five-hour lunch at the Gordon Biersch restaurant in Washington in the spring of 2015. The restaurant has since closed. President Trump has since given Laffer the Medal of Freedom, which is America's highest civilian honor.

Tim Boyle and I spoke about the damage of Trump's trade and immigration policies for his company, Columbia Sportswear, in its Portland, Oregon, offices, and on the phone. Some of our conversations first appeared in a story for the *Times*.

CHAPTER 11

I have worked with the polling firm SurveyMonkey on a monthly economic confidence survey going back to the start of President Trump's time in office, first at *Vox* and now at the *Times*. Laura Wronski and Jon Cohen have conducted the polls, rotating in new questions each month to supplement our long-running, repeated series of questions that gauge Americans' faith in the current economy and its prospects for the future.

One such survey is cited here. Others have informed the conclusions of this book.

Marianne Wanamaker and I spoke by phone and in person several times in 2019, including about the refugee family in Knoxville that Marianne's family has befriended and helped.

CHAPTER 12

I returned to Winston-Salem to interview Ed Green and his family in July 2019. I interviewed William Darity on the phone that same month.

The Pew Research Center's report *Race in America 2019* was published in April of that year. Statistics on wealth by race are drawn from the Federal Reserve's Survey of Consumer Finances, and from an analysis of those statistics published by the Federal Reserve Bank of St. Louis, *What Wealth Inequality in America Looks Like: Key Facts and Figures*, by Ana Kent, Lowell Ricketts, and Ray Boshara.

Marianne Wanamaker and William Collins's study on the lack of intergenerational mobility for black men, "Up from Slavery? African American Intergenerational Economic Mobility Since 1880," was published as a National Bureau of Economic Research working paper in 2017. The Republican staff of the congressional Joint Economic Committee have published multiple reports on so-called social capital in America; the map overlaying low social capital in the South with the antebellum-era maps of cotton production was sent to me by Scott Winship, a sociologist who is now the Joint Economic Committee's executive director.

Data on racial and gender underrepresentation in academic economics and comments about its prevalence, here and elsewhere in the text, are drawn from the American Economic Association's 2019 Professional Climate Survey, a voluntary (and nonrandom sample) poll of economists who were currently or in the recent past members of the association. Ben Casselman and I wrote about the survey and its findings for the *Times* when it was released to the public. We also wrote extensively about issues of discrimination and harassment in the profession, as did several reporters at competing outlets, notably Soumaya Keynes of *The Economist* and Heather Long of the *Washington Post*.

Census data shows the persistent geographic segregation by race in Winston-Salem. It is presented in striking detail by the Racial Dot Map, a project of researcher Dustin Cable and the University of Virginia's Weldon Cooper Center for Public Service. Estimated property values are from the online real estate sites Zillow and Redfin, accessed in fall 2019. The Brookings Institution report on disparities in property values by racial characteristics of neighborhoods is *The Devaluation of Assets in Black Neighborhoods*, by Andre M. Perry, Jonathan Rothwell, and David Harshbarger, published in 2018. Data on relative poverty in majority-black neighborhoods in Winston-Salem is from the 2017 *Forsyth County Poverty Study*, from the group Forysth Futures.

CHAPTER 13

I first wrote about Deborah Jackson for the fourth chapter of my 2014 series for the *Washington Post*, "Liftoff and Letdown," and I interviewed her again in person and over email in 2019. Her life story is drawn from her recollections. Data on women founders receiving venture capital and representation of women in the technology industry is drawn from Crunchbase News and the National Venture Capital Association, as presented in a 2019 slide deck by Jackson's firm, Plum Alley Investments.

Calculations about the potential gains from employing and paying women equitably in the United States are mine, using population and salary data from the Census Bureau's Current Population Survey and American Community Survey, as previously indicated. The bureau reviews some of that data in a 2019 report by Jennifer Cheeseman Day, *Among the Educated, Women Earn 74 Cents for Every Dollar Men Make*. The 2014 *Wall Street Journal* op-ed that dismissed evidence of gender bias in compensation as "illogical" was written by Mark J. Perry and Andrew G. Biggs.

Heather Boushey's work on the benefits of government paid-leave policies for labor-force participation and growth is summarized in her 2019 book, *Unbound*. Aparna Mathur has written frequently for the American Enterprise Institute on the benefits of paid leave, including in a 2019 AEI blog post, "Addressing Libertarian Concerns About Paid Leave."

Northwestern University investigated its representation of women in faculty in a report made public in 2017, *Women Faculty at Northwestern: An Overview*. It detailed its quantitative study of bias in hiring and retention in the *2018 Report of the Pipeline Advancement of Women Faculty Research Subcommittee*, which to my knowledge has not been made public as of this writing. For more generalized data on bias against women advancing in the workforce, see *Women in the Workplace 2019*, a report by McKinsey & Company.

Morgan Stanley's report on the "trillion-dollar" potential from investing in women entrepreneurs, dated 2018, is titled *The Growing Market Investors Are Missing*. The International Monetary Fund's 2018 study on potential productivity and growth gains from empowering women is *Economic Gains from Gender Inclusion: New Mechanisms, New Evidence*, by Jonathan D. Ostry, Jorge Alvarez, Raphael Espinoza, and Chris Papageorgiou.

CHAPTER 14

The history of the battle between English settlers and native tribes at what today is called Turners Falls was first related to me by Kevin Hassett, then the chairman of the White House Council of Economic Advisers, in a 2019 visit to the falls. My detailed account of it is drawn from several sources, including *Battle of Great Falls / Wissatinnewag-Peskeompskut (May 19, 1676)*, a study for the United States Department of the Interior conducted by Kevin McBride, David Naumec, Ashley Bissonnette, and Noah Fellman, and published in 2016; *The Present State of New-England with Respect to the Indian War*, published in 1675 by Roger L'Estrange; and "Village of Turners Falls History and Culture," published online by the Town of Montague, Massachusetts, which also provides other history about the village referenced here.

Hassett's boyhood memories are his own, though supplemented by interviews with Montague city officials and the town's online history. The history of the Greenfield Tap and Die is from "Greenfield Tap and Die: Economic and Historical Analysis," by Rebecca Ducharme, published in the *Historical Journal of Massachusetts*. Issues of Tap and Die's

World War II newsletter are collected and displayed online by the Museum of Our Industrial Heritage, in Greenfield.

Federal Reserve officials worried about geographic inequality in the recovery from the Great Recession in their February 2019 *Monetary Policy Report*. Significant work documenting that inequality has been conducted by the Brookings Metropolitan Policy Program and the Economic Innovation Group; I have relied on both groups' data and analysis for news stories in the *Washington Post*, *Vox*, and the *New York Times*, and for this chapter.

Olugbenga Ajilore's work on the demographics of rural areas is contained in the series "Rural America," published online by the Center for American Progress. Adam Ozimek's proposal for place-based immigration visas, *From Managing Decline to Building the Future: Could a Heartland Visa Help Struggling Regions?*, was published in 2019 by the Economic Innovation Group with coauthors Kenan Fikri and John Lettieri.

Anne Case and Angus Deaton have summarized their "deaths of despair" work in papers such as "Mortality and Morbidity in the 21st Century," published in 2017 by the journal *Brookings Papers on Economic Activity*, and their 2020 book, *Deaths of Despair and the Future of Capitalism*. Their 2018 response to a critic is titled "Deaths of Despair Redux: A Response to Christopher Ruhm."

The National Academies published its exhaustive study of immigrants and the American economy, *The Economic and Fiscal Consequences of Immigration*, edited by Francine D. Blau and Christopher Mackie, in 2017. The 2019 study that found that previous immigration restrictions did not help native-born American workers is *The Effects of Immigration on the Economy: Lessons from the 1920s Border Closure*, by Ran Abramitzky, Philipp Ager, Leah Platt Boustan, Elior Cohen, and Casper W. Hansen.

CHAPTER 15

The friend who drove me around Washington on my first night in town was M. E. Sprengelmeyer, who was then the Washington bureau chief for the *Rocky Mountain News*. I am taking him at his word that the sport coat really did belong to Jack Abramoff.

The 2012 International Monetary Fund analysis showing that the financial sector had grown to a size that slowed growth was *Too Much Finance?*, by Jean-Louis Arcand, Enrico Berkes, and Ugo Panizza. Thomas Philippon's "Has the U.S. Finance Industry Become Less Efficient?" was published in 2015 by the *American Economic Review*. The Organisation for Economic Co-operation and Development published *Under Pressure: The Squeezed Middle Class* in 2019.

Wealth statistics are from the Federal Reserve's Survey of Consumer Finance.

Policy prescriptions from William Darity, Heather Boushey, Melissa Kearney, Raj Chetty, Matthew Mitchell, Dean Baker, and Marianne Wanamaker are drawn from their published work and from interviews over the last several years with each of them.

You can read a sample of William F. Woo's lessons for journalism and life in the book *Letters from the Editor*, first published posthumously in 2007.

Index

Jim Tankersley, a tax and economics reporter for the *New York Times*, has written extensively about the stagnation of the American middle class, the decline of economic opportunity in wide swaths of the country, and how policy changes in Washington have exacerbated those trends over the past few decades.

Prior to joining the *Times*, Tankersley was the policy and politics editor at *Vox*, economic policy correspondent for the *Washington Post*, and economic and political reporter at the *National Journal*. He started his career at the (McMinnville, Ore.) *News-Register*, *The Oregonian* (Portland), the *Rocky Mountain News*, and *The Blade* newspaper in Toledo. At *The Blade* he was a member of the Coingate team that was a Pulitzer Prize finalist. He and a *Blade* colleague won the 2007 Livingston Award for Young Journalists for a series of stories demonstrating how and why the Ohio economy declined so dramatically over the course of a generation.